ERP

The Future of Business Automation

ERP

The Future of Business Automation

Zubair H. Shaikh

ATLANTIC
PUBLISHERS & DISTRIBUTORS (P) LTD

Published by

ATLANTIC

PUBLISHERS & DISTRIBUTORS (P) LTD

7/22, Ansari Road, Darya Ganj, New Delhi-110002
Phones : +91-11-40775252, 40775214, 23273880, 23275880
Fax: +91-11-23285873
Web: www.atlanticbooks.com
E-mail: orders@atlanticbooks.com

Printed & bound in India by Atlantic Print Services

Acknowledgements

It is a privilege to dedicate this page as a token of gratitude to all those who directly or indirectly participated in the development of the knowledge I have acquired and which ultimately gave me the courage to write this book.

I gratefully acknowledge a debt to all my teachers and professors in different parts of the world. I am grateful to late Dr. Shaukat (Sir), Prof. Verma and Prof. Dr. John Turner.

My heartfelt gratitude to H.E. Sheikh Waleed Y. Zahid (Hon. Consul General of Sweden in the Kingdom of Saudi Arabia) and President of the ZAHID Group of Companies, for graciously giving me opportunities to serve his companies. I am also grateful to the former senior executives in ZAHID Group, Mr. Sajid Mahmoud, Mr. Roland Pflaumer and Mr. Steve Butler for giving me opportunities to grow career-wise.

I am thankful to those who have supported me during my business career and they include eZeesoft customers, associates and business partners. My special thanks are due to Mr. Terry Duff, Mr. Phil Duff, Mr. Vikas Agarwal, Mr. Atul Gupta, Mr. Dinesh Kavoor and Mr. Dhananjaya Reddy.

I am also thankful to all my friends especially Mr. Rafie Khan, Director, Pre-Sale SAP Pakistan; Mr. C. Kumaresh, SVP, Tata AIG-India; and Mr. Javed Sheikh, CEO, Samreen Software, for their review and expert comments during the development of this book.

This acknowledgement will not be complete without expressing my gratitude to all my students and my juniors in different parts of the world. They might not be aware how much I learnt while teaching them.

Zubair H. Shaikh

Foreword

The author of this book is an ERP consultant having more than 25 years experiences in Computer Software, ERP solutions and business management and has worked for renowned international brands in different parts of the world. He is the founder and CEO of eZeesoft (P) Ltd., Mumbai and is also serving as a Senior Vice President, ERP, Nexxoft Infotel Ltd., Bengaluru, India. The author is a visiting lecturer on ERP & PM in management institutes in Mumbai.

The book explains the technicalities and functionalities of ERP solutions and illustrates different business scenarios to explain how ERP can be used as a tool for business automation. It also discusses in detail the reported problems and myths about ERP solutions. This book may not tell much about the ERP market and ERP business as such. However, the author has tried to epitomize the ERP market in general and ERP software solutions in particular.

This book is a complete guide on ERP and will be useful to companies planning for ERP solutions and equally beneficial to the students in management studies.

The book is largely based on the practical experiences of the author, but there are several books, articles and business literatures that have caused great impact on author's writing and they all have been mentioned in Bibliography of this book.

Prof. Anuj Mishra
Director, DGMTC
(Dr. Gazi Management &
Technical College),
Thane

Contents

Overview

Sixties and seventies was the era of mainframe and mini computers, and PC was under research and development phase. Large size companies were using full-fledged business automation whereas small and medium size companies were relying more on manual or semi-automation system. The software requirement was primarily fulfilled through customization. Large companies were using multiple software solutions in non-integrated mixed environment of customized and off-the-shelf package software. It was nearly impossible to get an integrated off-the-shelf software solution which could meet the total requirements of four primary business operations, i.e. Finance & Accounting, Sales & Distribution, Production & Planning and PR & HRMS. The software packages available at that time were predominantly focused on finance and accounting functionalities.

It was early seventies when the buzzword ERP (Enterprise Resource Planning) was first heard. ERP has originated from MRP (Material Requirements Planning) which is the fundamental aspect of production management, planning and control. Later it became MRP-II which includes purchase, inventory, logistics and distribution. The significance of integrating MRP with Finance & Accounting and Sales & Distribution system was felt at an early stage and the idea emerged as ERP software solution. Initially it was called IIS (Information Integrated System).

ERP software solutions have gone through over 35 years of evolution. They have been growing along with the rapid technological growth and have seen the development from Mainframe to PC networking, Monolithic to GUI, Floppy drive to Optical Disc, Mega to Terra bytes storage, Hubs and routers to Switches, ASCII file to XML & HTML format, DBMS to RDBMS, X.25 and Analog to Digital and Frame Relay, Periodic data update to Real-time online, NETBIEU to TCP/IP Protocol, Pier to Pier to Client/Server architecture and finally it has reached a new paradigm and is now called ERP-II. In view of the development in business concepts, ERP software has adopted different methodologies that have emerged with the facilities such as web-enablement .Net framework, DFM, COM, XML, XBRL, E-commerce, B2B, B2C, CRM, SCM, PLM, APS, ECC, SOA, among others.

It was essential that ERP software maintains its compatibilities with different interfaces such as Bar-coding, Web Browser, Shop Floor Terminal, Mobile, GSM, WAP, Smart Phone, Pocket PC, etc. and world-class ERP solutions have successfully achieved these compatibilities during evolution process.

SAP™, BAN™, Oracle™, PeopleSoft™, JDE™, Syspro™, IFS™ Sage™, Great Plains™, Navision™, and many others have been considered the marvels of ERP software solutions, providing the brilliance and continuous dedication of teamwork the corporate world has seen during the past three decades.

During the last one decade many ERP software brands vanished from the market. They were unable to cope up with the rapid technological enhancements and regular change in business concepts. Those who continuously invested in upgrading their solutions have not only survived but also capitalized on the technological growth and were later on accredited, applauded and ranked by prominent international institutions/surveyors.

Current ERP market is vibrant and gradually growing. In recent years it has witnessed many mergers, demergers, acquisitions, arch-rivalries, bankruptcies, scams, competitions as well as associations. ERP or ERP-II or whatever name it is given, the fundamental concept of ERP will remain the same and the future business automation solution lies in ERP.

ERP

1

Introduction

Chapter 1 start with an argument called 'Why ERP?' and explains the difference between ERP and non-ERP system environment. The first couple of pages will give you a graphical view to understand the business, goods and information workflow typically applied in different business disciplines.

This chapter takes you through the basics, fundamentals, definitions and benefits of Enterprise Resource Planning software solution.

The most important topic in this chapter is the 'Benefits' of ERP solutions, discussed in great detail, where you will find different scenarios depicted from the real life operations. Different operations from non-integrated environment are compared with the operations in ERP environments. This chapter is also important because it enables you to understand the ROI on ERP and sheds lights on some outstanding ERP functionalities. It also describes the qualities of an ERP solution that make an ERP worldclass.

Different diagrams outlined in this chapter will enable you to have a clear picture of ERP modulation and integration.

Why ERP?—An Argument

Before we study ERP in detail, it is necessary to know about non-ERP software solutions and their roles and significance in business world. The term 'non-ERP' used in this book to distinguish between ERP a seamlessly integrated system and all other software solutions and systems that work in non-integrated environment of mainframe, mini and micro computers.

If it is not ERP software then one has to go either for customized and/or readymade accounting package. Accounting Packages support limited functionalities. Customized software solutions were predominantly used before the emergence of the

ERP. Customized Software solution leads to endless programming and developments, therefore it has not been considered a cost-effective solution. It does not allow business to follow Industry Standard Practices. Both customized solution and off-the-shelf accounting packages do not provide seamless integration, therefore leads to duplication of works, lack of efficiency and accuracy. They do not grow as and when the business grows.

From the advent of PC in early eighties, small and medium companies (SME) have started using several different kinds of application software and small accounting packages in PC environment. Many of them have successfully been using Off-the-shelf software packages such as SBT™, Peachtree™, Macola, DacEasy™, Tally™ CODA™ and many such great solutions. Along with these packages, they have also been using spreadsheet application software such as VisiCalc™, Lotus™, Symphony™, Cross-Tab™, MS Excel™, MS Access™, etc. to produce different analytical reports. Many large size companies too started using such applications in PC environment in addition to the customized solutions they have been using in mainframe environment. Customized software solutions were developed in-house using different programming languages such as BASIC™, COBOL™, C™++, Dbase™+, FoxPro™, Visual BASIC, etc., by SME and large size companies.

All the above-mentioned software solutions are having great functionalities and during particular period of time they were the only available solutions of their kind. In many aspects these software have set good examples of human genius. In some cases these solutions are still the best solutions for some of the small companies. The question arises then why ERP? And the answer is discussed in great detail ahead in this book.

By analyzing above scenario we can easily understand that both the large and medium size companies have been using more than one software solutions in non-integrated environment. In mainframe environment, the integration used to be created manually through EAI (Enterprise Application Interfaces) system. All these companies have been trying hard to achieve maximum automation for their business processes by using all types of software solutions they deem will serve the purpose. Yet, these companies have not been able to achieve more than 50 per cent of business automation after continuously investing enormous amount of money in multiple software license, designing and development, customization, training and hardware upgrading. It is true that these companies were able to sustain some benefits by achieving 50 per cent business automation.

A Case Example: During our business consultation in year 2002, we have recommended ERP solution to a chemical manufacturing company and the owner of the company asked **'Why ERP?'** He also said that without ERP he is making profit and therefore unable to justify the investment on ERP. We gave the following justifications:

- Profitability does not mean growth in the business and if business is not growing then it is stagnant and in competitive business world stagnant means 'going down'.
- It is essential for a company to grow at sustainable speed and speed is vital for competition and growth. Business pundits say that gone are the days when 'big fish' were eating 'small fish', nowadays it is the 'faster' which eats up the 'slower'.
- Always there are possibilities in achieving additional profits and high rate of business growth and to achieve these goals companies use different methods and tools and ERP is one of them.

The owner of the company got convinced to give second thought to ERP and after RDS (Requirement Definition Study) decided to go for ERP. I am sure that the above justifications are still valid and this book is comprised of many such justifications and arguments.

ERP software provides all those features that are not supported by non-ERP software solutions (such as customized and accounting packages). In addition to this, scalability, future upgrading, user friendliness, navigation, integrity, minimum administration and security are primary aspects of ERP solution. Modern business automation concepts such as CRM, SCM, PLM, E-Commerce, web and internet compatibility, interoperability, platform independency are built-in features of the world-class ERP solution.

At the early stage, the ERP packages comprised of Manufacturing, Financial & Accounting and Distribution modules and at the later stage the HRMS (Human Resources) Localization (local taxation, local language, etc.) modules were added in the ERP packages. The need to add innovation to ERP is continued and the facilities of web-enabled solution, CRM (Customer Relationship Management), SCM (Supply Chain Management), PLM (Product Life Cycle Management), e.Net, E-commerce, C-Commerce (collaborative-commerce), Advance Planning & Scheduling (APS), Engineering Change Controls (ECC), Business Analytic and Inventory Optimizer have recently been included in the ERP packages. This trend will continue and more innovated facilities may be added to ERP. The concept of ERP software solution is the last resort to business automation and will remain same. However, the name ERP may be changed to ERP-II or something else that reflects advancement in business automation.

Typical Business Process Workflow—A Glimpse

In order to have a comprehensive view of the ERP solution let's first have a glimpse of some business process cycles and workflows illustrated below:

(a) A 3-dimension view of Company, Customer and Supplier's involvement in business cycle. How a buy and sell work flows are used to anticipate customer needs, manage and plan order and logistic cycles. (Fig. 1.1)

(b) A complex operational process that reflects the flow of information and physical movements of the goods. It also illustrates the flow of Finance, Accounting, Marketing, logistic and Inventory Management. (Fig. 1.2)

(c) A complex workflow on how a 'make-to-order' production cycle works in conjunction with the product design, project & contract, materials supplies, customer delivery and accounting. (Fig. 1.3)

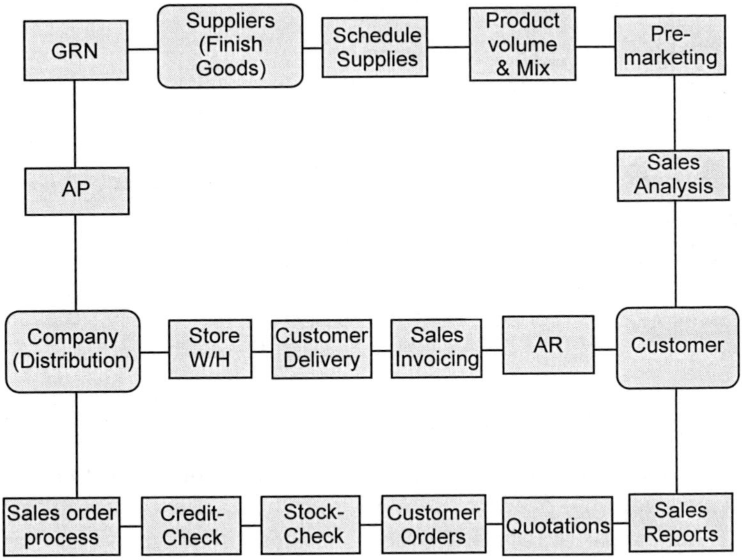

Fig. 1.1: Typical Buy and Sell Business Cycle

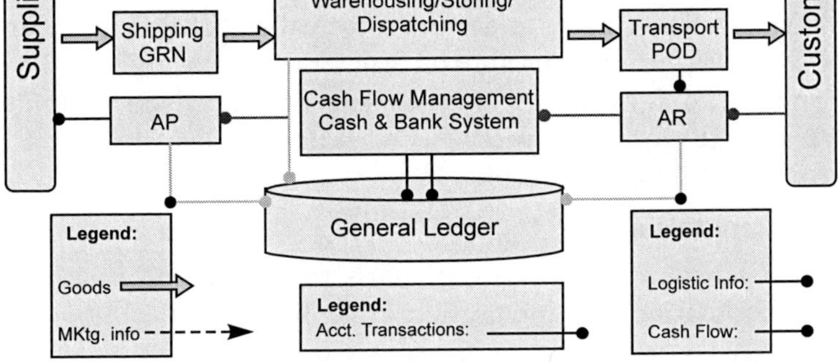

Fig. 1.2: Typical Goods & Information-flow

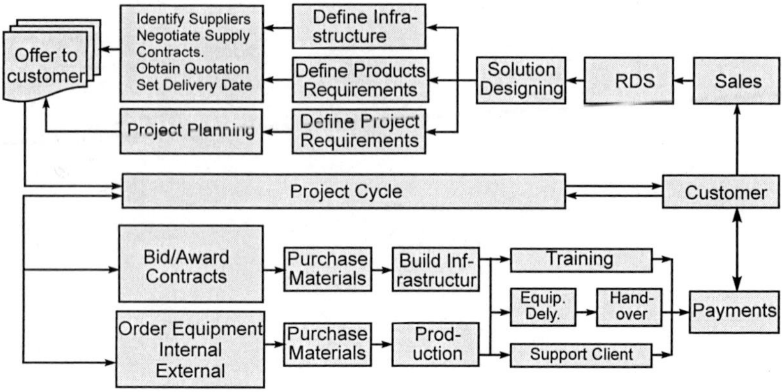

Fig. 1.3: Typical—Manufacturing Make-to-order Cycle

The above illustrations indicate the complexity exists in each operational process and workflow. In real life the complexity is much more than what is seen in these diagrams. There are multiple processes in each flowchart above and ERP solutions simplify and integrate them all by encapsulating each process in a module. This enables clients to choose required modules and finally acquire a business model that may suit their need. ERP Modulation and Integration is discussed next under the topic called 'Fundamentals of ERP', and sample diagrams are also illustrated below enabling you to compare and realize how ERP transforms the complexities of operational process into simple integrated system.

You will also find, under the topic called 'ERP Benefits and ROI' a written explanation on each process from the above graphical diagrams. A step-by-step comparison between operational workflow and ERP workflow is also discussed in great detail under this topic.

Fundamentals of ERP

Let's review the following charts to understand how basic ERP modulation and integration looks like.

If you compare and map the typical business workflow charts illustrated on previous pages with the ERP modulation and integration charts illustrated below, you will find how the complex business flow charts are encapsulated into the ERP

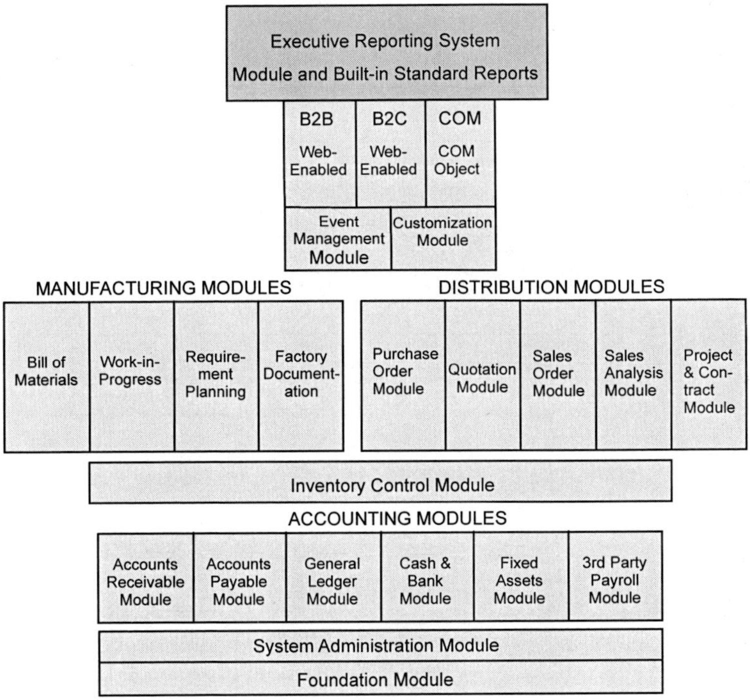

Fig. 1.4: Typical ERP Modulation I

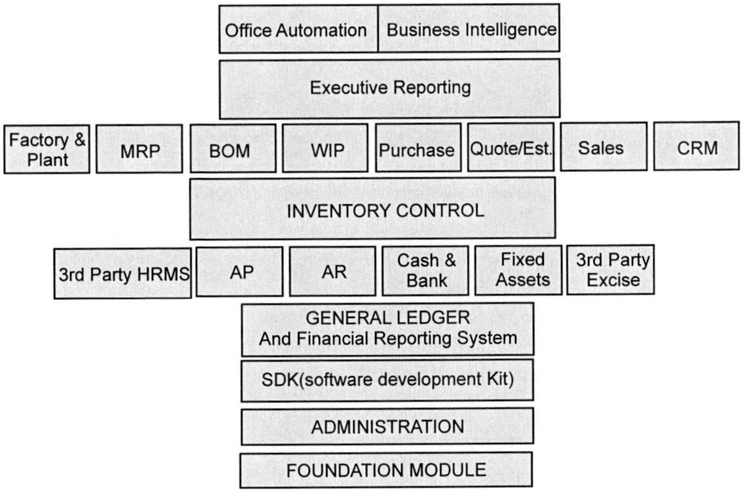

Fig. 1.5: Typical ERP Modulation II

modules (cubical/boxes in the diagrams below) and these modules are (1) Sales, (2) Purchase, (3) Inventory, (4) GRN, (5) MRP, (6) WIP, (7) BOM, (8) Project & Contract, (9) AR, (10) AP, (11) Cash & Bank, and (12) G/L.

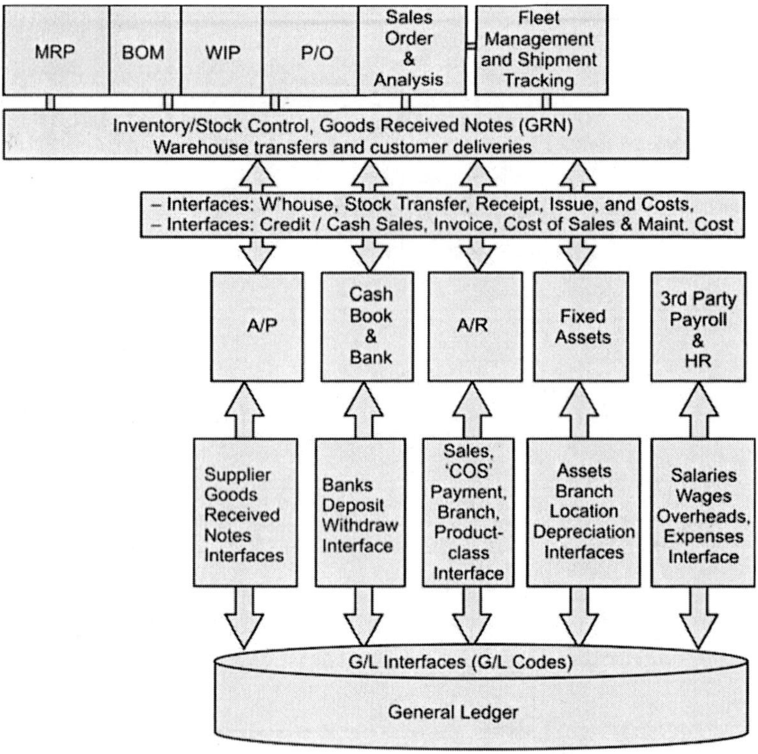

Fig. 1.6: Typical ERP Module Integration

ERP Definition

By definition it is Enterprise Resource Planning (ERP) software solution. An Enterprise is comprises of group of people with one common objective. Resources are vital to achieve that objective and they are finance, human resources, materials, infrastructure and all the other things that are required to run the enterprise. Planning is essential to ensure that enterprise resources are optimally utilized. In view of this, Enterprise Resource Planning or ERP software is a method of efficient planning and optimum utilization of resources in an automated environment. It is worth noting that ERP software packages are not just like any other products or commodities but it is a solution.

When we say ERP is a solution then the question arises: Do customers have any problem? I have experienced this during my early days of consultation services and found how the senior managers at the client's side got offended when I said we are offering ERP solution. They asked me "Do you think we have problems in our company?" and I confidently said yes, you do. In true sense ERP software is a solution to companies who have problems and these problems are discussed in this book under different chapters. This book also discusses why companies have problems even after having ERP.

Fundamental Aspects of ERP

Seamless integration plays pivotal role in preventing duplication of work process and increases level of efficiency and accuracy. The term seamless identifies that the integration is without requiring any manual interfaces as it used in earlier system environment called EAI (Enterprise Application Interfaces). Seamless integration is pre-defined and works automatically in ERP system. This can be best explained by creating a sales and accounting process scenario.

For instance; in non-ERP environment a sales invoice is printed (1 original + >3 copies) and distributed to Finance Accounting, Inventory, customer delivery and many other departments to process/update necessary transactions and entries in their relevant systems. In ERP solution, once a quotation or sales order is processed then the entries can accordingly utilized by all the relevant departments/entities without incurring duplication of works and without bearing risks of data inaccuracy. These departments and entities could be Sales, F&A, Credit Management, Payment process, Production and Planning, Procurement and also the executives.

Business Models: Different kind of business and operational work process are encapsulated into several modules. The modules are seamlessly integrated with each other. A group of modules forms a business model. These modules are ready to install but not ready to use and require certain implementation or business mapping procedures to be followed (discussed ahead in detail in chapter 4 under sub-title 'Roadmap-Project Management Based Implementation Plan for ERP'. These modules are grouped into five primary business operations (a) F&A—Finance and Accounting, (b) S&D—Sales & Distribution, (c) PP—Production Planning & Manufacturing, (d) HRMS—Payroll Human Resources Planning and other administrative functionalities are provided in a module called Utilities.

(a) F&A—generally comprises of following core modules:
- Account Payable (AP)
- Account Receivable (AR)
- Cash and Banking System (C&B)
- General Ledger (GL)
- Asset Register/Fixed Assets (FA)

(b) S&D—generally comprises of following core modules:
- Purchase & Procurement (PO)
- Marketing & Sales (SO)
- Inventory Management and Stock Control (INV)
- Transportation & Delivery System (TRP)

(c) PP & Mfg.—generally comprises of following Core modules:
- Material Requirement Planning (MRP)
- Bill of Materials (BOM)
- Work-in-Progress (WIP)
- Estimation (EST)

(d) HRMS—generally comprises of following major modules:
- Payroll System (PR)
- Human Resources Planning (HRMS)

Utilities—generally comprises of following functionalities:
- Executive Reporting
- Office Automation

- Integration and Interfaces
- User Security Access Control and Log
- 3rd Party Integration and Localization
- EDI (Electronic Data Interchange)
- Screen Customization and Translation
- SDK-Software Development Kits
- Taxation

Some other important modules are described below:

- Pre-Sales and Marketing
- Plant Maintenance
- Quote Writer
- Contact Management
- Return Merchandising
- Factory Documents
- Project and Contracting
- Servicing and Depot System
- Point of Sale System (POS)
- Net Landed Cost and Shipment Tracking
- Transportation and Fleet Management
- Electronic Fund Transfer
- Automatic Bank Statement Reconciliation
- Product Configuration
- EEC (Engineering Change Control)
- APS (Advance Planning and Scheduling)

Industry standard practice: is an inevitable part of ERP software designing and development. As discussed earlier, ERP software offers ready to install sets of business models, therefore it is essential that these models are designed and developed on the basis of Industry standard practices so that it fit for all. All types of small, medium and big companies nowadays inclined towards following standard practices and joining associations such as ISO certifications and many others and this indicates that industry standard practices are very important aspects of business process as well as business automation.

All the world-class ERP software manufacturers strictly follow the industry standard practices. Some of the Industry standard practices followed by world-class ERP manufacturers are outlined below:

- Standard accounting transactional process and implications
- Standard audit trail
- Double Entry Book-keeping System
- Concept of 'every Debit must have a Credit'
- Chart of Accounts
- Structured GL and sub-ledger System
- Pre-defined Account Types (i.e. Asset, Capital, Expenses, etc.)
- Concept of Balancing, Closing Books, Period-end and Year-end
- Process of Committed Transactions
- Concept of Journals and Posting
- Standard in-built formulas (Inventory Costs, Revenue, Profit and Loss)
- Monitoring 'T' account or transaction distribution before posting into General Ledger
- Transaction log and event log maintenance
- Amendment journal log (amendments made in the masters)
- Standard Financial Budgeting and Sales Targeting
- Facilities of predefined structuring and routing in BOM
- Rectifications of transacted entries through Dr./Cr., journals and log
- Standard in-built Financial and Accounting Reports (PNL, TB, BL)
- User Access and Security Controls based on segregation of duties
- RDBMS (Relational Database Management System)

Componentization or Modularity in ERP solutions is essential in order to enable the client to configure the ERP system as per his operational requirements. World-class ERP solutions are comprises of > 40 different components or modules and one can purchase different number and types of modules as per their operational requirements. Some of these modules are listed above. ERP solutions are designed and developed for all kinds of industries and business houses (Manufacturers, Distributors, Contractors, Traders, Importers/Exporters, Supply Houses, etc.). A manufacturing firm may purchase all the business models i.e. F&A, S&D, Manufacturing & PP and HRMS, however a distributor may require only first three sets of business models and not the manufacturing and PP. Likewise a retailer may require POS system instead of core sales invoicing module.

Upgradability: ERP software are designed and developed with the provision to upgrade and enhance as and when it is necessary. Upgrading is a gradual process in ERP development. It takes place in view of the technological development, innovation, change in business concepts and methods. In this situation the ERP developers introduce higher version. We have discussed the 35 years of ERP evolution in the earlier chapter called 'Overview' which indicates the significance of upgradability and you will find a detail on latest upgrading in ERP solutions ahead in this book under the topic called 'Enterprise Resource Enhancements—ERP-II'. Let's have a look on some other aspects of upgradability that is outlined below.

In late nineties ERP software were upgraded to meet the Y2K (Year 2000) date conformity and compatibility. During that time almost every software solution be it ERP or application software have undergone major upgrading to meet the Y2K conformity. During same period the GUI (Graphic User Interface) technology was emerged and most of the ERP software introduced the upgraded GUI version from Monolithic or character-based version.

During 2002-03 many renowned ERP software developers added new features such as E-Commerce, B2B, B2C, CRM and SCM. Similarly, during last couple of years the world-class ERP software developers have introduced new modules in view of the development in business process and they are APS (Advance Planning & Scheduling), ECC (Engineering Change Controls), Inventory Optimizer and Business Analytics.

One of the recent upgrading of ERP solutions are increase in the field-size (character length/width of a 'field'). The field could be a Stock Code, General Ledger Code, Customer Code or Name or any other field that appears on the ERP screens for users input and later on stored in the database.

Apart from major upgrading, ERP software developers continuously upgrade their system on port basis and they are called port-update. This covers small change/enhancements or sometime rectifications.

User friendliness: It is very important that ERP software is designed and developed with the concept of user-friendliness. ERP solutions are very complex and normally comprises of 40-50 different modules and each module consist of several options, sub-options and several screen-sets and screen-forms. Therefore, it is very difficult for users to remember all the names, labels and steps.

All the world-class ERP software solutions are intuitive, easy to navigate and very user friendly. Most of them have adopted the look and feel of universally used MS Windows interface and this provides consistency and uniformity in system environment.

ERP software are intuitive, therefore when a normal computer user press a key/option in ERP, he can easily guess the next option and screen-sets. Similarly, the navigation is so easy that a user remembers the start to end process in ERP software and never feel that he is lost in the midst of modules, options and screen sets.

In view of the segregation of duties and role of a system user, it is essential that ERP solution provides the facilities of user defined screens. Most of the world-class ERP solutions offer Screen Customization facilities where user can have a screen that reflects only those options which are related to his/her roles.

In addition to Customized Screen facilities, ERP software also offers the facilities of automatic execution of tasks. These tasks are automatically executed in batch process as per the pre-defined timetable.

Localization and 3rd Party Integration: It is very important that ERP solutions support 3rd party integration and there are many reasons to have this facility. Neither ERP can cover 100 per cent requirements of any specific business/discipline nor it is possible for any ERP manufacturers to design and develop solutions for hundreds types of business and industries. Maximum 80 per cent of the business automation requirements can be fulfilled by an ERP solution and this is the bench mark. The balance 20 per cent is normally part of localization/customization and can be achieved through 3rd party integration or customization support available in the ERP. Some of the world-class ERP software solutions offer the customization facilities through SDK (software development Kit), .Net and COM DCOM tools. Very recently, the ERP venders have introduced the concept of SOA (Service Oriented Architecture) and it is an easy and cost effective approach of 3rd party integration. (More detail on SOA is outlined ahead in this book.)

Generally, localization in ERP is applied for (a) local language support and called bilingual ERP solution, (b) support for local taxation, and (c) support for local HRMS system.

(a) *Bilingual ERP solutions*: Predominantly ERP software solutions are developed in English language where the scripts, dialogues, input and outputs, data storage and printouts are all maintained in English language. However, there are certain customers/users who would like to have ERP solutions that offer multi-language facilities for input and outputs (printouts). Such ERP solutions are available with necessary interfaces to select local language as second language option and it allows users to work in the language they better understand. Many a time the printouts, financial and audit reports, transactional documentation are required in local language as per the rules and regulations defined by the local governmental bodies and this require business houses to have multilingual business automation system. Many world-class ERP software offer Chinese, French, Arabic, German versions or bilingual ERP version.

(b) *Support for Local taxation*: It is nearly impossible for ERP developers to incorporate hundreds different types and levels of taxation systems used world-wide and frequently revised. Therefore, most of the world-class ERP solutions offer 3rd party integration. This integration could be created by in-built interfaces or by customizing a software solution using SDK module. Some world-class ERP offers basic taxation functionalities and options where simple Sales tax, VAT can be applied at the time of sales invoicing and purchasing/GRN/supplier payment. In ERP-II customization and integration can be easily achieved through .Net, XML, COM and SOA technology and ERP-II is discussed in detail in chapter 2.

It is worth noting here that the development of such complex taxation system is very critical and need special skills as well as authorization/certifications from local governmental bodies to use/apply necessary calculations and factors every time it is revised. World-wide Tax policies are frequently revised in view of the rapid economical changes. Therefore, when it comes to complex Tax, Excise, import/export duties and allowance calculations then it is recommended to have a locally well established and certified taxation software system that can be integrated with ERP as 3rd Party integration.

(c) *Support for Local HRMS system*: Unlike taxation, HRMS policies may not change frequently and do not require special authorities and certificates from government to define and apply HRMS policies in the software system. However, similar to taxation system the policies, terms and conditions vary from country to country. There are many world-class ERP software solutions offer in-built module or ready interfaces to instantly create 3rd party integration. Many world-class ERP venders tied-up with good HRMS software provider and the 3rd party integration is 100 per cent tested and integrated.

More detail on 3rd party integration is discussed in this book ahead.

Outstanding Functionality in World-class ERP

As we have studied the fundamentals of ERP solution, seamless integration and the core ERP modules. These modules are comprises of standard operational functions related to purchase, sales, services, inventory, production and so on. These functions are core functions and are identical in most of the ERP solutions, therefore they are not discussed in this book in detail. There are some outstanding functions available in world-class ERP solutions and it is necessary that we first study the qualities possess by a world-class ERP solution, or what makes an ERP world-class.

More than 500,000 different off-the-shelf business software solutions are available in the global market. There are >50,000 full-fledged ERP solutions available world-wide and fundamentally they are similar. However, there are several rankings given to them by renowned institutions and surveyors. Some are ranked world-class and some as 'Top 5' or 'Top 10', based on their qualities, performance and specialties.

Qualities of the World-class ERP Solutions

A world-class ERP solution must have the following qualities:

- It must have developed on the basis of fundamentals of ERP (detail on Fundamentals of ERP is discussed in previous topic).
- It must have developed on the basis of Industry Standard Practices (detail on Industry Standard Practices is discussed in previous topic).
- It should be compatible with all modern business concepts and technologies (detail on Modern Business Concepts and technologies discussed in next chapters ahead in this book).
- It must have a good network of professional consultants and support service providers worldwide and the vender must give guarantee of successful implementation.

– It must have sufficient number of reference sites and licensed users from different domain in different part of the world.
– It must have potentiality to upgrade and grow and at the same time let business grow.
– It must have gone through and still going through the R&D and evolution process.
– It must have been bench-tested/evaluated or recognized, ranked, awarded or recommended by at least one international financial institution.
– The vender must guarantee the accessibility on the source codes under ESCROW clause.
– It must be available on competitive pricing.
– It must allow buyer to choose the option of implementing it as business-oriented system or system-oriented business.
– It should allow buyers to plan implementation on the basis of company's budget and priorities.

Top 15 World-class ERP Software

Sl.No.	Brand	Market	Major Users
1.	BAN™	MLE	Global
2.	Cincom™	MLE	UK
3.	Epicor™	MLE	Europe
4.	Fourth Shift™	MLE	UK, US
5.	Great Plains™	SME	Global
6.	IFS™	MLE	UK, US, EUROPE
7.	JDE™	MLE	Global
8.	Mapics™	MID	Global
9.	MS Navision™	MID	Global
10.	Oracle™	MLE	Global
11.	PeopleSoft™	MLE	Global
12.	QAD™	SME	Europe, USA
13.	Sage Enterprise™	SME	Global
14.	SAP™	MLE	Global
15.	Syspro™	SME	Global

Some outstanding functionality available in world-class ERP solutions

Outlined below are some of the extraordinary functionalities offered by the world-class ERP solutions and most of them are optional:

- *Multiple Companies*: It allows a group or a corporate house to run different types of business from one ERP system. For example, a corporate firm deals in chemicals, fertilizer and pharmaceutical manufacturing as well as distribution and retail business can use one single ERP system and can add as many as 60 different types of companies. It is possible to have joint financial, auditing and executive reports for all the companies from one single system. The accounting books can be maintained separately or can be merged at the back-end finance system (Genera Ledger level).
- *Multiple Period Accounting*: This enables you to post transactions to previous months, effectively making it appear as if the transaction occurred in a prior period. This feature is useful for month end procedures where, typically, documentation relating to the current months business cycle has not yet been completed. You can close off the current months processing, complete all the procedures relating to a month end, and then at a later stage still post transactions to the previous month. It is for this reason that many financial reports allow you to produce reports for the current month, the previous month, or the month prior to the previous month.
- *Multiple Manufacturing Process*: World-class ERP addresses all aspects of the manufacturing process and provides the ability to integrate different types of manufacturing techniques. It supports both short and long production runs in the following manufacturing environments.
    - Make-to-Order—This production is usually a combination of standard and customized based non-specific customer requirement.

- Job Shops—Where similar equipment is used to produce different kinds of products.
- Make-to-Stock—Where the high volume based products are produced.
- Configure-to-Order—Where the production of discrete products has unique or custom properties that can be prototype parts or complete items.
- Assemble-to-Order—Where the product is assembled to customer specification using standard parts after receipt of a customer's order.
- Engineer-to-Order—Where products are produced according to customer specification involving unique engineering design or significant customization.
- Batch Process—Where parts are accumulated and products are processed together in a lot.

– *Multiple Currencies*: This facility allows users to buy and sell goods and services in multiple foreign currencies, however the primary currency will be 'local currency' defined in the ERP setup at the time of installation. All other currencies will be defined on the basis of currency conversion factors. These factors convert the foreign currency values into local currency at the time of transaction or transaction posting. These factors can be changed anytime as per the currency fluctuations and in some ERP it is automatically changed as it is linked with the local monitory and currency exchange system. Multiple currencies option also allows user to maintain bank accounts, cash and G/L in more than one currency.

– *Multiple Selling Pricing*: This enables company to sell a product at different prices to many different entities such as end-users, distributor, outlets, showrooms, shopkeepers and supermarket/Mall. It also allows selling prices to be maintained in multiple currencies. Selling prices can be pre-defined and controlled by assigning a price list code against individual stock item or even against individual customer or group of customers. However, if necessary the price control can be overridden by authorized users and an audit trail can be maintained for the same. Manual selling price option is also available and it can be assigned against any stock item and it will enable the user to enter the price manually at the time of sales invoicing or sales booking.

- *Multiple Units of Measurements*: This function plays important role in industries where the volume/quantity of the goods and materials are required to be calculated in more than one measurement. For instance, a company may buy or produce goods in bulk quantity/volume say in tonnes and may store it in different packets/boxes/cartons in small quantity/volume and may sell it according to the market requirements. The important point to be noted that multiple unit of measurement function automatically calculates, converts, update and maintain the value of the goods based on the pre-defined factors.
- *Multiple Warehousing*: It allows users to add/attach multiple warehouses to single stock item. Each warehouse, if necessary, can have different cost/value. These facilities are required in large companies where business is spread over regional and branch levels and each region has a warehouse and/or manufacturing unit which receives goods/materials from several local/overseas suppliers at different NLC (Net Landing Cost).
- *Multiple Costing Methods*: These can be categorized into (a) Costing at warehouse level and (b) costing at company level. Normally single costing method is applied across the company however multiple costing methods may be required in many cases especially if company is dealing in multiple product range and one of the range required average costing and another required FIFO/LIFO. Alternatively, various costing methods can be used within the company, by assigning a costing method to a specific warehouse.
    - *Average Costing*: This will average out the unit cost of an item that is received into stock and calculated as the average between the new cost and the existing cost of

the product held in the system. The average cost is calculated at the time the transaction is processed.

- *Moving Average Cost*: This costing method used under a perpetual inventory system whereby, after each purchase, average unit cost is recomputed by adding the cost of acquired units to the cost of units and dividing by the new total number of units.
- *Weighted Average Costing Method*: Weighted Average cost remains unchanged until the next purchase. This method is mainly used by companies that maintain very large stock of undifferentiated inventory items such as fuels and grains.
- *National Average Costing Method*: This method is not a conventional method and not generally practiced in accounting implications. This unique function was used in non-online environment where the data of inventory movement is replicated from mother warehouse to remote warehouses. For instance, a complex distribution business operates in non-online environment where the frequency of warehouse transfer is very high and the purchase price fluctuates on shipment basis. National Average Costing method creates uniformity in the average costing across the company warehouses and eliminates the gap between the average product costs at warehouses which may occur due to very high frequency of inventory movements i.e. purchase, stocked, transfers and sold.
- *Standard Costing*: This is normally used by manufacturer to maintain the inventory cost intact and separated from the production cost calculated and held in manufacturing modules. This cost will only be updated when a Cost change function is performed.
- *Last Cost*: This is used when the inventory valuation need to be based on the last cost that was entered for a product when it was received into stock.
- *FIFO (First in first out)*: This method allows products to move out of inventory (for sales or issues) on the

basis of oldest stock to be out first and newest stock to be out last.

- *LIFO (Last in first out)*: This method allows products to move out of inventory (for sales or issues) on the basis newest stock to be out first and oldest stock to be out last.
- *Activity Based Cost (ABC costing)*: This costing method is used to calculate the cost of non-product elements such as different kinds of activities in an operation. According to professors Robert Kaplan and Robin Cooper of Harvard University, "Cost accounting approach concerned with matching costs with activities (called cost drivers) that cause those costs. ABC states that (1) products consume activities, (2) it is the activities (and not the products) that consume resources, (3) activities are the cost drivers, and (4) that activities are not necessarily based on the volume of production. Instead of allocating costs to cost centers (such as manufacturing, marketing, finance), ABC allocates direct and indirect costs to activities such as processing an order, attending to a customer complaint, or setting up a machine. A subset of activity based management (ABM), it enables management to better understand (a) how and where the firm makes a profit, (b) indicates where money is being spent, and (c) which areas have the greatest potential for cost reduction."

– *GIT (Goods in Transit) System*: It enables company to monitor real-time inventory valuation that includes the value of goods in shipment, custom clearance or on the road due to warehouse transfers. GIT system play important role in providing the real-time inventory valuation at the time of period-end or month-end closing and it also increases efficiency in customer deliveries and production planning.

– *Lot Traceability*: This plays pivotal role in modern manufacturing where a quality assurance certification is essential, especially in Pharmaceutical, Auto, food and white-goods/electronic industries. This module records start to end movements of materials i.e. receiving, manufacturing, assembly, packaging, inspection, stocking, dispatching and shelving at customer's end. It is essential that this module is seamlessly integrated with all the other modules in distribution system. Bar coding, reading and serial numbering is essential aspects of Lot Traceability.

- *ABC Classification*: This function allows us to produce an analytical inventory movement report based on percentage breaks. The report will indicate the annual usage and frequency of sale along with the value percentage and classify them into different segment such as A, B or C.
- *Min./Max.*: This function allows us to set a re-order point. We can assign minimum and maximum quantity against a stock item for stock control and maintenance. For instance, in case of shortage of warehousing space we can set maximum number against a stock item and while printing purchasing worksheet it will indicate that this stock item has maximum volume and need not be ordered.
- *Safety Stock Level*: This function allows you to maintain the safety stock level and alarm when the stock is going below the safety level. This function also enables us to produce a positive purchase worksheet. This function is an antidote to 'out of stock' syndrome.
- *MPS*: Master production scheduling is a method used by the factory planner to schedule the production which is normally based on sales in process, allocated sales stock, sales forecast and current production pipeline. MPS system enables the production planner to generate a build schedule.
- *Cycle Time*: It is the time between receipt of the order and delivery of the product. This function allows users to create analytical reports on sales and delivery performance.
- *Lead Time*: It is the elapsed time between placing an order and receiving it. It plays pivotal role in analyzing purchasing, shipment tracking, production planning, customer deliveries and maintaining inventory control.

- *Back-flushing*: This function is used to record the manufacture of items without using a Work-in-Progress job. This enables production to issue, in one process, the materials from inventory, apply standard labour costs, and receive the finished good back into stock. This function is particularly relevant in situations where the benefits derived from creating a job to track the activity on the job floor do not justify the cost of processing all the data normally required for a job.
- *Back Order*: This plays pivotal role in booking sales, scheduled customer deliveries and maintain healthy customer relationship. This function allows users to process the sales in case of insufficient stock on-hand and automatically transfer the 'not available' quantity to back order. As soon as the quantity is available it automatically updates the sales process, replace back order quantity with 'ready to ship' and pop the user screen and notify about the action taken or to be taken. The back order quantity of an individual stock code can be seen during the queries from Inventory, Sales, Purchases and WIP modules.
- *ATP*: Available to Promise is very useful function that allows users to promise to customer certain volume of stock item. ATP is the uncommitted portion of inventory and production, maintained in the master schedule to support customer order promising.
- *DTF*: Demand Time Fence is very useful in make-to-order manufacturing. DTF is the time required to manufacture the part to order and is calculated by adding the number of days against the field available in the stock definition.
- *EBQ*: Economic Batch Quantity is the most economical order quantity and is calculated by taking into consideration inventory and production cost.
- *Parent and Son Customer Account*: In modern business world the large size companies are operating from different branches and regions and usually the purchasing process is decentralized, however the payment process is centralized through head office (HO). This requires the

suppliers to have parent and son account relationship in their ERP system which enables them to maintain controls on credit limit and follow-up AR.

- *Job Card*: This eliminates the manual job card system and provides an integrated automatic job card system linked with WIP, BOM, Company Calendar and MRP and in some cases with HRMS module also. It maintains the record of individual labour, group, job time, shifts and work centers.
- *Kardex System*: This eliminates the manual card system normally used at warehouses and storage to maintain the record of stock movements. It maintains the in and out records of individual stock item at individual warehouse and also give reports based on different criteria such as user/operator, transaction type and journals.
- *Operational Controls*: Following controls available in ERP solutions as in-built functionalities:
  - Automatic transaction journals and maintaining journal numbers. As part of accounting practice, this option automatically creates and maintains the record of journals against each transaction.
  - Automatic check on credit sales, terms and value. This protects credit sales invoicing if the accounts receivables are overdue by number of days or the value, meanwhile, allowing the authorized person to override this check/ control by using special password keys online.
  - Tracking lots in manufacturing place the controls and provides the ability to track the parent stock lot and serials back to the component lots and serials that were issued to the job at the time of receipting the job.
  - Disallow duplicate transaction numbering such as sales invoice.
  - Disallow imbalance posting in GL.
  - Audit Trail on stock adjustment, stock cost change, purchase variance.

- Automatic Contra A/c: This controls the liability balancing in AP and AR when a customer and the supplier is same.

– *Cross Reference of Customer and Supplier's Stock Code*: It is common practice that the manufacturers maintain their own stock coding called OEM (original equipment manufacturer) part number/code, the distributor maintains its own stock coding and the customer (especially large size companies) who buy from such distributors maintain their own stock coding. In this situation the distributor need a system which allows him to link his stock coding with the OEM codes as well as his customer's codes so that he can produce a Purchase Order indicating his own code as well as the Manufactures OEM code and can also produce a sales order indicating his codes, OEM part number as well as the customer's codes.

– *Predefined Accounting Implications*: This is the major concern for every junior or senior person in accounts department and the first thing they would like to see in ERP is the 'virtual reality' or how ERP does accounting implications. These implications in fact are the fulcrum of finance and accounting system, therefore the transactions must be concluded with 100 per cent accuracy. In order to follow Industry Standard practices, it is necessary that ERP solutions are developed on the basis of universally acknowledged accounting implications. For instance, as soon as a sales invoice is processed in an ERP system then the in-built accounting system must complete the transactional cycle automatically by debiting and crediting the relevant value in relevant account heads and type of accounts. To understand this better, let's review the following complete transactional cycle of purchase, goods receipt (GRN), inventory valuation, supplier payment and bank transactions:

	Transaction Processed	Action taken		
(1)	PO & GRN	Dr	-	Warehouse A/c
	PO & GRN	Cr	-	Suspense A/c

(2) AP Bill Booking	Dr	-	Suspense A/c
Bill Booking	Cr	-	AP Party A/c
(3) Variance in PO & GRN	Dr	-	Purchase Variance A/c
Variance in PO & GRN	Cr	-	AP Party A/c
(4) AP Payment	Dr	-	AP Party A/c
AP Payment	Cr	-	Bank A/c
(5) TDS Deduction	Dr	-	AP Party A/c
TDS Deduction	Cr	-	Tax-TDS A/c
(6) TDS Payment	Dr	-	Tax-TDS A/c
TDS Payment	Cr	-	Bank A/c

In above transactional cycle the debits and credits are automatically carried out by the ERP system when the transactions are processed by the users. In ERP environment, accountants do not need to bother about amount or value of transaction going to right type of accounts or not as normally they need to take care of these aspects while working in manual system or trivial accounting packages. There are several transactional cycles in an operation such as Sales and AR, warehouse transfers and GIT, issues and jobs, BOM, WIP, purchase of assets and payments cycles, etc. and every transaction in business operations require to go through with several stages of debits and credits and the complexity of such process are very well taken care by the ERP system.

– *EDI (Electronic Data Interchange)*: EDI is available as an in-built facility in most of the world-class ERP software solution. It enables customers to electronically transfer ERP transactional data from remote operational sites to the Head Office or central system. During past two decades, when broadband, DDN and high bandwidth communication systems were not available EDI was the only solution for database replication. ERP users worldwide used to have EDI facility to replicate transactional data from multiple remote sites. EDI enables the remote sites to export transaction database in a 'packet' (ASCII or XML file format) that can be sent to the central server using normal dialup communication line and in turn it is imported and updated at the central ERP server. The functionality is designed meticulously and it maintains the export and import log and transactional journals eliminating the duplication. In some ERP solution EDI also fulfils the basic requirements of SCM and B2B. EDI is a cost effective solution, however it is no more an efficient tool in view of the requirements of real-time online system.

Benefits of ERP

The modern business world is looking for an answer on the real benefits and tangible return on investment from ERP solutions, therefore, the benefits of ERP solutions are discussed in this book in great detail. You will find that different scenarios are created and practical examples are outlined below to justify the need and the benefits of ERP solutions.

Major benefits of ERP

- Eliminates duplication of works
- Increases work efficiency and accuracy
- Real-time reporting and data analysis
- Speed-up the management decision-making process
- Reduces Overheads
- Reduces Lead Time
- Reduces Cycle Time
- Maintains precisions in production, planning and scheduling
- Reduces Work-in-Progress
- Stock value reduction
- Facilitates JIT Inventory (Just in Time Inventory)
- Ease of warehousing and storage, binning shelving and tracking
- Timely Quality Control and monitoring
- Real-time monitoring of cost of material, labour, machine and energy
- Improved Customer Delivery time

- Instant Deal Profitability calculation
- Controls on Payables through GRN matching
- Controls Credit Sale and Account Receivable
- Produces timely Bank Reconciliation
- Provides ageing reports on Inventory, Accounts Receivable, Accounts Payable
- Provides ready to print standard in-built Reports
- Customized-Executive Reporting

It is a common phenomenon in business world to relate benefits with ROI (return on investment) and this means a tangible return. It is said in corporate world that gone are the days when business automation projects were approved based on 'guess-timation'. Nowadays, every project has to be justified with a solid business case that includes an estimated ROI, a tangible return on investment.

A Case Example (Inventory Valuation "As of Now"): Recently, during an ERP presentation, the MD of a traditional business house in India agreed to go for ERP solution only if we submit a ROI calculation on ERP. We assured him for the same but requested him to provide us "As of Now" total inventory valuation of the company. The MD turned his face toward his Finance Chief who uttered certain figures. We said to the MD that this figure must have a variance of +/- 20-30 per cent. [We said so because earlier we studied the RFP (Request for proposal document) of the company and found that they are using a trivial accounting package along with several parallel systems in non-integrated environment.] This led to a long argument, evaluation and to cut short the story after 7 days the MD called up and said that a variance of 22 per cent is found. The MD was very curious to know how we identified the problem and how to resolve that. The answer is given below and the ROI calculation is also discussed ahead in this chapter in great details.

There are hundreds of benefits in ERP solutions, however most prominent one is to get every single report based on 'As of Now' and not based on previous month-end closing. It is well-known fact in the world of F&A (Finance & Accounting) that month-end or period-end closing is never on time in manual, semi-automated or non-integrated system environment. It works 2-3 months behind the schedule because verifications, rectifications, manual integration and synchronization of different sets of databases in non-ERP environment take 30-45 days. In case of large and multiple operational sites the number of days could be more. This is explained below by exemplifying a case-study.

Case Example: (COS goes higher than Net Sales). During early nineties, I have witnessed a situation where a large size company, using F&A package + in-house customized distribution system in mainframe environment, was trying somehow to achieve month-end closing on regular basis and at each month-end the operating statement was indicating calculation variance between the Net Sale value and the COS (Cost of goods sold). Many a time we have seen that the COS indicated on the statement was higher than the Net Sales Value and this in fact was distorting the very purpose of operating statement which normally printed on the last day of the current financial month i.e. 30 days behind 'As of Now'.

The system analyst was aware about the root cause of the problem and each month tried to fix it but in vain. It was a mixed system environment where many application interfaces were used to synchronize the database updates. This happens typically in large companies where the sales, inventory and accounting activities are in very high volume and always there are 11th hour sales deal to be updated in the system due to the strict sales targets.

Referring above two different scenarios (the variance in inventory valuation and the difference in Net sales and COS in the operating statement), one can easily understand the complications in producing 'As of Now' reports in non-integrated environment and its consequences in competitive business world. An inventory valuation report based on As of Now can support decision-making in future purchase of raw materials, maintenance of stock turnover, Production planning, load levelling, Marketing and Pricing, Accounts Payable, Cash

Flow, credit sales and customer delivery commitments and many more. The corporate world especially the manufacturing segment and large size distributors are very well aware that inventory means lifeline and both surplus or insufficient stock of raw materials and finish goods means major setback in cut-throat competition. You must have heard companies got bankrupted due to inventory mismanagement.

Another scenario is when Account Receivables and Payables and Bank Reconciliations are not monitored on the basis of 'As of Now'. I have witnessed a large size distributor in India got major setback due to the delay in producing timely AR ageing report. The distributor was using a trivial accounting package + in-house customized programs. Mismanagement of AR and credit sales may be more disastrous then mismanagement of inventory because it can compel an organization to enter into vicious circle of AR-Inventory-AP and it will end-up in doubtful bad-debts, stock obsolescence, legal notices from the creditors and in some cases loss of market share too.

In view of above scenarios, the question arises if ERP is able to produce 'As of Now' reports then why some companies using ERP solutions are unable to produce it. The reason is either they are not using a world-class ERP solution or it was not professionally implemented, or solution has not been utilized optimally, or the company was not ready for ERP solution or 'corporate culture change', or poor infrastructure could be one of the reasons. To know more on this issue please refer the chapter 4 in this book under sub-title called "Roadmap—How to Plan Purchase/Select an ERP" and other related topics.

Apart from above scenario a case example is outlined below which will enable you to understand the significance of ERP and its impact on the total business operation.

> *A case example*: How a world-class ERP played effective role in quick decision-making in purchasing/bargaining and managing cash-flow of a company is seen in recent years. A leader in automobile industry in Europe came across a situation when the MD landed at the airport midnight hours and enquired his CFO and DSM (Director Sales &

Marketing) if there is any major problem that brought them to the airport. The DSM showed his concern over the overnight decision of the competitors on reducing their car prices. The MD enquired his CFO about the Cash-Flow status 'As of Now'.

Note: The above-mentioned company is using full-fledge world-class ERP solution coupled with well-equipped and efficient infrastructure. The ERP solution is professionally implemented, optimally utilized by >200 users from 15 different operational sites.

The CFO, via his mobile phone/pocket PC, logged on to the ERP server remotely located in Head office and got access on to the executive reporting module, which has pre-defined setup to produce necessary reports generated from the integrated modules such as Inventory, AR, AP, Cash and Banks. By the time the MD, DSM and CFO sat into the car the CFO gave the figure to the MD.

The MD reviewed the figures and discussed necessary financial aspects with the DSM and CFO and made emergency calls to couple of overseas tire manufacturers, bargained with them for bulk tire purchase, obtained 15 per cent discounts on cash payment terms and asked the tire manufacturers to apply this discount for the supply in the pipeline. Similarly, the MD called up couple of other auto parts manufacturers and got price reductions on cash payment terms. Finally the MD discussed necessary factors with the CFO and reached to the conclusion that they have managed to obtain 5-7 per cent discounts on the total material/parts supplies in the current pipeline and decided to reduce their car pricing by 5 per cent. The DSM gave cent per cent assurance on sales target achievements and 15 days payment terms instead standard 60 days credit term.

In an hour or so, by the time the MD reached his home, a major company decision is made with the help of ERP solution. Without ERP solution the decision could have been made little later, let's say couple of days later or a week or so on. But then neither the market nor the end-users wait so long for our decision.

Three different scenarios based on individual operation cycles are outlined below to explain how an approximate ROI can be calculated.

ROI Scenario 1: Purchase Cycle

This scenario will explain the process of purchases, stock receipts, inventory control, accounts payable in non-ERP and ERP environment. Purchasing requires lots of pre- and post-process activities, information tracking, internal document-flow, work-flow and materials handling. Purchase process is one of the complicated and lengthiest operational processes in the business.

Purchase cycle is categorized into following stages:

- Stage I, Purchase requirements and evaluation
- Stage II, PO processing and shipment tracking
- Stage III, Goods receipts and material handling
- Stage IV, Finance & Accounting (F&A)

Scenario 1—Purchase Cycle Process in Non-ERP Environment

Stage-I—Purchase Requirement and Evaluation

- Purchase requirement study is normally initiated by Planning or Procurement Departments. Following reports are produced manually or from different systems in non-integrated environment. Manufacturing industries produce all the following reports and Distribution industries produce last five following reports:
  (1) Material Requirement Planning
  (2) Pending Material Allocations
  (3) Pending Work Orders
  (4) Shop floor requirements
  (5) Inventory turnover
  (6) Cycle time and lead time
  (7) Safety Stock Level
  (8) Sales commitments
  (9) Customer Delivery Schedule

- Supplier's quotations are obtained and final purchase prices and terms conditions are agreed in view of the above evaluation.
- Purchase worksheet produced by Procurement Department. Cross checking and verification carried out by the F&A on expenses such as shipping, transportation, custom duties and insurance, etc.

Stage-II—PO Processing & Shipment Tracking

- Based on the purchase worksheet the PO is prepared manually or processed through the system. Most of the time it is manual.
- In some cases PO is initiated by the 'buyer' in procurement department and routed to different authorities for approvals. In manual and non-integrated system environment a lengthy documentation process is followed for the approvals from different authorities.
- After necessary approvals, PO is printed and distributed to:
  - Planning & Procurement Departments (for record and follow-up).
  - Finance & Accounting (for information).
  - Central/Regional Warehouse (for necessary preparations and actions).
  - Master File in Procurement Department.
- Follow up procedure is carried out by the procurement department and shipment tracking reports are produced and forwarded to warehouses, stores, and F&A department.
- Shipping documents such as manifest, B/L and/or invoices are received and copies distributed to all concerned department for their information and reference.
- In case of import, shipment tracking carried out and necessary arrangements are made for custom clearance, transportation, etc.

Above-mentioned process in manual or non-integrated environment cause negative impact on production, sales and customer deliveries and normally lead to delays, duplication of works and unnecessary overheads.

Stage-III—Goods Receipt and Material Handling

– Goods arrived at the warehouse along with the Delivery Note (D/N) and other shipping documents:
  - Goods unloaded in inspection area in the warehouse.
  - Necessary inspection documents are manually produced.
  - Goods are sorted, counted, inspected and accepted/rejected.
  - Shortages, excess and damages are noted down manually.
  - If necessary, insurance claim processed or damaged goods returned to the supplier. Updating such information is never on time in manual or non-integrated environment.
  - Accepted goods labeled and bar coded.
  - Goods are shelved/binned.
  - 'Kardex' system is updated manually and always there are chances of human errors. Kardex logs are very important for the auditing and accuracy is highly essential.
  - Computer system is updated by keying individual stock update and this is a tedious job.
  - GRN (Goods Receipt Notes) processed from the system or manually produced and the printed copies distributed to:
    - Procurement for necessary follow-up
    - Finance & Accounting for AP, claim, etc.
  - In case of Finish goods purchase:
    - Warehouse transfers takes place in rush hours which normally cause chaos.

  - Transportation and loading takes place and on many occasions trucks are queuing-up due to the above-mentioned documentation process. This cause protracted deliveries and ultimately it lead to mismanagement and mishandling.
  - Customer deliveries take place hurriedly and normally cause errors, shortages, excess, damages, returns and un-updated backorder and ultimately inventory goes out of control.
- In case of RM (Raw Material) purchase:
  - GRN is submitted to Production, Planning, Floor-shop for update and its all duplication of work-process.
  - RM issue process takes place.
  - RM supply processed in production line.
  - Necessary acknowledgement is obtained.

Stage-IV —Finance & Accounting

– A new work and document flow starts in F&A. Most of the part of the process is carried out manually and on many occasions these process causes duplication works.
  - GRN versus PO is matched manually.
  - Follow-up with the suppliers commenced. Credit notes are obtained in case of damages and shortages and in case of excess stock debit notes are obtained.
  - In case of CIF shipment term, insurance claim processed against damaged goods.
  - Product cost is assessed by the cost accountant team. This is a tedious task in manual and non-integrated environment and high level of accuracy is critical.
  - Inventory valuation is updated manually.
  - Supplier invoices sorted out and terms verified for payment.
  - Supplier invoices matched with the GRN manually.

- Cash flow reports produced. In manual and non-integrated system environment it is not possible to produce timely cash-flow reports.
- Bill booking processed referring supplier invoices and cash-flow.
- If necessary credit notes or debit notes are updated in non-integrated system.
- In case of importation of goods the foreign currency calculation made manually and necessary adjustments are made in the books in view of currency fluctuation.
- Payment processed by AP Department after referring the payment due date and necessary terms conditions.
- Cheques are manually issued, dispatched and acknowledged.
- Payment process and cheque issuance are not efficient in manual or non-integrated environment because the time gap between manual cash-flow and the payment process.
- In case of large number of payment process a team of AP section tries to make timely payments and normally fails.
- Bank accounts updated manually and in manual or non-integrated environment it is not possible to link or relate the bank transactions with supplier invoice, GRN and PO.
- Bank statement received and manually reconciled. Again it is very tedious task.
- At the end, the following accounting tasks are carried out purely in manual environment and normally it is all duplication of works:
  - Necessary journals are produced from different systems.
  - Posting is made in General Ledger.
  - Necessary adjustments are made through JVE in case of the variance in freight, transportation invoices received later stage.

- Necessary executive reports are produced by different departments manually or by using different application software.
- Necessary follow-ups are made in case of open purchase order.

One can imagine the volume of work-flow and mandays involved and low level of accuracy expected in non-ERP environment. Now let's see what ERP software can do.

Scenario 1—Purchase Cycle (Process in ERP Environment)

Stage-I—PO Process and GRN in ERP Environment

- Necessary purchasing analysis reports can be produced by just pressing couple of keys in ERP system.
    - PO, GRN, AP, Inventory, Sales, MRP and WIP are all integrated modules in ERP system and the databases are stored with the concept of RDBMS (Relational database management system) which enable users to produce reports in any combinations or sets of criteria.
    - Apart from several in-built reports ERP system also allows to produce any kind of evaluation reports that is necessary to meet the challenges in competitive edge. These reports can be generated by anyone who is authorized to do so.
- Purchasing worksheet can be printed for individual stock item which will be based on predefined parameters such as safety-stock level, Min/Max Qty, Re-Order Qty, etc.
- Once an order is processed from PO module all the authorized persons having necessary access can query or monitor this order anytime from anywhere.
    - The process of PO approvals can be maintained in well organized form through requisition and approval functionalities available in PO module.
    - A world-class ERP solution offer the facilities in office automation/business intelligence module to pop-up the screen of authorized personnel whenever a PO is produced or edited or changed and printed.

- The last moment change can easily be carried out with necessary access authority.
- In view of the advancement, a world-class ERP can produce an XML file and can directly send it to the authorized personnel through internet/email, anywhere in the world.
- Using E-Commerce, B2B facilities in ERP-II the same PO can be sent directly to supplier online and it will be converted as sales order at supplier's end if he is also using ERP-II.
- Above facilities in ERP eliminate the duplication of works, reduce human errors, increases efficiency and reduce involvement of large number of manpower resources.

– Shipment Tracking is part of PO and Goods Receipts and it allows users to track shipment based on PO, stock item, supplier and shipment.

– ERP solution efficiently and cost effectively handle the GRN process. It allows bar-coding and reading facilities and two-stage-goods receipt option where the system is automatically updated after inspection, counting and sorting process.

- In-built stock receipt and goods inspection forms are available in the ERP system and it helps warehouse team to perform different stages of inspection and receipts.
- Authorized personnel from different departments can make queries, produced necessary reports and take necessary action on the GRN processed by a warehouse which in many cases remotely located away from F&A, Procurement and Planning departments in Head Office.
- Documentation, distribution and manual verification can be eliminated and the efficiency and productivity can be increased in view of the above facilities.

- Using hand-held PC, bar reader and coder, warehouse staff can do faster and accurate counting sorting and system updating.

Stage-II—F&A in ERP Environment

F&A department can utilize the PO/GRN information updated in the ERP system (as described above) and can process GRN match, bill booking and payment process by just pressing couple of keys and without incurring any duplication of works.

- Once the GRN is processed the following tasks are automatically carried out in ERP system with 100 per cent accuracy:
  - Stock availability and quantity-on-hand updated in warehouse.
  - Back-order qty. converted into order/ship quantity in sales order.
  - Job status updated by materials allocated in WIP.
  - Inventory cost updated.
  - Inventory valuation updated.
  - GRN is matched with PO and Payable is processed accordingly.
  - Cash-flow reports and report on allocation of funds are ready to be printed in Accounts Payable and Cash Module.

  There are several other reports that will be ready to produce efficiently and without requiring large number of personnel.

(In view of the above scenario a company can reduce minimum 5-7 per cent of total operating expenses and can increase efficiency in production, sales and customer deliveries.)

Scenario 2: Production Cycle

The tasks described in this Scenario are mainly related to manufacturing operations. In this scenario we will also discuss how material handling work is carried out and warehouse transfers of finished goods takes place in both non-ERP and ERP environment. Warehouse management and production planning are crucial aspects in manufacturing industries and unlike PO/GRN these functions are an internal process, except in the case of sub-contracting.

Production Cycle is categorized into following stages:

- Stage I, Planning & Designing
- Stage II, Estimation & Scheduling
- Stage III, Production & Warehouse Management
- Stage IV, Finance & Accounting (F&A)

Scenario 2—Production Cycle Process in non-ERP Environment

Stage-I—Planning & Designing

- The Planning Department initiates designing and structuring of the product and document the routings and different stages of the production process. Manual Bill of Materials are developed and documented. Breakdown of every single job is documented with step-by-step process of every individual component and parts being produced. They also prepare the breakdown of the cost of elements, components, materials, labors, tools and energy that are required to manufacture a product. In such a manual calculation it is difficult to maintain the efficiency and accuracy especially if the company is dealing in hundreds of different types of products and components. It requires lots of human resources and incurs heavy overheads. Consequently the production cost goes high, the profitability reduces and the overall operation and business growth is affected.
- Planning department makes necessary production schedule based on MRP, lead time and cycle time, sales forecast and customer delivery schedule, availability of resources and project and contracts. They use different methods to monitor and control the production schedule. The entire process goes through rigorous manual exercise and several key management players dedicate time to develop a viable production schedule.

- The draftsman in Engineering department produces necessary diagrams and charts manually or using CAD programs:
  - The designs are reviewed and approved by different departments including Production & Planning and Sales & Marketing. It goes through manual process and finally copies are distributed to the concern departments with a copy to master file.

Stage-II—Estimating & Scheduling

The cost accountants team calculates the costing of each element and work center separately and achieve estimated production cost. In case of sub-contracting, it is an additional operational process and a separate project plan and estimation is required and in manual and non-integrated environment it is difficult and time consuming to achieve appropriate estimation of production cost. Again efficiencies and accuracies cannot be maintained in view of the complexity, volume and size of the production.

- Production Schedule is defined based on different methods and techniques (discussed in next chapter). A production calendar is manually designed to monitor and control different stages of the production schedule.
- The costing and evaluation reports are sent to the Production Managers and Marketing Managers for review and comments. In turn, they produce necessary executive reports and evaluations for the review of higher management.
- Once the plan and costing is approved, the physical movements of the materials and goods take place.

Stage-III—Production & Warehouse Management

- Manual documentation and monitoring system in different work centers in WIP (Work-in-progress) takes place including the shop floor.
- The production managers initiate the process of material requisitions and obtain necessary materials from warehouse. Warehouse transfers and issue takes place

and the manual Kardex system (stock in and out log) is maintained.

- The jobs are created based on the approved planning, structure and routing:
  - Jobs may be created with or without bill of materials respectively for stocked or non-stocked items.
  - A manual job progress tracking system is used.
  - Necessary resources are allocated to every individual job and they could be materials, labour, machines, tools energy.
  - After going through different stages a job is completed and routed to next stage. Sometime multiple jobs are completed in one stage.
  - Once a job is completed then stated as closed.
- Different components and parts are produced in different work centers under different jobs incurring different types of costs. The cost factors such as time, labor, energy, raw materials and wastage are calculated on the basis of estimation made prior to the production and they are not based on actual value. It is not possible to achieve accurate value in manual environment. It is difficult for the production management team to take decisive action to control the production, to perform load-leveling, to slow down or speed up the production by optimally utilizing the resources such as labour, energy, raw material, etc.
- The finish goods are processed through several stages and finally reach to assembly and quality check section. Once again, lots of documentations, approvals and certification works are carried out before the finish goods reaches to packaging area.
- Necessary packaging, wrapping, labeling and bar coding works carried out either in manual or non-integrated system environment. This lead to several duplication of works where information and data updating carried out by different departments such as production, warehousing, inventory control, sales and marketing and F&A.

- The finish goods are transferred to relevant warehouses through warehouse transfer option. The finish goods are shelved and binned and are ready for sale.
- The production and planning manager produces the final report on the production costs, loss of time, waste of materials, cost of labors, material cost, energy and packaging expenses involved and submit it to F&A for their review and update.

Stage-IV—Finance & Accounting

The F&A department update the records and manually achieve the production cost. In non-integrated system environment the 'actual' production cost cannot be achieved. There are many reasons for this and the main reason is time synchronization. Always there are possibilities of delays in reporting actual production cost and by the time the calculated cost of goods is taken into consideration the goods are booked or sold. Such charges/discounts or reduction in production costs are adjusted/updated in the books at later stage. In the arena of cut-throat competition the sales and marketing department are much dependant on the calculation of individual deal profitability and if actual cost of the product or COS (Cost of goods sold) is not available at the time of sales invoicing then this may distort the profitability and may also cause loss sales.

Let's study how the above process works in ERP environment.

Scenario 2—Production Cycle (Process in ERP Environment)

Stage-I—WIP, BOM, MRP & Inventory in ERP

The Planning Department design and structure the products and their routings in BOM (Bill of Materials) Module. This is one time task and the information is editable, changeable and even they can be duplicated to create many similar structure and routings for hundreds of different products.

- The product designed and developed in any CAD software system can be stored in BOM module as bitmap file and can be linked with the relevant structure and routing process for future references and records.
- The product structures and their routings are linked with different work centers in WIP (Work-in-Progress modules) which in turn linked with MRP.
- ERP system allows users to define a company calendar and this enables the planning department to define different schedule for different production line including project outsourcing and subcontracting.
- MRP (Material Requirement Planning) module, linked with BOM, WIP, Inventory, Sales & Purchase modules, plays pivotal role in enabling inventory, warehouse and purchase process to act on timely basis and create real-time monitoring system. The MRP module creates different evaluations on availability of RM, lead time, cycle time, ATP (Available to Promise), etc. The estimated production cost is achieved without any difficulty.
- Due to seamless integration in ERP, jobs created in WIP are linked with Purchase and Sales modules hence these modules are automatically updated when the jobs are created or completed. When a job is issued the system automatically takes into consideration the structure and routing and assigns relevant elements to such structures and routings. The production manager uses different options to produce necessary evaluation reports for monitoring and instant decision-making. The whole or partial process can also be monitored by the authorized persons from the management team, F&A, Sales & Inventory departments. Based on the system security levels they can participate in the change/update/review or approval of jobs in the WIP.
- Authorities in Production and Planning department can take timely decisions on load leveling and can optimally utilize raw materials, labor and energy. They can take decisive actions with the instant involvement of

managements from sales & marketing, warehousing and executives to speed-up or slow down the production or divert the process when needed.

- Necessary documentations are instantly available by just pressing couple of keys. ERP system produces complex evaluation reports based on the pre-defined formulas, factors and universally approved accounting laws. In-built functionalities such as Job Card, Kardex, Cost explosion, ATP, Lead time, Cycle time eliminate duplication of works and increases levels of efficiencies and accuracy.
- The finish goods processed through several stages of production are ready for scheduled warehouse transfers, transportation and customer deliveries.
- In ERP-II, APS functions produce the simulation of shop floor and creates live scenario of production line. This enables the management to take necessary decisions on timely basis.

Stage-II—F&A in ERP

The F&A department can instantly generate necessary evaluation and valuation reports. The 'actual' production cost can be achieved and the finish goods cost is available in the warehouse at the time of sales booking. Actual COS is available to calculate the deal profitability.

- Following reports are instantly available:
  - Analytical reports on Production Capacity Plan and Schedule.
  - Gantt chart and analysis on allocation of resources in WIP; elapsed time, Capacity Planning, Scheduling and Load Leveling.
  - Analytical reports on scrap and waste of materials and productive and non-productive labor time.
  - WIP valuation.
  - Job Variance analysis.

- In view of the advancements in business concepts, ERP system offers following advanced functionalities which are not possible to acquire in manual, non-integrated or mixed environment:
  - Inventory Optimization
  - Co-products and by-products process
  - Advance Planning and Scheduling (APS)
  - Multiple Inventory Costing methods
  - Engineering Change Control (ECC)
  - Supply Chain Management (SCM) system
  - Product Life-cycle Management (PLM) system
  - Co-Product and By-product functionalities

(In view of the above scenario a company can save minimum 5-7 per cent in Inventory and production cost and can have positive impact on profitability and minimum 5-10 per cent increase in sales.)

Scenario 3: Sales Cycle

Scenario 3 will focus on different types of sales, pricing, deal profitability, customer delivery, transportation, Accounts Receivable Ageing, Credit Sales, Cash and Qty Discounts, etc. In order to create a complex scenario the credit sales process is taken into consideration rather than cash sales which is normally a simple process.

Production cycle is categorized into following stages:

- Stage I, Pre-Sales Process
- Stage II, Sales Process
- Stage III, Delivery and Transportation
- Stage IV, Finance & Accounting (F&A)

Scenario 3—Sales Cycle Process in non-ERP Environment

Stage-I—Pre-Sales Process

Sales and Marketing Department develops studies on market trend, sales forecast, product placement, competitive pricing, products' classification and consumer's behaviors and finally documents them for record and references.

- Planning and Purchase departments produce cost evaluation of the finish goods and/or raw materials.
- Based on the sales studies and production costing the Cost Accountants produces analysis on pricing and profit. Theses analysis are comprises of breakdown of manufacturing cost, list-price, MRP/retail prices, discounts, dealer net, sales commissions and other factors to reach estimated profit percentage.
- All the above studies and evaluation reports are manually produced in non-integrated system environment and later on reviewed and approved by different managers, senior managements and the executive directors. The approved documents are circulated manually to all the concern managers and the key players for record and reference.
- Based on the approvals, Sales & Marketing Managers define weekly, monthly and yearly sales targets and produces List Prices. The list prices could be of different types such as Distributors List Price, Retailers List Price, showroom list price and many a time list prices for different regions and branches.
- The above documentations are produced manually or using different application software and spreadsheet programs. These documents are distributed later to the sales-force, point of sales, showrooms, outlets and the channel partners.

Stage-II—Sales Process

The sales-force brings the different sales deals and as per the levels of discount authority and List-price they process quotation/sales booking/sales invoicing. During the process, lots of queries are made and communications and discussions take place back and forth in between the salesman, managers, accountants, warehouses and sometime the senior managements. These queries are mainly related to the pricing, customer credits, discounts, stock availability, delivery and transportations. Lots of ideas, information and decisions are captured and transferred internally during these queries and such information documented sometimes on slips or sometimes as 'internal memos'.

- Tracking past records such as customer sales, stock sales, invoicing and pricing are very time consuming and efficiency and accuracy cannot be guaranteed in manual or non-integrated environment.
- Finally, the sales invoice is printed with 1+4 or 5 copies for the following distribution:
  - The original + 1 copy goes to the customer whereas the copy is signed by the customer as acknowledgement and returned back to the warehouse and filed as POD (proof of delivery).
  - One copy goes to F&A for update, record and follow-up of receivables if the sale is a credit sale.
  - One copy goes to Inventory warehouse master.
  - One copy goes to the Sales/Customer Master.
- The entire process, as mentioned above in Stage I - II, is full of complications and in non-integrated system environment it does not work efficiently:
  - There are possibilities of duplicate sales, Debit Notes, wrong entries of number, date and value and wrong calculations.
  - There are possibilities of delay in customer deliveries and consequently cancellation of sales deals.
  - Many a time the customer credit limits are overridden without any controls and this may cause huge bad-debts, surplus in production, stock obsolescence and mismanagement of cash-flow.
  - Many a time, the selling prices are manipulated in order to achieve the sales target and this occurred despite proper manual controls on pricing and discounts.
  - It is not possible for production, planning, procurement, warehousing and inventory departments to coordinate

and harmonize the decision-making on sales and customer deliveries in non-ERP environment.

Stage-III—Delivery and Transportation

- Companies normally outsource and rely on external transportation services for customer deliveries and in the absence of an integrated system it is difficult to synchronize the timing of sales processing and timely customer deliveries. Companies who have in-house trucking and transportation operation face similar problems.
- In non-ERP environment, transportation management is manually carried out without any link with the sales, warehousing and inventory, documentations. Truck loading notes and Truck allocation documents are made and used manually and which normally lead to delays, inefficiency and inaccuracy in customer deliveries.
- There could be more complex process of sales invoicing where a delivery note (D/N) is printed and goods are delivered either by internal transportation department and/or external transportation service providers.
    - In some cases D/N is printed by the warehouse department and the sales invoicing is processed by the sales marketing department.
    - In some cases the sales invoices are hand-carried to the warehouse by the delivery man for customer deliveries.
    - In some cases the invoices are sent electronically or through EDI to warehouse to make necessary preparation for the customer deliveries.
    - In view of above, there could be complex workflow process in large warehouses where the D/N or invoice copy is submitted to the 'pickers' who brings the goods in inspection area and from there it goes to delivery area/loading area. The level of accuracy in counting and loading is critical in both the cases of internal or external transportation services.

- In case of value goods the important aspect is to check and verify different type of verifications of serial numbers, references and inventory valuation.
- In case of volume goods it is crucial to maintain the accuracy in counting and measurements and delivering right kind of goods. Always there are possibilities of return merchandising or part returned un-used. In non-integrated system environment these situations creates more complex scenario of taking back goods into inventory, crediting appropriate sales invoice and customer account.

– Let's assume the credit sales invoice is produced, goods are delivered and POD is obtained

Stage-IV—Finance and Accounting (F&A)

– Now, the F&A department follow-up the receivable from customers:

- Periodic customer statements are produced by F&A department.
- The 'collectors' team follow-up and collect the cheques.
- Either cheques are deposited directly in the bank or submitted to the 'payment process' section in F&A for necessary updates.
- In some cases the cheques are deposited directly into a centralized bank account by the local branch and the 'deposit slips' are sent to the F&A for necessary follow-up.
- Based on deposit slips the accounts staff either update the receivable against the relevant invoice or in some cases update these entries in the suspense A/c and wait for the bank statement and/or bank confirmations that the cheque is 'honored' and not 'bounced'.
- In case of parent and son customer account it is difficult to manually maintain such account and place necessary credit control. This process is very complex where the sales deal is closed at the customer's branch

and the payment is received from the customer's head office and the customer has several branches.

- In case of contractual sales and pricing it is very difficult to manually apply the credit control which should be in line with the customer delivery schedule.
- In case of large volume of credit customer base it is very difficult to apply credit control policies in manual or non-integrated system environment.
- Delay in AR is common phenomena in business worlds and manual or non-integrated system environment does not support the complexity of this process. It is really difficult to codify and maintain the customer's payment behavior or patent in non-integrated system environment and this normally lead to loss sales and doubtful bad-debts.
- PDC (Post dated cheque payments) is a common practice worldwide and manual or non-integrated system does not support efficiently high volume credit sales and PDCs.
- Once the cheques are cleared in the bank then accordingly the customer account, bank account, sales account, branch account and many other accounts are credited/debited in view of accounting implications.
- The AR ageing reports are produced and the follow-up is continued by the collectors or sales-force.

– Finally, AR Payments is received and customer account is updated.

– The entire process goes into loop and Stage IV is repeated. Efficiency and accuracy is at stake in the manual and non-integrated environment. Enormous amount of duplication of works occur and it cost unnecessary overhead expenses.

In non-integrated system environment the AR section in F&A prints and reprints customer statements obtaining necessary data information from different sources and monitor the due dates and produce payment reminders manually. The payment updating is also painstaking tasks in a situation where the 'RTs' or 'PRTs' (customer payment receipts) never get tallied with the customer statements and bank deposit slips and enormous amount of time is spent in non-integrated system environment to reconcile these documentations.

– At the end, thousands of man-hours are spent to produce different types of report by different entities in different departments.

Let's review the above process in ERP environment as described below:

Scenario 3—Sales Cycle (Process in ERP Environment)

Stage-I—Pre-Sales Process

– Sales & Marketing Department develop market studies, market trend, product placement, competitive pricing, product classifications and consumers behaviors and finally update the stock masters, customer masters and other relevant modules in integrated ERP system. This allows sales team to update/change anything they want and it maintains the event-log on such updates.

  • ERP solution provides total access controls based on levels of user authorities and the information will be accessible by planning, production, F&A and other departments and their staff for queries and reporting purpose.
  • For instance, the pricing evaluation report can be produced by the Cost Accountants based on the breakdown of manufacturing cost, list-price, MRP/ retail prices, discounts, dealer net, sales commissions and other factors to reach estimated profit percentage. Meanwhile, the executives can produce necessary reports to take appropriate decisions on high levels in regard to price calculation factors.

– ERP solutions allows predefined multiple selling pricing, discount levels, qty discounts, sales target, salesmen commission, customer credit limits and payment terms, delivery schedule and can place necessary controls on pricing and discount authorities. This eliminates duplication of works and increases level of efficiency and accuracy that is essential for the growth of the company.

- CRM module in ERP-II facilitates users to develop customer relationship in an organized form. This allows online customer support services and make customers feel as part of the business process.
- SFA (Sales Force Automation) module enables the sales team to participate in the operational process anywhere away from the office.
- POS (Point of Sales) module enables remote outlets, showrooms and warehouses to efficiently process instant sales and handle cash and online credit cards payment process.
- Due to the seamless integration in ERP, the sales process is linked with Inventory, WIP, Purchase, MRP and BOM. This provides real-time 360 degree operational view and helps instant decision-making in the entire operational process. A sales order or sales invoice processed in the ERP system automatically updates stock, allocation/back-order, job in WIP/BOM and MRP/Purchase requirements.

Stage-II—Sales & Delivery Process

Different types of sales leads/deals brought by the sales-force can instantly be updated in the system and based on pre-defined factors the quotations and sales order can be processed while the other authorities can monitor and control the pricing, discount and delivery elements. The sales process can go through automatically without duplication of works and a quotation can be converted into sales invoicing. There are different stages where a complete process cycle need to be performed especially the queries on pricing discounts, report on deal profitability, report on production pipeline, reports on stock movements, queries on stock availability, credit availability, transport availability, sales scheme and delivery schedule, and all the authorized users from different department can participate online in this process.

- During above-mentioned cycle process, on one hand ERP system restricts unauthorized process and decision-making and on the other hand it allows authorized entities and decision-makers to release or override the controls in ERP system. For instance, a sales deal is at the credit check stage and system is not allowing the process to go ahead as the customer's credit limit is over and this require special authority to override this control. In this situation, the salesman/sales administration can simply send a message, being in the ERP system, to the authority to approve/override the control and release the sale. The authority will receive a pop-up message on his screen, use his/her password, put some comments and release the sale.
- With the help of modern technologies, ERP system produces individual/batch printout of sales invoices or delivery notes. It can be printed locally and/or in remote warehouses in DDN WAN environment and if necessary it can be dumped periodically through EDI system. The business intelligence module can pop-up the screen of warehouse user and inform them well on time about the printing of invoices and delivery notes and if necessary the entire customer delivery schedule.
- It is not necessary to produce several copies of invoice and delivery notes. In ERP-II environment the POD (proof of delivery) can be obtained online and one original for customer and one copy as POD is sufficient for record and reference purpose.
- On the basis of POD, F&A and other departments can follow the next process without incurring any duplication of work. The AR and credit control department can follow-up the next cycle of producing reports, printing customer statements, bank deposit slips, post dated cheques update, cheques in suspense a/c, cheques clearance, etc. A world-class ERP offers automatic bank re-conciliation facilities to eliminate the manual verifications and reconciliation of banks accounts.

Stage-III—Finance and Accounting (F&A)

At the end, necessary 'As of now' evaluation reports can be printed by just pressing couple of keys. Some of the essential reports are QOH (Qty-on-hand), GIT (goods in transit), Fast movers and slow movers of the stock, Goods in dispatch or loading area, AR ageing, Inventory Ageing, Cash-flow, customer performance, deal profitability, sales and profit analysis on different types of products, regions and branches. All these reports are management decision-making tools and it also helps to place an accurate monitoring system in the operation. Seamlessly integrated system enables management to take corrective measures in purchase and production planning.

(In view of the above scenario a company can increase minimum 5-10 per cent sales and also save additional 2-5 per cent in operating expenses.)

In order to have a comprehensive view of the above three complex scenarios you may once again review the diagrams (Figs. 1.1 - 1.3) and compare it with the ERP modulation and integration diagrams (Figs. 1.4 - 1.6).

Conclusion

In general, the above scenarios portray how ERP solution can make positive impacts on production cycle, sales performance, efficiency and accuracy in operations. It also indicates how ERP solution will directly/indirectly increase the profit by 10-15 per cent, sales by 10-15 per cent and save inventory, production and operating expenses by 10-15 per cent. The conclusion is illustrated below in a comparative operating statement summary. It illustrates that due to ERP solution the sale is increased by 10 per cent, production cost or COS is reduced by 5 per cent, operating expenses are reduced by 5 per cent and consequently the Operating Profit is increased from 8 per cent to 18 per cent. The illustration is based on extremely minimum calculation and could be more than what is calculated below. It constitutes to a total of 2.36 Mil as an additional profit in first year of ERP implementation. Small and medium size companies can easily go for a world-class ERP by investing maximum 2.5 Mil and within a year time will have tangible benefits/ROI. It is worth noting that the benefits/profits and ROI increases as per the size of the organization, larger the organization higher the profit/ROI in ERP.

Non-ERP Environment:			ERP Environment:	
Net Sales	20 Mil	⇧	Net Sales	22 Mil
COS (Prod. Cost) 45%	9 Mil	⇩	COS (Prod. Cost) 40%	8.8 Mil
Operating Expenses 25%	5 Mil	⇩	Operating Expenses 20%	4.4 Mil
Other Expenses 22%	4.4 Mil	=	Other Expenses 22%	4.84 Mil
Operating Profit	1.6 Mil	⇧	Operating Profit	3.96 Mil
Opr. Profit %	8%	⇧	Opr. Profit %	18%

Fig. 1.7

One may say that the above calculation looks good on paper and practically it is very difficult to achieve. Yes it is difficult but not impossible and we all know that increasing profits and sustaining business growth is not easy either. Companies take different measures, use various tools and apply different methods to achieve these goals. ERP software is the best tool and a tested method which enable companies to achieve these objectives. It is true that it is difficult to successfully implement an ERP solution and it is more difficult to optimally utilize it. However, let's evaluate ahead in this book how to minimize or eliminate such difficulties and ensure cent per cent successful ERP implementation.

There are following non-tangible benefits one can realize only after successful implementation of a world-class ERP:

Brand goodwill in the market and customer satisfaction

Increase in quality control

Trust of shareholders

Organized and harmonious work environment.

In addition to above-mentioned benefits the extended enterprise version called ERP-II offers everything that a modern business requires. Let's study in next chapter what extended enterprise solution or ERP-II is all about and how it supports Modern business concepts.

CONCLUSION

We have learnt in Chapter 1 important aspects of ERP software solution and how one can be benefited out of it. We have learnt in this chapter the evolution process of the ERP and have noticed that the ERP evolution is an ongoing process, therefore, it is important to know the next step in the ERP evolution process which is discussed ahead in the Chapter called "ERP-II".

ERP-II

2

Introduction

This chapter is supplementary to previous chapter and is concisely focus on the characteristics of ERP-II. For elaboration purpose, we have catagorized ERP-II into 5 major categories (1) ERP (as discussed in previous chapter), (2) E-commerce, (3) APS, (4) Business Analytics, and (5) SOA, the most recent advancement in ERP.

This chapter talks about the significance of modern business and the role played by ERP-II to meet the modern business requirements.

This chapter also illustrates different diagrams enabling you to understand the system architecture used in different elements in ERP-II. You will find in this chapter that primarily ERP-II evolves around the compatibility and advancement of ERP solutions with Internet and Web technologies.

Modern Business Concepts

Modern business concepts played pivotal role in development and growth of ERP solutions and ERP market. Rapid development in technology, change in global economy and change in consumer's behavior making it necessary for businesses to think and perform strategically in order to remain competitive and profitable. In compare to the traditional business environment the modern business environment is getting more complex day by day. At one end every business aspect evolves around customer satisfaction and at the other end the manufacturers and suppliers would like to have accessibility and total control on the supply-chain. Market share is much dependent on better customer service and long-term customer relationship be it end-users or channel partners. This required business pundits to think beyond ERP solution and that is how the concept of Extended Enterprise Solution or ERP-II emerged.

Modern business concepts demand total integration of five pillars of the extended enterprise solution emerged as ERP-II. ERP-II opens up possibilities of increase in efficiencies and productivity with respect to real-time decision-making in purchase, sales, production and Supply Chain Management (SCM).

The following are the five pillars of the extended enterprise solution which provides total integration in ERP-II:

1. ERP (Enterprise Resource Planning)
2. E-Commerce:
   a. Web-enablement
   b. B2C (Business to Clients)
   c. B2B (Business to Business)
   d. CRM (Customer Relationship Management)
3. APS (Advance Planning and Scheduling)
4. Business Analytics
5. SOA (Service Oriented Architecture)

1. ERP (Enterprise Resource Planning): Discussed in previous chapter.

2. E-Commerce: E-commerce means all type of online business transactions or transactions that carried out electronically in online environment. This includes the complete SCM (Supply Chain Management) through B2B & B2C and Customer relationship through CRM systems. The following diagram illustrates a complete system architecture how E-commerce works.

(a) Web-enablement

Emergence of Internet, WWW, dot.com and mobile/cell phone technologies have changed the landscape of the IT and caused incredible impact on the business automation system. These technologies have revolutionized the whole information management system across the world and companies started using these technologies to boost their business, explore new

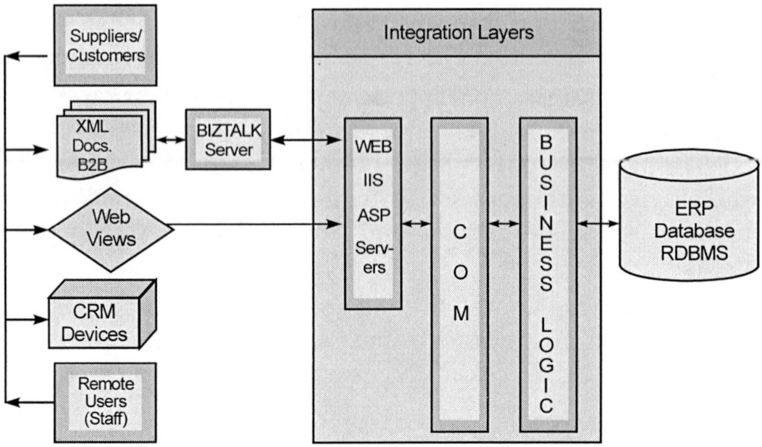

Fig. 2.1: E-Commerce System Architecture

avenues and move forward with strategic advancements. User friendly web browsing features attracted computer users in the corporate world and even the mainframe users migrated from terminal system to PC system. More and more personal computers, notebooks/laptops, handheld PC, pocket PC, Mobile/ Cellular phones are used in the corporate worlds and new business concepts and trends are introduced such as Sales Force Automation (SFA) system, Mobile-commerce, Contact Management systems, Wireless Networking system, Mobile User Access system, Universal Access system, Online ordering and so on.

In view of above, it was essential that ERP manufacturer enhance their system and create compatibilities with emerging technologies. It was during 2001-2003 when ERP venders introduced web-enabled features along with B2B (Business to Business) and B2C (Business to client). Web application interface was developed by the ERP manufacturers using ASP and .Net technologies. The user interface was designed to meet screen customization and to suit user requirements.

Web-based applications are easy to use and can be accessed from anywhere by any user who has Internet Browser facility on his/her PC, Laptop, Cellular Phone, handheld device, etc. The functionality is very simple and by using any web browser the users can access ERP system without finding any difference in look and feel. The accessibility and security controls are administered from the central ERP server.

Imagine a salesman sitting at airport or railway platform with a notebook on his lap or a Cellular phone in his hand and making real-time online queries on stock in production or stock in pipeline, quantity-on-hand, discounts and list prices. In another scenario, imagine a team of engineers working in a mine accessing on to the BOM, WIP and MRP modules through ERP server and making necessary queries and performing transactions. Such an environment was a dream couple of decade back in corporate world. This could now be achieved easily by web-enabled ERP system or ERP-II.

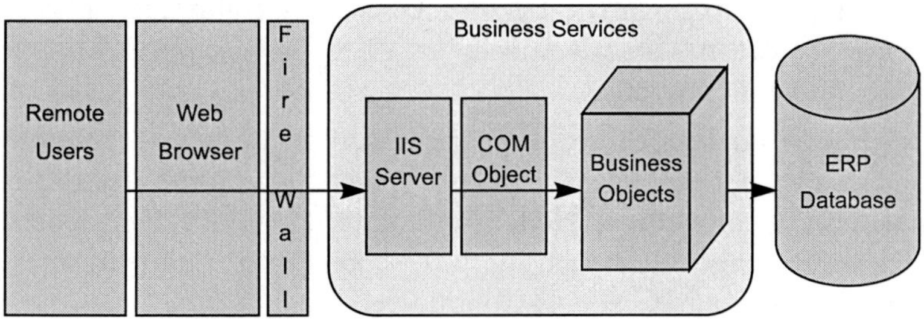

Fig. 2.2: Web-enabled Application Architecture

A website serves up an HTML form, created from Active Server Page (ASP) code. This form is rendered within a web browser on user's laptop/pocket PC or cell phone. Users can make any query or even perform online transaction and the browser sends the request back to the IIS server running ASP code, which in turn loads the appropriate COM based component and give users an access on the business objects. The ASP code delivers Wireless Markup Language (WML) code back to the notebook or mobile phone and the users can see the results in the form of options on their laptop/notebook/pocket PC/cell phone.

The COM specification is widely supported by the industry and most of the world-class ERP products are COM based and therefore allows remote access on the business objects. ERP-II makes extensive use of XML (Extensible Markup Language) as a means of exchanging data, either by exchanging documents between companies over the Internet, or as a messaging mechanism between different types of applications. A component based framework is provided by the ERP venders that makes integration to the core ERP system. In a nutshell, the product opens ERP interface to grant access to a remote user.

(b) B2C (Business to Clients)

B2C stands for "business-to-client(s)" and applies to any business or organization that sells its products or services to consumers or end-user over the Internet. In addition retailers, B2C includes services such as online banking, travel services, aviation, online auctions, hospitals, health and real estate, etc. Even small flower shopkeepers, medical stores and grocery outlets participate in the B2C process. B2C technology played major roles in the advancement of SCM (Supply Change Management) system.

Retail businesses although operates on low profit margin and could be low value business however the volume size of the business is enormous. Hence, manufacturers and medium to large enterprises are planning to enter into retail business capitalizing on B2C and E-Commerce.

SCM is the centrifugal point of the manufacturing and distribution industries and B2C coupled with the core functionalities of ERP solutions offers total SCM and e-fulfilment. Manufacturers looking for a total solution that allows them to track record of every individual piece of product, from its raw material purchase to manufacturing and from channel partner's shelves to the end-user's usage and records of warranty and after sales support system. Monitoring and controlling all these process introduced the concept of PLM (Product life cycle management system) and it became the integral part of B2C E-commerce.

How a world-class ERP-II solution supports E-Commerce requirements of its clients is described earlier in this chapter. ERP-II, with its compatibility with the .Net and COM technology, allows users to design and attached necessary applets, XML documents and accessibility controls where the end-user/

consumer can access to the required information. The information available in ERP database can be utilized to provide necessary access to the end-user/consumer via E-Commerce system architecture as explained in the diagram.

While going ahead with B2C one should ensure that he/she has a business plan that includes profitability not too far down the road. Opening an e-commerce site is not a difficult task but getting visitors to the site is major task. Whether they buy something or not is what determines if you win. Therefore, large investments need to be planned to compete the fierce battle of market competition. For example, hundreds of travel agents worldwide have personalized their website and also rented space in other renowned WWW sites so that more and more visitors view their schemes and get attracted to their offers. The site must have increasing number of visitors and to achieve this, different associations with different products are required in the world of WWW.

B2C to great extent depends on reaching millions of end-users through successful Ad and Promo. Like other business tools it is all about how fast one can make presence in the market and how long one can survive in the market. B2C businesses operate on high risk and it is a long-term investment and the success is depended on many factors as discussed and explained in above paragraphs.

(c) B2B (Business to Business)

B2B stands for Business to Business automation solution normally provides through Internet and Intranet communication system.

It is companies buying from and selling to each other online. But there's more to it than purchasing. It evolved to encompass supply chain management as more companies outsource parts of their supply chain to their trading partners.

B2B services can be obtained either through Public or Private Exchange. Public exchanges are owned by industry consortia or independent investors and have their own boards of directors. Though each exchange sets its own rules, they are generally open, for a fee, to any company that wants to use them. Private exchanges are run by a single company for doing business exclusively with established suppliers and customers (although the systems that support it may be outsourced).

B2B e-commerce can save or make your company money. Some ways companies have benefited from B2B e-commerce includes managing inventory more efficiently, adjusting more quickly to customer demand, getting products to market faster, cutting the cost of paperwork reigning in rogue purchases and obtaining lower prices on some supplies.

One of the risk factor in B2B is failing to understand its true and long-term requirements in context with the nature of business, products, ROI. One of the major dependency is it really takes time to establish full-fledge B2B e-commerce especially if hardware compatibility is not met and necessary technological awareness are not created among the staff.

B2B is all about sharing data between trading partners. For instance, a sales order received through e-mail into your back office system may prompt a request to process a PO. Hence, you have a sales order received and a PO going out to the supplier. It is necessary to make proper information available online with easy access and in user-friendly manner that too keeping the necessary security controls. The most time-consuming aspect of building B2B systems is mapping your business processes to those of your trading partners. The major dependency is to make the trading partners and associates ready to do business online.

B2B becomes very productive tools in a situation where a modern company and its trade partners utilize the DFM (Document Flow Manager) technology. DFM allows easy exchange of documents such as sales and purchase orders and forms a key part of facilitating collaborative commerce. It allows you to automate the document flow as documents can be retrieved automatically and instantly as they electronically arrive at a company. Incoming documents in XML format can be tracked and posted directly into the ERP-II. Documents can be transformed from one format to another using DFM. The DFM provides an automated global business-to-business and business-to-consumer gateway.

You may refer the above diagram 'e-Commerce System Architecture' to understand the technical setup of B2B.

At the end of this topic, it is necessary to distinguish between B2B electronic process and EDI (Electronic Data Interchange). Normally people mix up B2B with EDI, EDI is an outdated concept and unfortunately couldn't fulfilled its promise for a variety of reasons, not least of which is the cost of implementation and maintenance, and typically remains the domain of larger enterprises. We have discussed the significance of EDI in previous chapter.

(d) CRM (Customer Relationship Management) System

CRM stands for Customer Relationship Management. In my personal opinion, CRM is not merely a customer relationship management but an overall relationship management between everyone involves in the business. CRM somehow enables a company to develop, strengthen and manage the relationships between every entity that involved in business process and this includes end-users, customers, channel partners, employees, managers, executives and suppliers.

The emergence of computer hi-tech, E-commerce, Internet and Collaborative commerce brought significance change in customer's behavior and consequently company started looking for a solution to have mass customization of customer related activities as discussed above.

CRM is a strategy used to learn more about customers' needs and behaviors in order to develop better relationships with them. After all, good customer relationships are at the heart of business success. There are many technological components to CRM, but thinking about CRM in primarily technological terms is a mistake. The more useful way to think about CRM is as a process that will help bring together lots of pieces of information about customers, sales, competitors, marketing effectiveness, responsiveness and market trends.

CRM software solutions are designed to allow companies to quickly put their customers at the center of their business. The concept is to create a company-wide database of every customer, vendor, prospect and anyone else with whom you do business. By sharing information about your business contacts throughout all of the departments of your company-marketing, sales, service, mail fulfilment and accounting—you can improve your customers' experience and maximize your sales opportunities. The most common approach to becoming customer focused is to invest in CRM software. CRM programs typically consist of different software modules for each department.

The total activities related to customer sales and services may be small or large in volume or may be of poor or high quality depends on the existing resources, infrastructure, business methodologies and most importantly automation environment. The customer related activities epitomizes as follows:

- Marketing; exploring, visiting, advertising, etc.
- Communication means: Telephone, correspondences, Internet.
- Maintaining Customer profile of different types of customers.
- Categorization: Distributor, Reseller, POS, End-user.
- Periodic evaluation by performance, relationship and behavior.
- Terms & Conditions: Selling Price, Delivery, Discount, Credit, Contracts.
- Transactions: Sales, Service, Campaign, Contract.
- Special Events: Campaign, Seminar, Conference, Promotion, Launch.
- Reports on: Statements, Credit, Ageing, Product, Price.
- Maintaining history and producing analysis.

The following are the minimum pre-requisite for CRM solution:

A. EAI (Enterprise Application Interface) or ERP environment (preferably).

B. Web-based or Web-enabled Applications.

C. RDBMS, Historical database, and Data Warehousing.

D. Communication Channels: Networking, CTI & IVR.

E. Business Intelligence Applications.

Planning for CRM:

(a) Bring awareness and study customer behavior.

(b) Requirement definitions and Proposals.

(c) Evaluation and Software selection (Customized or off-the-shelf).

(d) Implementation through phase based Project Management.

(e) Go-live CRM solution, maintenance and future upgrading.

The idea of CRM is that it helps businesses use technology and human resources to gain insight into the behavior of customers and the value of those customers. Once CRM solutions are properly implemented and optimally utilized that it surely will give the following benefits:

- Develop, enhance and maintain quality customer services.
- Develop, increase and maintain efficiency in staff.
- Provide necessary information access to the customers online.
- Creates more customer bases.
- Obtain customers feedback and place necessary controls.
- Increase efficiency in customer deliveries.
- Monitor close market competitions and have instant evaluation.
- Provide fast and efficient Management Reporting.
- Enhance management decision-making.
- Increase productivity, sales and profit and reduce cost.
- Create Global links with Supply Chain Management System.
- Make customer feel as part of the business.

Generally, CRM solutions are a costly solution. It requires corporate cultural to change and sometimes leads to major re-engineering in the company. Most of the Risk and Dependencies in CRM solutions are same as in ERP solutions.

The great amount of risks exists in implementing CRM if efficient and skilled staff are missing, if compatible hardware, LAN, WAN and communication setup is not available. However, the risk is minimized if a good ERP system and organized and cultured environment exists. Companies planning for CRM must realize that CRM is basically a front-end business tool and need powerful and well-organized back-end Accounting and Logistic system or database which normally exists in a good ERP environment.

The biggest dependency in implementing CRM solutions lies in bringing awareness among the customers and employees. It demands a change in the customer's operational process not whole but to certain extent and which initially causes lots of hassles, however, once the understanding is developed and necessary awareness is created it works fine.

Most of the world-class ERP solutions offer best of breed CRM system fully integrated with the core functionalities with the ERP system. Any company using ERP for past couple of years can easily get ready for CRM system. For technical aspect you may refer the following diagram.

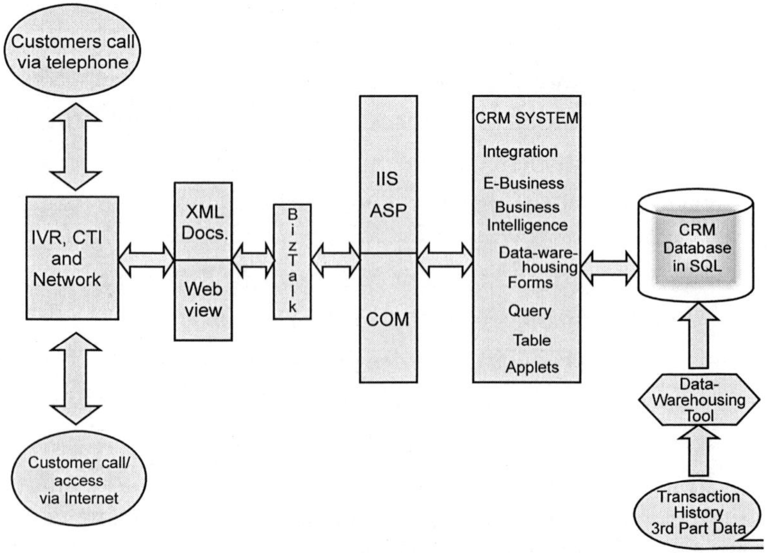

Fig. 2.3: Typical CRM System Structure

3. APS (Advance Planning & Scheduling): APS provides outstanding facilities for shop floor in manufacturing. In fact manufacturers have been desperately looking for a real-time monitoring system that can eliminate the unpredictability commonly encountered by the manufacturers in the midst of production. Although, there were different features available in earlier versions of ERP solutions which have been utilized for scheduling, monitoring and controlling product quality however, these functions were not able to create and provide real-time picture of the shop floors.

APS is a module dedicated for shop floor. It provides management with a comprehensive, real-time view of the shop floor in any dynamic manufacturing environment. APS provides a graphical image of the shop floor in real-time and measures productivity accurately before even the product reaches to the packaging area as finish goods. Different ERP solutions offer different functionalities in APS module. Generally, APS is comprises of the core functionalities such as (1) Planning, (2) Designing, (3) Scheduling, (4) Tracking and (5) Evaluating. Although these functionalities are very much part of the MRP module in any ERP solutions however, the difference between MRP annd APS is that MRP creates factual scenario annd APS creates actual scenario.

Planning

Planner assists users in planning workload against available capacity. Capacity is derived from the number of available machines and its working hours. Load is calculated using the standard structures and routes.

Designing

It allows users to create integration with CAD systems and maintain records for the design change. It allows users to attach the necessary production details with the product designs and archive them for reference purpose.

Scheduling

Scheduler allows individual manufacturing unit to be scheduled independently with user-defined rules. It generates

Gantt charts to show a time-based view of scheduled operations for the machines in each unit. Additional requirements of labors, operators, equipments and tools are shown when calculating the schedule. The Gantt chart create live scenario even in a situation if any changes occur in demand and the resources.

Tracking

Tracker is a touch-screen compatible, graphical shop floor application that supplies operators with current work to list. It also supplies a list of required materials and any text or diagrams associated with each job.

Evaluating

Evaluation functions allow users to produce necessary evaluation in data and graphical formats and produce necessary reports and documents.

4. **Business Analytics:** We have assessed earlier in this book how ERP software solution has gone through >35 years evolution process and reached to extended enterprise solution and ERP-II. On one hand this has provided lots of facilities to efficiently manage the business and increase the productivity and on the other hand it has created enormous amount of complex databases. Consequently, this has opened several new avenues and new dimensions for business analysis and business decision-making process.

In view of above, it was essential to find out or develop a tool that can handle, maintain and utilize the complex databases. The most important task was to convert the data storage system into data warehousing system and then find out the tool which will facilitate users to process online analysis. That is how the concept of 'Data warehousing' and OLAP (Online Analytical Processing) came into existence.

Although, the above situations led to another problem i.e. 'data-traffic jam/bottleneck' in WAN environment, however, now this issue can be resolved in view of the broadband and high bandwidth DDN (Digital Data Networking) communication system.

ERP-II offers BA (Business Analytical) module that provides necessary facilities to create different types and sizes of 'cubes' (small data warehouses). The BA functions are very easy to use and can be linked with any good report writer program or even with commonly used MS Excel™ spreadsheet. It can also be linked with any 3rd party database or RDBMS.

BA works on the basis of FTP (File Transfer Protocol) technology and converts data to and from ASCII file to any RDBMS system. BA allows data filtering and purifications and transforms the sets of databases into mini data-warehouse cubes through OLAP. It allows users to apply necessary analytical rules and these rules and definitions can be stored for future use.

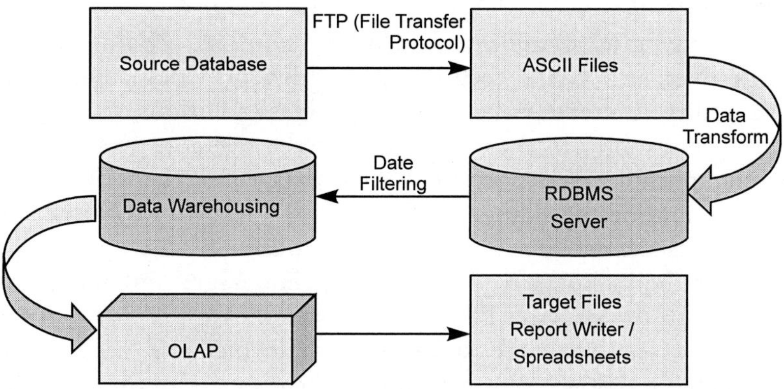

Fig. 2.4

Let's take a look how it was difficult to produce a report on 100 different stock items, their purchases and stock movements, sales and delivery movements, their actual cost and price on which they were sold, their exact profit and profit percentage. It is really difficult to drill down into the complex transactional databases with hundreds of data relationships to remember, map them and then create 3-4 different reports and transform them into desired spreadsheets and tables and finally produce the required analytical reports which will be based on several mathematical factors and formulas. It is a rigorous exercise and very time consuming too and only possible to be performed on stand alone PC system and not in LAN or WAN environment.

Now with the help of BA, the above exercise can be carried out by pressing couple of keys and the required report is ready in WAN environment within no time. The following diagram illustrates how Business Analytics works.

5. SOA (Service Oriented Architecture): SOA is the next evolutionary step in business automation and extended enterprise software solution. It is a business driven IT structure based on the creation of business software components that function as services on a computer network. Gartner analysts predict that by 2008, 60 per cent of enterprises will use SOA as their "guiding principle" when creating applications and processes. SOA reduces the risk and cost in the business world where business expansions, optimal utilization of resources and globally distributed operations are the keys to profitable service delivery.

Today, most of the world-class ERP solutions are compatible with .Net and COM technologies which provides companies the ability to create custom made business solutions, especially those solutions which caused 'gaps' in the business process due to change in business concepts, expansions, rules, methodologies, culture and/or the change in HRMS. SOA allows ERP users to develop necessary business module or business object with the help of their choice of programming language, and integrate them with the existing ERP system. This means companies can build services that are specific to their business needs and accessible to other systems and applications. Companies can create any programs or systems that integrate other programs, share data with other applications, communicate through e-mail and are available wherever there is an Internet based connection.

A Case Example: A pharmaceutical group in India who has been using a world-class ERP system for past several years, recently planned to extend their SCM system to their distributors and channel partners. The group has arranged a distribution system developed in .Net and integrated without any problems with their existing ERP system. The distribution system is installed at >15 different sites of the 'super distributors' and at another 10 sites of the channel partners. All these sites are remotely located. The distribution system is successfully integrated with the ERP RDBMS with necessary controls. This would have not been possible a decade back when the concept of SOA was not existed and the ERP users were reluctant to have such integrations as it was a costly and risky IT affairs and was not possible without the involvement of ERP venders or their developers.

CONCLUSION

So far we have learnt the basics of ERP and ERP-II and how a company can utilize the power of ERP and ERP-II for its growth, productivity and profitability. It is necessary that we find out the problem and issues in ERP software and they are discussed in next chapter.

Issues and Concerns

3

Introduction

In this chapter we have discussed, argued and clarified the doubts, issues and misunderstanding about the ERP solution. Like any other valuable commodities ERP too has issues mainly on its cost and we have made necessary arguments and justification and left the decision on the reader.

We have also discussed the impact of business process re-engineering and issues such as concurrent users, 3rd party integration and continuous enhancement in ERP functionalities as well as the increase in total cost of ownership.

Is There Any Disadvantage in ERP Solutions?

According to past studies and surveys, as such there is no major disadvantage reported in ERP software solution. However, there are few concerns, issues and misunderstanding people have about ERP solutions and they are discussed below:

ERP Demands BPR?

Although we are focusing in this book largely on ERP and not on BPR, however, it would be in the fitness of the subject matter to review the necessary aspects of BPR and its relationship with ERP. People say that ERP implementation compels the buyers to go for BPR (Business Process Re-engineering). In fact BPR has always been a controversial topic in business world. As such there is no conflict between ERP and BPR and both have their significance and are different from each other. I do agree that some high-end ERP solutions may compel a company for BPR and a positive change in corporate culture as a result of

BPR is always good for the growth. It is necessary to determine well on time that at what scale the BPR is required.

BPR or re-engineering of business process means great level of changes in human resources, organizational structure, workflow and operating cost, etc. It is necessary that we understand ERP solution as a tool for BPR and not *vice versa*. BPR could possibly be a requirement and part of ERP implementation process. This is one angle of looking at ERP & BPR and another angle is BPR is the first step that comes prior to ERP implementation.

Following explanations and scenarios clarify that BPR and ERP is two separate processes, two separate tools and methods that do not create any conflicts or inflict anything on each other.

It has been seen that many companies who have already implemented ERP system and have been using it for past several years now found the need for BPR. One of such company is a large group of companies in Middle East who have been using the 'Rolls Royce' of ERP package for past more than 10 years. The BPR requirement was crucial in the company due to vast business expansion plan and acquisitions and it was conducted by an international consulting firm. It was successfully carried out and existing ERP package played pivotal role in the success of BPR process.

Another example is a company who has been operating in non-ERP mainframe environment recently gone through ISO certifications and simultaneously carried out BPR.

In large size companies BPR may be essential while planning for successful implementation and optimum utilization of an ERP solution. The necessity to go for BPR can be determined during the RDS Phase as to what scale the BPR is required. Sometime it may cause confusion whether to restructure the business process first or implement the ERP, however, this is all part of good RDS and project management planning discussed ahead in this book.

BPR could be a 'stitch-in-time'

During our consultation services in 2003, we have witnessed a large multi-national breweries group in India decided to go for phase based and priority based ERP implementation solution and successfully achieved it during the business expansions and acquisitions process. Three-year ERP implementation plan was made taking into consideration that at the later stage BPR will be required. In this situation the MNC did not bother of BPR and focused on business development and gradual ERP implementation process. In the midst of the business expansion and ERP implementation they realized the need to have corporate culture transformation. Predominantly their business philosophy was the Internationalization of the company. Since the ERP plan was a phase based and priority based implementation, therefore, the BPR process successfully carried out at later stage without any conflict with the ERP implementation.

Nowadays, many local and international companies are going through the process of mergers and acquisitions and BPR is imperative despite the fact that the company is well organized and has been using ERP solutions for past several years.

The most painful and risk bearing element in BPR is to bring changes in the workforce. Companies usually make changes in workforce without BPR however at the time of ERP implementation it can best be justified.

In BPR, it is necessary to distinguish between the change and downsizing (It should be down-right-sizing). In corporate world the BPR is mistakenly considered as an alarm for 'layoffs', 'firings' salary reduction, etc. Therefore, most of the prestigious business groups hire consulting firm to professionally carry out the re-engineering process. Ultimately BPR brings change and in modern business world this could be 'corporate cultural change'. In business consultation, recommendation of an ERP solution could be one of the outcomes for BPR.

ERP Inflicts Down-Sizing?

The term 'downsize' applies to many things or let's say anything that is larger than the requirements. It applies to Information Technology, workforce, operations, sites, plant tools, machineries and all other resources and sometime it relates to the business as a whole.

Let's take this on face value that ERP solution reduces the size of the workforce for the very simple reason that it eliminates the duplication of works and to some extent unwanted work process. However, a good organization and management knows how to utilize the workforce and increase the productivity in long run and they normally do not drastically reduce the size of the manpower. Organizations normally retain the 'performers' and utilize them in other areas as per their capabilities, however, some organizations replace the 'non-performers' with 'performers'. Shuffling, reshuffling, transferring, training of workforce, planning and developing a long-term 'capital intellectual' has been considered as concrete approach of workforce re-engineering.

Infrastructural downsizing could be another element in BPR. Downsizing in IT infrastructure could be recommended during the time of ERP project planning. Advent of PC technologies have compelled companies to think about downsizing where many medium size companies realize that in the name of business automation they have been investing more than what is necessary. In fact, many companies have made their automation setup much lager than the size of their business setup. Especially, before the advent of PC, some of the highly profitable small and medium size companies opted for mainframe and mini computers with in-house customized software solutions and ended up in spending millions. What they have spent must have justified but what not justified was the ongoing and increasing maintenance and service costs in accordance with the productivity. It was just impossible for such companies to 'jump the gun' and overnight plan for ERP. For them it was adding an 'elephant' to existing fleet. Hence, many such companies have decided to go for a world-class ERP with system down-right-sizing and many are still finding themselves in dilemma what to do with their existing mainframe and mini computers.

The Cost is a Major Disadvantage in ERP?

People may say that the ERP cost is the biggest disadvantage but then it is the economic term 'demand' that applies on ERP purchase. ERP too is a commodity and all that matter is the 'demand' (Necessity + Power to Purchase + Willingness to pay). The necessity for ERP is justified in previous chapter. The purchasing of ERP is discussed in next chapter.

ERP costing is based on number of users and number of modules selected by the company. Other aspects of ERP costing are discussed subsequently in the chapter 4 that will enable you to understand that the ERP cost is not really a disadvantage as far as ERP solutions are offering you to choose the right size that best fit into your need and the budget.

The disadvantage exists only when a company decides to go for ERP without proper planning and RDS (Requirement Definition Study) and then it is not only the disadvantage but may lead to 'failure' and could be a 'disaster'. (ERP failures are discussed ahead in this book in chapter 'ERP Project Failures in the Past'.)

Unwanted Functionalities and Modules

ERP venders normally offer package deal and many a time unwanted modules or functionalities are part of such package deal. For instance, a vender is offering ERP package deal comprises of 20 modules including Fixed Asset, Plant Maintenance and Fleet Management modules that may not be required by the buyer.

Sometimes clients find difficulty in selecting required modules from >60 different modules and mapping functionalities with the operational requirements. There are modules which are dependant on other core modules and one cannot simply avoid them. However, there are very few such modules and the concept of module dependency varies from vender to vender. Many a time an individual module required to be selected for few important operational needs and may be utilized partially. Similarly, many a time the modules selected are not immediately utilized and later on the buyer feels that such modules could have been purchased/added after sometime. All these issues can be resolved in RDS and project management planning process as discussed ahead in this book.

It is recommended that small and medium size companies should opt for priority-based and phase-based implementation plan where only core functionalities are part of the ERP plan. This is necessary because small/medium size companies normally encounter budgetary restrictions and most of the time finds themselves in the midst of business expansions and organizational setup works.

A Case Example: In recent years we have recommended total 18 core modules to a small company who deals in manufacturing of plastic products. The solution was comprises of the following:

- 10 modules, S&D + Executive Reporting for Phase-I.
- 3 modules (F&A) Phase II i.e. after 3 months of above implementation.
- 5 modules (PP & Mfg. + Payroll + BI) Phase III i.e. after 12 months from implementation of above 2.

Above recommendations were based on the RDS and the company's approved budget. As per the RDS it was found that the Inventory, Procurement and Sales were the 'bleeding areas' and their existing system (bunch of non-integrated software + manual document and workflow) was unable to resolve the problems and issues.

The accounting package was up and running but was causing problems which are part of Journal Voucher Entries in trivial accounting packages. The package was allowing the client to make rectifications in entry errors without any 'amendment journals' or audit trail or user log report and that was causing inefficient, inaccurate and protracted financial and management reports. Despite of such severe problems the accounting area was not considered in RDS as 'bleeding area' and it can be addressed at the later stage in view of the budget.

Apart from the accounting package they were also using many other software applications, spreadsheets and it was non-integrated software environment. As per the RDS an annual loss of 1.5 Mil was estimated due to the mismanagement of

Inventory and customer deliveries. Therefore, the priority based ERP implementation plan was recommended and it was successfully achieved.

It is worth noting here that the requirement of system users defined in above-mentioned RDS was 20 and in view of the priority and approved budget, the number of concurrent users recommended was 6, 10 and 4 respectively for Phase I, II and III. (More detail on concurrent users is discussed in next topic.)

It is the beauty of ERP solution that it allows buyer to buy what is priority and gradually go for the total ERP solutions. Thus unwanted modules and functionalities can be discarded as explained in next chapters under the topics 'Purchasing & Implementing ERP', 'RDS Process' and 'Project Management based implementation plan'.

ERP Solutions Restrict Concurrent Users

Some ERP pricing are based on concurrent users and some are based on named users. Very few venders offer unlimited users or offer pricing without restrictions on number of users.

For concurrent users pricing, it is recommended to conclude in RDS the number of system users required. Small/medium size company may start with 50 per cent of their required number of users and can gradually increase the numbers during and after the implementation phase as described in previous topic. To optimize the usage and minimize the ERP pricing it is possible to assign access time-table for the users and user group. Usually, all the system users are not required to access concurrently. The concept of concurrent number of user facilitates you to define as many users identification as you want but the concurrent access will be limited to the number of user's license purchased by the client.

For named users pricing, the ERP license are issued as per the named users. This allows only named users to get access on the system and this may cause problems for the client especially if he/she has human resource crises. However, such problem can be resolved by naming a 'group' instead the actual name of the user. Five six users can be accommodated in a group. It is necessary to define grouping during the solution designing phase or prototyping phase of ERP implementation plan discussed in next chapters.

As explained earlier the number of concurrent users or named users can be managed according to the budget and size of the company and what is essential is to properly define the size of ERP in view of the client's budget.

ERP Solutions have Similar Problems as Non-integrated Packages

Many people say that ERP has similar problems as other non-integrated software solutions but this is a misunderstanding. There are certain aspects which might have some similarities in both ERP and other solutions. These aspects are discussed below to clear the misunderstanding:

Limitations in ERP and 3rd Party System Requirement

It is said that like non-ERP solutions ERP too required many other 3rd party software to sustain total business automation and ultimately this creates mix environment of business automation. If we analyze this notion in right perspective we will find that an ERP fulfils 80 per cent of total business automation requirements and as far as non-ERP solutions are concerned they can meet maximum 30-40 per cent of total business/operational requirements and combined with all other software solutions they can meet maximum 50 per cent of the requirements (as discussed earlier in this book).

We have also discussed earlier in this book that there are many reasons to have 3rd party integrated software solutions. It is true that no ERP solution can fulfil 100 per cent requirement of any company. The bench mark is 80 per cent and most of the world-class ERP solutions have been bench-tested by renowned institutions and found that they can meet 80 per cent of the requirements. Some of them are able to fulfil even 90 per cent requirements in view of the total solution offered in conjunction with their business partners and associations.

We have also discussed earlier in this book and justified how one can fulfil balance 20 per cent requirements through 3rd party integration. It is worth noting that 5-10 per cent requirements are usually of trivial nature and evolves around change in the look of the screens and report, colors and designs, etc. and these requirements are considered as wish-list or sometime considered as user's resistance to cultural change. Other 5-10 per cent requirements are usually non-functional, technological and infrastructural. The nonfunctional requirements can be fulfilled through BPR at necessary scale and technological/infrastructural requirements can be fulfilled in view of the budget and priorities.

Third party integration may require in the following situations:

- In case of localization as described earlier in this book in chapter 1 under subheading 'Definition and Fundamental of ERP'.
- In phase based implementation plan where part of the ERP solution is planned to implement with the existing system. This is planned on temporary basis until such time the client is ready for the additional ERP functionalities and features.
- In case of industry specific requirement where a company plan to go for ERP with some special front-end software system such as in hotel, building construction and hospital industries.
- In a situation where a company wants full ERP-II solution without F&A modules as they are satisfied with their existing in-house customized F&A solution developed with diligence and lots of investment of time and money and it may not be a wise decision to scrap it. This situation normally arises in company who has been working in mainframe environment for past several years and may not find system down-sizing as feasible option.

The above arguments indicate that there are hundreds different types of business models required by the industries and an ERP solution cannot fulfil industry specific requirements of all kinds. Third Party software requirements and its integration with ERP is an ongoing process. This is one of the reason we have considered 3rd party integration support as a fundamental aspect of ERP solution, as described earlier in this book.

Endless Programming and Enhancements

It is said that like any other solution ERP software also follows endless programming and developments. As discussed previously (under the topic 'Fundamentals of ERP' in chapter 1), that it is the fundamental aspect of ERP and the responsibility of the ERP developers to continuously upgrade their system in view of the developments in technologies and change in business concepts and for which these developers charge 10-15 per cent annual license fees. The port update and major enhancements are provided to the users free of charge. Unlike non-ERP solutions, ERP users need not incur any overheads and expenses on R&D and they do not bear major risks of errors, failures and dependability on human resources.

Hence, it is true that enhancements in ERP solutions are tend to endless programming and development but it is the responsibility of the vender and not the end users or ERP clients.

Endless Investment—Yearly Renewal Fee

This is a fear factor found among small and medium size companies and to some extent people rightly feel that the ERP venders should find out some solutions to eliminate this fear factor. For medium to large size companies it is not a big issue to invest >10 Mil on ERP and pay every year >1.5 Mil as License renewal fee because they can have optimum utilization as well as good ROI. Whereas, small to medium companies are reluctant to invest 2-3 Mil for the license purchase and suppose if they agree somehow to invest 70-80 per cent of this sum then they may not agree to pay yearly 200-300K as renewal fee. Many ERP consultants have tackled this situation by suggesting priority and phase based implementation plan, where ERP license is purchased for minimum number of modules and minimum number of users. By doing this they are able to minimize the total license purchase cost, the annual fee and the implementation and training charges. However, this approach may not attract the market by and large.

In general, this is a marketing issue and a 'market issue' whether it is genuine or fake must be resolved otherwise it remains an issue. A futuristic approach to resolve this issue is ERPO and discussed ahead in chapter 4.

Who Should Not Go for ERP and Why?

There are many companies who are dealing in millions but the volume of workflow or numbers of business activities are insignificant. For instance a realtor or estate agent in New York, Mumbai and Hong Kong may not require traditional ERP package although their business turnover goes into millions.

During our consultation services for a European engineering firm we were developing a RDS and found feasible that the client should enhance the existing customized software and continue with it without going for an ERP solution. Although the company's turnover was in millions and they were doing lots of business activities. However, they were just playing a role of a mediator in exporting machineries and outsourcing installation, maintenance, shipping and transportation. The existing accounting system was an in-house customized solution and required certain enhancements in view of the modern technological developments and modern business concepts.

Another case example is: We have recommended a diamond trading company, in India, not to go for ERP and just install bar-coding system and continue with existing customized software package. They too were dealing in millions with lots of operational activities, however, they were not doing purchases, production, inventory/stocking, credit sales, etc. but just contracting designing and cutting diamonds. Their major requirement was physical count or real-time control on inventory/stock movements, therefore special bar-coding system was recommended for them which fulfilled the requirements.

Conventional off-the-shelf ERP package may not be suitable for the financial institutions such as Banks, Insurance, Shares, Stock and Commodity market, therefore, special dedicated ERP systems are used in this domain. Similarly conventional ERP may not be suitable for NGOs, Governments and Charitable institutes and housing societies. Many governmental departments, especially municipalities may acquire ERP software solution in conjunction with E-Governance program available off-the-shelf. Generally, 99 per cent of the industries including manufacturers, distributors, services, retailers, wholesalers, exporters, importers are all required ERP software solution for their business automation.

CONCLUSION

From this chapter, it is clearly understood that as such there is no disadvantage in ERP solution. Except ERP cost all other issues are just a misunderstanding and as far as cost is concerned it is all depend upon the size of the company and operation and the compatibility and quality of the ERP solution.

Now, let's study how to plan, purchase, install, implement and utilize ERP software solution and it is discussed in great detail in next chapter.

Purchasing and Implementing ERP

4

Introduction

Last three chapters gave us a clear and positive view about the ERP software as a solution and business tool. However, the most important aspect in ERP study is the selection of an ERP solution and most difficult aspect is the planning and implementing ERP. The success and the failure of ERP is all depend on the implementation and utilization.

We have started this chapter with an alternate solution to ERP purchase called ERPO and which could be the future of ERP in Small-Medium Enterprises (SME) and hopefully which would resolve the cost issue discussed in previous chapters.

This chapter covers minute detail of the purchasing, planning and implementing ERP solution and outline step-by-step guidelines on subject matter.

Like other chapters, you will find here different scenarios created from the real life case studies, graphical illustrations, arguments and explanations which will enable you to have better understanding of the topics.

You will find an in-depth discussion and explanation on the Project management based ERP planning which is the key for the successful implementation. This chapter also describes roadmaps for both the selection process and implementation process.

Purchasing or Outsourcing—An Argument

Before we go forward and study in this chapter the purchasing and planning ERP implementation, it is necessary that we study the possibilities of having an alternate to ERP license purchase.

Generally, ERP software solutions are available in the market on purchase of software license. The 'Software License

Purchase Agreement' in principle allows the customer to install selected ERP modules on his computer server and use it in LAN/ WAN environment. It is necessary to renew license on yearly basis by paying 10-15 per cent annual renewal fee. This fee/charge justified by the venders stating that it enables the venders/developers to invest on continuous R&D, enhancement and upgrading of the core systems and functionalities and it is rightly justified. However, this justification is unacceptable for the SME segment by and large (as discussed in previous chapter).

Acquiring an ERP software solution is quite a difficult and lengthy decision-making process for the customers. In fact small companies considers ERP solution is an exorbitant and time consuming business matter and thinks that it is meant for large size companies only. They have this impression that implementation cost, ongoing maintenance cost, administration costs are very high and also that ERP demands major change in corporate culture. On top of all these the 10-15 per cent annual fee is the major concern for SME segment. Slow response-time in communication lines, User's training and change in management reporting are few other factors that creates dilemma in decision-making. There are other issues and concerns discussed in previous chapter. If the 'bone of contention' is the ERP cost in SME segment then an alternate approach need to be found because SME incorporates >70 per cent potential market and both volume and value wise it is much larger than the large enterprise market segment.

In view of above, the only possible alternate solution to the ERP License Purchase is 'ERP on Rent' or ERPO (ERP outsourcing).

Outsourcing always looks attractive, however outsourcing critical business activities is a difficult decision and need to study and assess several factors such as risks, profitability, commercial and legal viabilities, data communication, administration and so on. Let's analyze all these factors and the possibilities of defining the future of ERPO.

In recent years, some ERP venders have offered ERP solution on rent, however, the attempt was not successful as the scheme was not attractive for SME. It was vague as far as the ROI and legal viability of the rental scheme is concerned. The ERP rental scheme currently offered in the market enables the client to use the ERP system installed on his/her own computer in similar manner as it applied in ERP license purchase. All the aspects of planning, selecting, purchasing and implementing ERP solution will be similar to what we have discussed ahead in this book, except that the ERP system will be rented by the client instead purchasing software license. The client and the vender will agree on certain annual rental charges/fee. This may not be as cost effective and attractive as the ERPO.

Definition of ERPO: ERPO stands for Enterprise Resource Planning & Outsourcing services provided individually by the ERP vender or in association with their authorized channel partners or VAR (Value Added Resellers) and communication service provider and/or financial service provider. All these entities will form a group and will be considered as an ASP (Application Service Providers).

In ERPO, the ERP system will be rented by the client and the access will be given to client's users in WAN, internet or web environment. This scheme can be divided into (a) Partial ERPO or (b) Full-fledged ERPO.

(a) *Partial ERPO Services*: The client will perform all the business transactions online. This includes accounting transactions, reporting and periodic accounting tasks and administration tasks, etc. This scheme will be comprises of the following facilities:

- Complete ready to use online ERP system tailored as per the client's requirements will be made available by the ASP. This includes the communication line and the remote ERP server.
- Necessary RDS, process mapping and other implementation and user training tasks to be carried out or arranged by the ASP.

- Online transaction process will be carried out by the users preferably in web-enabled ERP environment.
- Database information will be owned by the client.
- All the accounting administration and reporting works will be carried out online by the users.

This scheme will not provide zero administration facilities to clients and the client will perform all administration tasks online. The major problem in this scheme will be the data communication line, bandwidth and 'data traffic bottleneck'. This is due to the fact that online administration and executive reporting, in addition to the routine transactions, will require high bandwidth and the scheme may not be feasible and may not be justified by the ASP.

(b) *Full-fledged ERPO Services*: This could be an ideal scheme provided the ASP and the client reached to some mutual agreement in order to cover the legal and commercial viabilities. This scheme can be based on the following terms:

- Complete ready to use online ERP system tailored as per the client's requirements will be provided by the ASP. This will include communication line and remote ERP server.
- Necessary RDS, process mapping and other implementation and training tasks to be carried out by the ASP.
- The only tasks will be carried out by the client is online transactions from his/her operational site(s), preferably in web-enabled ERP environment.
- Backup service will be provided by the ASP in case of communication online failure.
- This scheme will offer 'Zero Administration' at customer site.
- Any one or more than one special services may be offered from the following:

- Administration tasks such as daily, monthly, yearly, balancing, closing will be carried out by the ASP.
- Online auditing and taxation support services will be provided by the ASP.
- Online chartered accounting, taxation and banking tasks will be carried out by the ASP and his associates.

Value Proposition

Acquire a leased based ERP solution, process the financial transactions online and outsource routine tedious tasks such as IT administration, Accounting administration, Management Reporting, Internal and external auditing, etc. The resources are outsourced but the database and its controls are owned by the customer. This will offer high rate of ROI in compare to the software license purchase which incurs additional costs of implementation, training, consultation and ongoing administration. Outsourcing ERP solution means 40-50 per cent ERP cost-saving and 10-15 per cent saving in recurring IT expenses.

Rationale

Typical ERP cost and annual expense calculation is outlined below:

• An average ERP software license purchase cost (for 20 modules, 5-10 users is approx.)	US$ 1.5 Mil.
• An average ERP implementation and training costs @ 40 per cent over the software license	US$ 600K
• An initial investment on hardware, server, accessories, O/S and and RDBMS license purchase	US$ 200K
Total investment on ERP implementation	US$ 2.3Mil.

- An annual license fees over the license Purchase cost @ 15 per cent — US$ 225K
- Communication line, annual charges — US$ 100K

PLUS:

- Overhead expenses for an IT team per year estimated — US$ 200K

Total annual expenditure approx. — US$ 525K

(There are other costs that are not taken into calculation here and they are cost of office space, furniture, electricity, auditing and other administration cost may incur for IT team and this could be an additional 150K.)

The above estimation constitutes to US$ 2.8 - 3 Million.

Conclusion

The concluding part of this rationale is that a SME client instead of buying ERP license at 2.8 - 3 Mil may have an ERP solution by paying annual rental charges of approx. US$ 500K and can sign an agreement with minimum 1.5 to 3 years advance rent. Special services can be charged separately by the ASP as per the size and scale.

The above rationale indicates that on one hand the SME can have a feasible and affordable ERP solution and on the other hand the ERP venders can have major increase in sales and market shares. ERPO will eliminate major issues and concerns as discussed in previous chapters. In general, it will bring the long awaited ERP market boom.

Issues and Concerns

Some clients may disagree to give total access or control of their transactional database to an ASP. Yet there are possibilities of resolving this issue through some legal procedure and/or with the involvement of the chartered accountant firm. This can also be resolved through different technology where the client's database residing on ASP's server can still be protected from unauthorized access of the ASPs. Generally, companies for many reasons rely on their Chartered Accountant and External Auditors when it comes to accessing the company information and the ERPO can be offered as a combined solution for outsourcing the ERP services plus Auditing, Chartered Accounting and Management Reporting services.

The ERP vender and its VAR need to form an associated service network system and make a tie-up with the communication service provider and an auditing and financial service provider to offer total solution with zero administration. There is sufficient scope of business and profits for each one of the entities in this scheme.

One possibility is that the client agrees to install the ERP RDBMS on the computer located in his/her offices and the business logic and ERP programs are installed on the ASP's computer. However, this is not a cost effective approach and the very purpose of renting ERP or ERPO will be defeated.

There could be many other approaches and different schemes that can be studied and offered to the clients as part of ERPO.

Roadmap—How to Plan Purchase/Select an ERP

In different situations a company may think of going for ERP. Selecting right ERP package is one of the crucial aspects. There are many ways to select and purchase or rent an ERP package and one can follow the similar procedure used for the purchase and renting of any high value goods or assets of the company. These procedures might be well tested and may be successful for the purchase of a commodity or asset in the company, however since ERP is not only a commodity but also a solution, therefore, it is recommended to follow the specific procedure based on the RDS (Requirement Definition Study).

Significance of RDS

RDS is an important study and document which clarifies following points:

- It indicates if the company is really in need of an ERP solution and if yes then of what size and type of ERP solution is required.
- It gives an idea if the company is ready for the ERP and what should be the approximate timeframe of ERP implementation project. And if it is essential that company

should go for priority and phase based implementation plan.

- It enables company management to understand the real problems and gaps in existing system and operational workflow. Normally what individuals or departments think and discuss may not be the fact or may not be the exact problems. It is also possible that a requirement of an operation or a worker or a department may be the problem for other operation or department.
- It tells if the company need down-right-sizing.
- It gives an early indication if the company requires BPR and if so then at what scale.
- A good RDS developed and documented in-house by the key players, helps management to decide whether a business consultant is required or not and if so at what scale. In some cases where the company possess 'capital intellectual' and a team of professionals from F&A and IT then both RDS and ERP implementation project can be carried out by them.
- It facilitates the company to ascertain the finance, budget, timeframe and resources required for an ERP solution without hindering the business development, growth and in some cases long-term business expansion plan.
- Based on the RDS a company can speed up the RFP (Request for Proposal) process with the ERP venders and ERP consultants.
- It indicates how many modules for how many users are required and during what phases. This is very important aspect of RDS because the ERP software license costs are generally calculated on the basis of number of modules selected + the number of users who will be concurrently accessing these modules (across the board).
- It covers the primary phase of project management based implementation plan. The significance of the project management based implementation is discussed ahead in this chapter.

– Last but not least, a professionally organized RDS development process will give your entire company a feeling of re-discovering yourselves.

RDS Check-list

Following study and documentation will be prepared during the process of RDS:

A. *Executive Summary (Company Information document)*

Note: The following documents must cover both the current setup and future requirements.

B. *General Documentation*

1. Organization structure (Chart)
2. List of Departments and Divisions (Table)
3. COA—List of accounting activities (Table)
4. Product list, categorization and classification (Table)
5. List of Branches, Warehouses and depots (Table)
6. Operational sites structure (Chart)
7. List and total number of Suppliers, Customers, Distributors, sub-distributors and Sales Reps and other elements (Table)

C. *Operational Work-Flow Charts*

1. Production and Planning
2. Purchasing and shipment tracking
3. Stock management and warehousing
4. Sales Services and Customer Delivery
5. Finance and Accounting
6. Others

D. *Detail Functionalities in Each Operation*

1. Purchase (Types of PO, Import, Local, Open, Schedule order, etc.):
   i. Buyer types and purchase authority levels and 'Requisition Cycle'
   ii. Suppliers classification
   iii. Avg. No. of PO printed per day/month

2. GRN Matching Process:
   i. Integration with AP
3. Inventory, Stocking and warehousing:
   i. Physical Cycle counts in a year
   ii. Movements, IBT, Safety, Re-order, Costing methods
   iii. Costing Methods, Current cost and last cost
   iv. Unit of measurements and conversion factors
4. Sales (Types of Sales: Local, Foreign, Export, etc.):
   i. Customers classification
   ii. Quotations, sales, transportation and delivery
   iii. Avg. No. of sales invoices printed per day/month
5. Production:
   i. WIP
   ii. BOM
   iii. MRP
6. Accounting:
   i. AP
   ii. AR
   iii. Cash & Bank
   iv. General Ledger
7. Other functionalities.

E. Print Document Forms/Formats

1. Sales Order, Sales Invoice, Dr/N, Cr/N Delivery Note
2. Purchase Order, GRN/IGR
3. Customer Statement of A/c
4. Others.

F. Report Formats (Sample Reports)

1. Sales pipeline
2. Deal profitability
3. Customer delivery status
4. Purchase pipeline or On-order
5. Re-ordering sheet
6. Stock movements.

G. Utilities

1. Web Interfaces
2. Third party solution or Interface for 3rd party solutions
3. Data Export/Import (periodic)
4. Customization
5. Business Intelligence, Office Automation
6. Users security access, audit trail and log report
7. Spreadsheets.

H. System Information—Current and Future Planning

1. Software system, language, tools, database
2. Hardware, communication system
3. LAN/WAN system setup
4. Storage and backup system
5. Number of system users
6. Number of sites
7. Users groups and security access control.

RDS Process—Important Aspects

- If necessary, appoint a business consultant to develop RDS. It is preferable to have an external business consultant or professional project management team in the absence of in-house 'capital intellectual'.
- In view of the budget, it is recommended to have a preliminary discussion with the management on different option of purchasing ERP licenses or renting, leasing or outsourcing ERP as discussed in previous chapters.
- It is recommended to form a committee comprises of a team of 'think-tank'. This committee will participate in the RDS process and take necessary decisions in view of the outcome.
- A circular from MD may be issued to all departmental heads defining clear objectives and goals and announcing the appointment of key management players or a Project Manager to develop the RDS and in case of external business consultant it should be one internal key player +

the consultant. The circular should clearly state that necessary support and cooperation must be provided to these key players in any circumstances.

- It is recommended to establish an e-mail communication and messaging system for RDS process.
- Referring the RDS check-list, the project manager (PM) should ensure that he develop an action plan and scheduled timetable for every department and every single workflow and document flow. It is recommended to set a timetable after office working hours or if possible before working hours. This is to avoid disturbance in daily routine works which may also affect the RDS process.
- The PM should very patiently sit and follow the RDS process with the departmental heads or if be needed with the front-end workers. The RDS process should be carried out at grass-root level.
- It is necessary that the project manager should avoid any chaos and process the RDS in harmony and healthy environment. He should explain the objective of this RDS and should not offend anyone or should not make anyone feel insecure about his/her job.
- The PM and his team should visit all the operational sites and carry out the documentation as described in the RDS check-list.
- The PM should prepare necessary notes, diagram, workflow, document flow and maintain the records of current document forms and formats as described in the RDS check-list.
- The PM should separately write all the concerns and complaints made by individual players and these concerns and complaints should be taken into consideration in complainer's perspective and his level of understanding. This is the key aspect of RDS development as this will support the next crucial steps in RDS called 'Gap Analysis'.
- If necessary, PM should explain the operational staff how his/her work is interrelated with other departments and other business process and should also ensure that he/she

is aware about this interrelationship of the business operation.

- The PM should ask the complainer if he can suggest some solution to the problems or the complaints he/she made. These suggestions should be an integral part of the complaints. It is possible that the complaint made and the concerns showed by the front-end player is personal or not related to the operational process and in such situation it is recommended to maintain a separate document for such complaints.
- It is recommended that all such reports must be copied to the relevant departmental heads and the door should be kept open for more complaints, suggestions or changes he/she would like to make within a week time. This gives opportunity for people to think and rethink about their complaints and suggestions and later on they feel like part of the RDS process. This way one will follow 'peoplistic' rather than 'individualistic' approach in the development of RDS.
- The Project Manager should avoid quoting/informing the complaints/suggestions of one person to another. He may discuss the interrelated business process and workflow of one department/person to others.
- It is recommended to start the RDS process with F&A and end with F&A in the following sequence:
  - Finance & Accounting
  - Production & Planning
  - Procurement
  - Sales & Marketing
  - Delivery & Dispatching
  - Warehousing and Storing
  - Executives and Management
  - Finance & Accounting.

Selection Process of ERP Software/Vender

- Form an evaluation committee based on senior and junior management key players. This committee can be the same committee as stated above in RDS process.
- Review RDS document and analyze the operational 'gaps'. Gaps in what you have and what you have not and would like to have as part of business automation. These 'gaps' are the complaints documented in RDS and related to operations and business process and/or workflow. (Gaps are discussed in detail ahead in 'Gap Analysis' topic.)
- Find out the best of the breed ERP solutions available in the market or search them on Internet. (Sample online ERP evaluation is illustrated in next chapter. Website such as www.technologyevaluation.com will be helpful in this regard.)
- For an up-to-date ERP survey report you may also log on to many independent ERP surveyors' websites.
- Develop RFP (Request for Proposal) document based on the RDS. (RFP-check-list is outlined in next chapter.)
- If necessary, along with normal ERP license purchase scheme ask for ERP on Rent or ERPO option.
- Send the RFP to the venders of best of the breed ERP solutions.
- Obtain and study the preliminary proposals and evaluate the demo version of the ERP software CD submitted by the venders.
- Do not allow ERP venders at this juncture to give you presentation and map your requirements with their ERP as you will get confused.
- Short-list best of the 5 ERP solutions.
- Check if any vender is offering prototype testing and if he has a ready business model that match your kind of business or falls under your industrial domain.
- Check there are some world-class ERP venders who arrange ERP training program prior to finalizing the

project deal or selecting ERP solution. The PM and couple of other key players, especially from F&A background may participate in such training program. (In recent years, the author recommended this concept to one of its client and the end result was very productive and satisfactory. In fact the recommendation was not only for the training but also for a prototype testing and later on the Project Manager was able to confidently handled the project and have successfully achieved the milestone without depending much on the external consultants.)

- Now call the vender's functional and technical team for discussions in view of the RDS documents and ask them to map your RDS with their ERP system. This session may be prolonged for couple of days. The first thing you should manually map your operational workflow charts (available in RDS) with the workflow charts provided by the ERP venders. You will compare these two charts based on the individual operation and will note down the missing functionalities as gaps in ERP system. You will find the functionalities encapsulated in individual module as described in previous chapter 'Fundamental of ERP'. Please note that this mapping will be based on business model and not on individual functionality or operational steps. It is not possible at this juncture to map the complete business process. The business process mapping will be carried out in Operational Analysis phase discussed ahead in next chapter.
- Visit reference sites of all 5 venders (min. one from each).
- Obtain a final proposal from the vender based on above mapping, modulation and integration. If there is any gap found at this point of time then it would be a major gap and the vender must give appropriate solution or alternate to fill the gap without asking you to compromise on operability, quality and integration.
- At this point of time you may bargain prices in view of 'value for money'.
- Produce a document, mapping RDS with the functionalities offered by all 5 ERP solutions. The bench-mark is

'minimum 80 per cent of your operational requirements must be fulfilled'.

- Produce a comparative study on strengths and weaknesses of the shortlisted ERP solutions. This report will be produced in view of the RDS, budget, resources, priorities, guarantees, support services, discounts and other facilities offered by the venders and which safeguard your investment. This report will enable you to define necessary evaluation criteria for the final selection of ERP solution.
- Do not follow the concept of 'Something is better than nothing'. For ERP purchase the only approach is "nothing is better than nonsense".
- Select the one which is the best among five shortlisted solutions and which offers best suitable price for ERP software license costs, implementation, training and setup charges and first year free AMC, and if possible first year (after project handover) free of charge on-site support service by one ERP consultant.
- Check the possibilities of ERPO as discussed in previous chapter.
- Sign necessary legal documents and agreements. Make sure that the software license purchase agreement or ERP rental agreement is signed directly with the vender and not with the distributor or consultants.
- Ensure that necessary guarantees with the ESCROW clause are covered under the terms and conditions.
- A separate agreement to be signed with the ERP consultants/ consulting firm or distributor. (Sample-scope of consultation works are illustrated below.)
- With the help of the consultants, choose a suitable project management implementation plan (a) composite or (b) simple plan, as discussed in next chapter.

Check-List—RFP (Request for ERP Proposal) Document

RFP document can be generated out of the RDS. RFP speed up the ERP selection and bidding process and facilitates the ERP venders to understand requirements and submit a suitable

ERP proposal. You may define or just cut and paste the following aspects from the RDS document and e-mail or dispatch to ERP venders:

- Summary-Introduction of the company.
- Primary goals and objectives of implementing ERP solution.
- General terms and conditions of the proposal.
- Option of ERP license purchase, ERP rental and/or ERPO.
- Standard clauses of the agreement and scope of works recommended by your company legal advisor.
- Evaluation criteria on which the ERP solution will be evaluated by you.
- Company Organization and operation structure chart.
- The business process chart and workflow to map with the ERP solution.
- The business model and number of modules required.
- The detail functionalities required in each module.
- Services such as business, users, data and integration required in ERP solution.
- The implementation methodologies required.
- Training methodologies required.
- Consultation, local support, after sales support and future planning.

Sample—Scope of Consultation and Implementation Works

It is recommended that ERP consultants hired for the implementation project. It is necessary to understand the minimum scope of works ERP consultants can cover during the course of project implementation. ERP consultants:

- Shall form an implementation team comprises of client's staff/management who will be able to take the "project ownership" during the implementation and "system ownership" after the ERP go-live.
- Shall install and setup ERP products and ensure connectivity and initialization of data model.

- Shall install and setup relational database where it is necessary and make 3rd Party Integration in SQL.
- Shall provide the initial test of application and data communication in LAN and WAN environments. This will be subject to the availability of appropriate network LAN/WAN infrastructure.
- Shall, assist clients in designing element codes. The designing and structuring of the modules will be based on the business study provided by the client.
- Shall study and design necessary stationary forms, tables and reports in Report Writer Module.
- Shall ensure that the implementation covers the G/L integration and smooth functioning of transaction process, G/L Distribution, Postings, Registering, Purging, Balancing and Period and Month-end.
- Shall design appropriate file structure table and user access rights in accordance with established IT department standards.
- Together with the client's staff shall perform testing and certification on successful and complete delivery of each milestone of the system implementation discussed and agreed.
- Shall study and identify the problems that may cause delay in implementation, hinder to the impact functionalities and directly or indirectly affects the usage of selected ERP.
- Shall ensure that the standard practices are followed during the project implementation and necessary measures are taken to avoid any loss of time and money to the project stakeholders.
- Where necessary, shall propose additional modules and or customized solution which is suitable and meet the current and/or future requirements.
- Shall assist in finding 3rd party software solution that can be best fit into the budget, project planning and integration with the Syspro business model.

Sample-online ERP evaluation from
www.technologyevaluation.com Page 1/4

The following evaluation has been carried out for an Automotive and manufacturing industrries. (Make to order, Make to Stock, Repetitive, Process, etc.)

ERP Discrete

The Discrete ERP Knowledge Base will help manufacturers research vendors that support a range of production capabilities such as production planning, shop floor control and product costing. The knowledge base also provides information on financials, human resources, and other enterprises management modules.

ERP Process

The Process ERP Knowledge Base anticipates as many factors as possible that will assist businesses in the process manufacturing field. The knowledge base includes criteria for determining batch control and reporting, formula and routing, and material management capabilities. It also provides information for other enterprise management modules.

Results

Although the results lists >300 venders, however, given below are the top 5 venders that best match a low cost, high performance, fully integrated Financial, Manufacturing, Distribution ERP solution with necessary provision for the future upgrading to .net, CRM, SCM and E-commerce solutions.

Rank	*Products*	*Best Match Factor**	*Weighted Average**
#1	SAP—mySAP ERP	94.2	97.0
#2	Jeeves Information Systems—Jeeves Enterprise	87.7	93.3
#3	SYSPRO-SYSPRO	78.7	88.0
#4	Epicor-Vantage	67.4	80.4
#5	Scala Business Solutions—iScala	66.4	80.2

* View ranking methodology

(*Contd.*)

Chart of A/c Parameters			
Rank	*Products*	*Best Match Factor**	*Weighted Average**
#1	SAP—mySAP ERP	100.0	100.0
#2	Scala Business Solutions—iScala	95.0	97.5
#3	SYSPRO-SYSPRO	92.9	96.4
#4	Jeeves Information Systems—Jeeves Enterprise	92.2	95.8
#5	Epicor-Vantage	74.7	85.4

* View ranking methodology

- The vendor is amenable to work with 3rd-party tools and software.
- Mobile access to enterprise data in the product offering is available.
- There is total portal access to the system, role-based and customizable.
- There is "rich client" web browser access to the Internet and use of selected system areas.
- There is HTML (zero client footprint) web browser access to the Internet and selected system areas.
- There is a thin-client link to the Internet and selected system areas.
- There is collaborative sharing of system data, automatic processes and workflow.

Technical Parameters Applied for the Evaluation

Please indicate the degree to which statements about a prospective product, pertain to your business (select all that apply)

- There is tight native integration between each functional module.
- There is tight native integration between each of the supported industry standards.
- There is flexibility between functional modules (i.e., modules can be implemented incrementally and can be interfaced to 3rd-party modules) between each of these areas.

Roadmap-Project Management Based Implementation Plan for ERP

Let's first review why project management is essential for ERP implementation and what a 'Project and Project Management' means in business operation. Project Management altogether is a different and very vast subject therefore in this chapter you will find the basics and important aspects of the Project Management that are relevant to ERP implementation.

Significance of Project and Project Management: ERP implementation is a transient task unlike regular and monotonous operational tasks carried out in the organization. Therefore, it is imperative that ERP implementation is carried out with the concept of the project management.

Project means a temporary task undertaken by group of people to achieve pre-defined objectives in pre-defined timeframe, at an estimated cost. Projects vary in size and duration and require few selected skilled personnel from the organization to start and finish the specific task in given timeframe.

Project Management means planning and managing a project in highly organized manner by using standard project management tools and methods, by adhering to company's business strategy, objectives and philosophy taking into consideration the available organizational resources, the risks, constrains and dependencies factors.

In view of the RDS and depending upon the nature and size of the business you may choose one of the following plans for ERP implementation:

(a) Composite project management plan (recommended for large size company)

or

(b) Simple project management plan (recommended for small/medium size companies).

(a) Composite Project Management Plan are normally required a business consultant/consulting firm to involve from day one and in some cases even before the RDS process is initiated. Composite Project Management Plan life cycle may be categorized into following phases:

Phase 1: Definition

- Define scope of the project
  (Objectives, goals, requirements, budget, etc. in the RDS)
- Define project estimation and scheduling
  (Discussed in detail under next topic)
- Identify risks, assumptions and dependencies
  (Discussed in detail under next topic)
- Define project organization and responsibilities
  (Discussed in detail under next topic)
- Define current business process
  (Discussed in detail under next topic)
- Define the future business model
  (Discussed in detail under next topic)
- Define technical infrastructure requirements
  (Discussed in detail under next topic)

Phase 2: Operations Analysis

- Develop proposed business model
  (Based on the RDS)
- Business process mapping
  (Discussed in detail under next topic)
- Identify gaps and perform gap analysis
  (Discussed in detail under next topic)
- Develop solution for the gaps
  (Discussed in detail under next topic)
- Develop migration strategy
  (Discussed in detail under next topic)

Phase 3: Solution Design

- Commence training
  (Discussed in detail under next topic)

- Design coding and structure
  (Discussed in detail under next topic)
- Design and develop solution prototype
  (Discussed in detail under next topic)
- Design and develop data conversion, interfaces
  (Discussed in detail under next topic)
- Finalize the technical infrastructure
  (Discussed in detail under next topic)
- Design recovery plan
  (Discussed in detail under next topic)

Phase 4: Development

- Develop programs (in ERP)
- Perform program tests (in ERP)
- Perform Integration tests (in ERP)
- Develop user's documentation
  (Discussed in detail under next topic)
- Test data recovery

Phase 5: Transition

- Setup parallel system environment
- Conduct end-users training
  (Discussed in detail under next topic)
- Perform data conversion from Live to New system
  (Discussed in detail under next topic)
- Start parallel run
- Go live

Phase 6: Production

- Discontinue old system
- Perform audits and performance reviews
- Refine the new system
- Plan future business and technical requirements

(b) Simple project management plan:

1. Pre-implementation phase:
   - Develop RDS documentation
   - Form Project team
   - Define Project Scope
   - Define 'Risks and Dependencies'
   - Gap analysis
   - Identify 'trouble areas' and set priorities
   - Define proposed Business Model
   - Define Integration and Migration Strategy
   - Define coding structure
   - Define project time-line
2. Implementation phase:
   - Pilot Project kick-off
   - Commence training with the concept of 'Train the Trainer'
   - Design Proposed Business Model in ERP
   - Prototype testing in LAN/WAN environment
   - Test conversion, migration and integration
   - Design and develop necessary forms and formats
   - Update opening Balance and reconcile with old system
   - Catch backlog and Go-live
   - Obtain user's appreciation
   - Intensify user access controls, data and system security
   - Prepare data disaster recovery plan, training notes
   - Roll-out
   - Project handover
   - Post project assignments and adherence

Important Aspects of Project Management and Planning

Discussed below are the important aspects that must be taken into consideration while planning project management based ERP implementation.

- Methods and Tools for project planning
- Business Process Mapping
- Gap Analysis
- Risks and Dependencies
- Project Timeline Plan
- Project Organization Plan
- Structure and Coding
- Data migration and Historical record updates
- Prototype-tests in different LAN/WAN environment
- User Training Program (Train the Trainer)
- Knowledge Management
- Disaster Recovery Plan
- Data Communication System

Methods and Tools for Project Planning

The evolutions of the project management have gone through different stages in history of human kind. According to the researchers the earliest project management concept can be seen in the construction of the Great Pyramids of Egypt and the Great Wall of China. During past few centuries the evolution is more evident from the 'seven wonders of the world'. It is a mystery that very little is known about the project methods and tools used in constructions of these marvels. During past few decades the project management has been given utmost importance in different business domains, industries, engineering, construction, IT, Military and infrastructural projects. Different methods and tools have been discovered and applied in the project management and they are discussed below:

- Estimation and Scheduling: Project estimation/costing and scheduling are the most important aspects of project management. The project estimation allows you to know the cost of different resources required and the project scheduling enables you to define the timeframe in which different project tasks and milestone events need to be achieved.

Project estimation and costing covers every single amount of money required to spend on the project resources. This includes direct and indirect expenses, asset purchase, labor, energy and materials cost, consultation and legal fees and banking charges.

Project scheduling allows you to define the process timeline. The project schedule is categorized in (a) Project Master Schedule, a high level plan and scheduling done by the managers and (b) Project task scheduling are specific tasks to be carried out by the project team.

- Gantt chart: is also called Bar Chart, introduced by management consultant Henry Gantt in USA Army, during World War I. Gantt chart is widely used by the industries in different forms. Generally Gantt chart illustrates the time (hours, days, weeks, months) on the horizontal scale and the project activities or tasks on the vertical scale. It is necessary that the sequence is maintained in both the horizontal and vertical scales. Several project management software programs are available in the market which allows you to produce different types of Gantt charts along with other related diagrams discussed below:
  - AON (Activity on Node) & AOA (Activity on Arrow) Diagrams: The Gantt chart does not indicate the relationship between the tasks, therefore, a logic diagram is used by the project managers. AON diagram indicates different 'task-boxes' or nodes linked with each other and creates a network whereas the AOA diagram indicates different tasks are linked using arrows.

Certain rules and methods are used to create the linkage between tasks and subsequently create a network of task boxes. These rules and methods are discussed below.

- PDM (Precedence Diagramming Method): This method is commonly used when designing task-box network diagrams. Primarily PDM allows you to have overlapping between two tasks and this is called as 'lead time'. The delay time between two tasks is called lag time. For instance the system designing task takes 10 days and from 8th day onward the user training task will be started and this will create 2 days overlapping period. Similarly, suppose the system designing tasks take 10 days and after 2 days i.e. onward 12th day the training task is started then this will create 2 days lag time.

  Many a time the relationship in the task-box network creates complexities and to make these relationships comprehensive the following tools are utilized in PDM:

  - Start-to-Start/SS or EST/(Early Starting Time)
  - EFT (Early Finishing Time)
  - LST (Latest Starting Time)
  - LFT (Latest Finish Time)

  The Gantt chart, logic diagrams and PDM as discussed above are straightforward methods and tools in project management planning, estimation and scheduling. In these methods, you assumes that the resources, cost and time are going to be met without major variances and fluctuations. However, in large project the scenario will be different than what you have assumed in the planning, estimating and scheduling. The fact is that, as and when the project goes through different stages of process, the estimation and scheduling gets change and some technique is required to monitor and control such unexpected changes and uncertainties. That is how Program Evaluation & Review Technique (PERT) and Critical Path Method (CPM) emerged in project management planning and they are discussed below.

- PERT (Program Evaluation & Review Techniques) & CPM (Critical Path Method): These techniques facilitate project managers to measure the uncertainty related to the cost and time and monitor and control them during the project process. PERT is primarily used to measure the uncertainties in project time schedule especially the project delays which may lead to project failure, whereas the CPM primarily used to measure the possible risks factors for both time and cost of the project. CPM is based on mathematical calculation and is an advanced technique that facilitates the project managers to reallocate the resources and apply load leveling as and when necessary.

Business Process Mapping

Mapping the business process with ERP functionalities is a tedious job. A portion of this task is normally covered during the ERP selection process as discussed earlier. It is very important that the mapping is carried out in great detail and gaps are found by taking into consideration every individual steps in operational process and matching them with the functionalities available in the selected ERP system. It is worth noting here that this gap is different from the gap analysis you have done in the RDS phase. Those were the gaps found between what you have and what you don't and would like to have. This gap analysis should be achieved with an 'apple to apple match' to find what you want and what is available and if not available in the ERP solution then note down as a 'gap'.

During the selection process you have already mapped your module requirements and the selection was finalized on the basis that minimum 80 per cent of your system requirements can be fulfilled through selected ERP. And if you have undergone training through ERP vender and have carried out the prototyping test during that training then you must have already made your assessment about the gaps.

Now, this is the time to document every single operational function and cross check in the ERP solution as to where it is available in the ERP module, under what name or caption and what are the accounting implications. This need to be documented as per the sample Table on next page.

Function Name in the RDS	*Operation Name in the RDS*	*Name/ Caption in the ERP*	*ERP Module Name*	*Integration with other Modules*	*Accounting Implication*
Stock Transfer	Warehouse and storage	Stock transfer W/H to W/H	Stock Management	Purchase GRN Sales MRP	Debit to Receiver's A/c
		GIT Yes/No?			Credit to Sender's W/H A/c
Material Issue	Shop Floor	Stock Issue	WIP & Stock Management	MRP Inventory BOM	Debit to WIP work center
					Credit to Issuing W/H
Electric Bill Expense	JVE	Expense Journal Voucher	General Ledger	N/A (Not Applicable)	As per pre-defined COA.
		OR			
		Recurring Expenses			
Supplier's Quote updates	Procure-ment	Not Available	N/A	N/A	GAP

You may add couple of extra columns in above table such as 'Remarks', etc. to have more and more information and comments in regard to mapping.

Please ensure that you enter, without missing a single operational step, all what is defined in RDS as your system requirements and what the ERP is offering. Any operation function not available in ERP is a gap and an alternate solution need to be found.

In above example the gap is an entire module. Suppose it was not in the list of priority or the gap was ranked as 'good to have' function. For this one single function the entire module is not required to be purchased as it will hamper the project cost.

Despite the fact that the above gap is not a critical one but still need to be counted in the total gaps calculated from the above table and later on if possible an alternate solution or option can be found from the ERP. For instance, in case of this gap called 'Supplier Quotation updates' one can use the alternate option called 'Temporary Purchase Order' and can easily update the information related to the quotation submitted by the supplier(s). This can be edited and deleted and if necessary any reports can be printed out of such updates.

Business process mapping documentation may create hundreds of pages. This document is the most important portion of the knowledge management as discussed ahead in this chapter. This document will also be used for the 'gap analysis' tasks discussed in next topic.

Gap Analysis

Gap analysis is the most critical part of ERP implementation and an in-depth gap analysis plays pivotal roles in successful ERP implementation. For documenting the gaps you need to refer the Business Process Mapping table as described above.

Gap analysis process is all about exploring, identifying and listing the problems, defects and missing aspects in the different areas of your business and operational workflow. Identifying the gaps (right gaps) means you are halfway through in solution designing and development. It is good to give some type of ratings to individual gap. These ratings could be 'High priorities', 'Low priority', 'somewhat essential', 'essential', 'highly essential', 'a wish-list' or good to have. These gaps could be functional, technical, infrastructural or of trivial cosmetic nature.

It is very important to ascertain that all what you 'do not have' are not necessarily the requirements in your business or all that have been listed as gaps are not necessarily your utmost requirement. If a gap is not causing a loss or incurring major expenses and can be fulfilled by certain changes in documentation and operational workflow then it is recommended not to put this in the list of priority or rate them as highly essential.

The above recommendations are primarily made for those companies who are planning to migrate from non-ERP environment to ERP environment. In rare case a company may think of migrating from one ERP to another and in such a case the gaps are very narrow and usually filled-up by customization using SDK or by 3rd party solution. It is also possible that these gaps might have developed long after the project implementation, due to the reasons such as; drastic changes occurred in the company's business or operation or management or human resources or geographical setup or technologies, etc. It is also possible that the gap is less than 20 per cent and the ERP system was in fact implemented professionally with 80 per cent benchmark and the system users are still having the impression that ERP solution means 100 per cent fulfilment of the requirement. If the gaps are very wide (say more than 20-30 per cent) between the existing ERP system and the required system then it indicates that the ERP system was not professionally implemented or the selection was wrong. A case study in this regard is outlined in next chapter called "ERP Project Failures in the Past".

Case Examples on Gaps Analysis: There are certain requirements which considered as gaps by the clients and they are discussed below by giving examples from real-life scenarios and case studies:

- *Case Example I*: A world-class ERP solution was professionally and successfully implemented in a company and the users for some reasons could not perform the daily balancing tasks and period-end regular basis. This led to enormous amount of backlog in GL posting and the managers demanded that the system should provide a facility to perform more than 180 days' balancing, more than 6 months' month-end processing and it must also allow the users to produce necessary financial reports without month-end closing. Although the justification for protracted daily balancing and period-end given by the users was valid in their perspective but in view of the fundamentals of ERP it was not an industry standard practice which demand strict adherence to the balancing and period-end tasks. Finance & Accounting people can better understand this situation as a case of non-accounting practices. This was considered by the client as a 'gap' in the ERP system, however there was no other alternative but to follow the ERP guidelines and later on the client streamlined the system.

- *Case Example II*: A company, during midst of the implementation, decided to migrate from an ERP to non-integrated system environment because the ERP was unable to function in dial-up communication mode and this has been considered as a 'gap'. The client has two major sites using ERP in WAN environment 64K DDN communication line plus seven remote sites (branches, depots and distributors) in remote locations where DDN communication facilities were not available. The ERP vender and the consultant recommended periodic data update through dial-up mode and asked the client to change the necessary aspects in the RDS where executive reporting system will be provided in non-online environment. The client is still looking to fill-up this gap. Truly it is a gap, not a functional but an infrastructural gap.
- *Case Example III*: During 1997, a Managing Director with marketing background, rejected couple of world-class ERP solutions stating that he is looking for a business-oriented system and cannot have system-oriented business. The company was looking for an ERP system which allows freehand customization during the transactional process. The company was in the process of rapid market exploration that too at grand scale hence were unable to accept a software system that impose any kind of restrictions or cause limitation in such exploration. This was a gap in almost all the ERP solutions available at that time. Recently some of the world-class ERP venders have introduced freehand customization functionality and cost effective add-in functions through SOA which allows users to customize anything they want in the ERP system.

It is true that a company has to do business in a way best suited their objectives and plan and ERP solution should not cause any impediments in business growth. However, in modern business environment it is always good for a company to consider best business standards and practices.

Many companies may find ERP solutions restricting their business practices, and therefore may opt for legacy system depending much upon the customizations and the impacts of customized solutions in long run are discussed earlier in this book.

Risk and Dependencies in ERP Implementation Project

Projects are planned with some risks, constrains, dependencies and assumptions. Risk is everything that could cause any type of impediment in meeting the project expectations. Constrains are the restrictions imposed on the project in view of the available resources and capacity. The elements on which the success of the project is much depended on are all project dependencies. Assumptions are the unknown aspects of the project which is listed during project planning and they are limited to some logical assumptions and not to be based on 'God's Act' or 'Force Majour'. This type of assumption can be covered separately in 'Disaster Recovery Plan' as discussed ahead in this chapter.

Risk management is an essential tool for the successful project implementation. Therefore, a risk identification exercise is necessary where the project team members perform a brainstorming session to list down 'what and when could go wrong to the project'. Each risk identified shall be ranked in terms of "probability" of the risk and its impact on the project. Each risk, when identified, must be placed on a grid as exemplified below in a diagram. Also outlined below are some sample risk elements, assumption and dependencies.

Risks Analysis

A sample risk analysis exercise is illustrated below along with necessary explanations.

Please note that each risk required to be analyzed thoroughly by defining its consequences, contingency and early mitigation as explained below. The risk analysis must be carried out by the project manager with the help of team members and if necessary executives and it is normally carried out in a brain-storming session. Please study the different risks taken into consideration below and note that risks are vary from time to time, place to place and project to project.

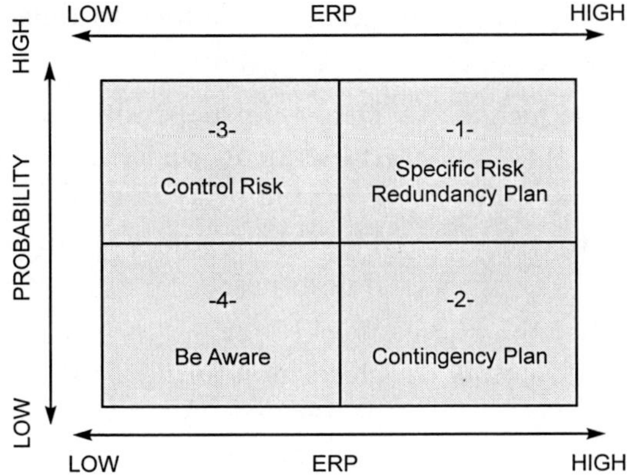

Fig. 4.1

Information gathering is incomplete: Information gathered from the RDS is used during the Operations Analysis phase to ensure that all of the business requirements of the company are investigated and addressed. There is a chance that this information is inadequate.

- Risk Category: Contingency Plan (2)
- Consequence: Delay of project, possible additional costs, as operational analysis sessions may need to be interrupted while specific operational analysis is undertaken.

  Unknown business requirements may not be addressed and become evident as issues only during integrated testing of the Business Systems Test.
- Contingency: Operations analysis and prototyping would be delayed pending completion of this activity or the requirement would be targeted for a subsequent phase of the application implementation.
- Early Mitigation: The project teams review the state of the requirement definition output. The team will review this documentation to ensure completeness.

Project phase takes longer than planned to finish.

- Risk Category: Be Aware (4)
- Consequence: Delay in dependent tasks and/or subsequent phases of the project. Potential delay in go-live.
- Contingency: Flexible project plan with firm milestones.
- Early Mitigation: Weekly review of project status and close monitoring of the tasks being performed. An appropriate project tools and methods need to be applied in project planning and scheduling.

Significance changes in the scope of the project: There may be some changes to existing business process within the company. The assumption is that these changes will be identified during Operations Analysis phase and completed by business in time.

- Risk Category: Contingency Plan (2)
- Consequence: Possible restating of project objectives, recalculation of costs, redefining milestones.
- Contingency: Move non-critical project components to subsequent phases.
- Early Mitigation: Ensure that all principals agree on project scope at time of Project initiation.

Selected ERP cannot meet 100 per cent requirements: The project assumes that the business requirements of the company can be met by selected ERP with a minimum of 15-20 per cent customization of the base package.

- Risk Category: Contingency Plan (2)
- Consequence: Delay in delivery of the project. Possibly a 3rd party software is required, additional cost to the business.

- Contingency: Look for solution outside the core product.
- Early Mitigation: Review during gap analysis and thorough study of the gaps and viability of alternate solutions.

The selected server is not sized to handle the production load or performance specifications are not met. Although preliminary sizing has been undertaken, an actual determination of the specific volumetrics for the applications will only be known after the appropriate application configuration options are selected. At the time, it will be possible to model the ERP 'xyz' on volumes and the resulting consumption of the disk, CPU and memory resources.

- Risk Category: Contingency Plan (2)
- Consequence: Unacceptable performance in the live environment.
- Contingency: Upgrade hardware or acquire additional hardware resources.
- Early Mitigation: Undertake a perpetual detailed sizing process throughout the project as volumetrics become more evident. Determine production hardware environment as part of the technical design. Monitor performance during acceptance testing and manage user expectations.

Hardware setup is not available when required for testing: The project planning and scoping indicates that the system architecture will be ready prior to the solution designing and prototype testing phase.

- Risk Category: Contingency Plan (2)
- Consequence: Delay the testing of the applications and go-live.
- Contingency: Careful planning for test environment set-up. Additional hardware to be acquired on rental basis. The existing

users PCs could be used for setting up a test environment.

- Early Mitigation: Obtain required development and test environment. As soon as possible after hardware requirements and sizing is finalized.

Data conversion of existing data to new system is not transferable: Data in existing system to be converted to new format as per new ERP set-up will require clean up in some cases. Assumptions will need to be made during data migration with respect to the consistence and accuracy of this cleaned up data. Often, ongoing problems with converted data will occur following conversion:

- Risk Category: Be Aware (4)
- Consequence: Possible ongoing problems with converted data in New environment resulting in additional maintenance of data following go-live.
- Contingency: Clearly defined data conversion plan. Test data conversion in dummy environment.
- Early Mitigation: Early identification of data problems and clean up to conversion to the new applications.

People competency is inadequate: Assessment is made during the project planning process as to the training requirement, aptitude and capacity to contribute for all project personnel. From time to time, this assessment may be incorrect.

- Risk Category: Contingency Plan (2)
- Consequence: Slippage in deliverables due from personnel, or inadequate level of participation in decision-making.
- Contingency: Careful selection of project team members. Initial coaching following by escalation to project sponsor for direction.

- Early Mitigation: On project commencement, review with each individual the expectations for their involvement. Seek agreement with the individual.

Retention of project team members during the implementation: From time to time, key project personnel may reassigned to other enterprise initiative or leave THE COMPANY.

- Risk Category: Be Aware (4)
- Consequence: Possible significant Syspro to project tasks, key deliverables, project milestone achievement and subsequently budget. Loss of key skills during critical timeframes.
- Contingency: Careful selection of project team leaders and members. Replace personnel as quickly as possible, seek transition where possible.
- Early Mitigation: Ongoing initiative to augment user and technical procedures, and prepare an in-house training program.

Dependencies

Some of the dependencies in ERP project plan are outlined below:

- Software functionality support
- Hardware and Communication Infrastructure
- Bandwidth
- Technical Support
- Training

Assumptions

The following list of assumptions are typically taken into consideration for ERP project planning:

i. Requirement Definition Study is the base of the project.
ii. Management is fully supportive to the project.

iii. Management is committed towards the successful delivery of the project.

iv. The Core Project Team remains the same throughout the entire project life cycle.

v. This project will be run using standard Project Management principles.

vi. This plan will be communicated to the project team and all other interested parties.

vii. The plan will also be delivered to the Steering Board.

viii. Changes to the plan must be made through the Project Management.

ix. The Project Team will hold weekly review meetings and be of limited duration (one hour) sticking strictly to Project Progress matters. A typical agenda may include:
   - ensure knowledge imparting
   - review project progress
   - agree and set actions
   - close completed actions
   - mark as complete, all activities completed in the previous week
   - confirm the detail the coming week's planned work
   - identify any project issues
   - review objectives and progress in achieving them
   - review the quality plan
   - review the risk plan

ERP Project Timeline

Project Time is very crucial in ERP implementation. Most of the ERP failure reported in the past was due to project delayed and time factor that was not analyzed well in advance. Project Timeline can be defined depend upon the priorities, resources, size of the project and availability of the 'capital intellectual' in the company. If necessary, overlapping factor must be taken into consideration as shown in the sample chart below. Overlapping may be required in simple project management based ERP implementation, especially in small industries. However, the float time is necessary in composite project management planning. Float time is the time gap in between the end of one activity and start of another activity and also called Lag time, as discussed in previous chapter.

Timeline is very much part of the planning and scheduling as discussed in last topic in this chapter. A sample timeline plan is shown in Fig. 4.2.

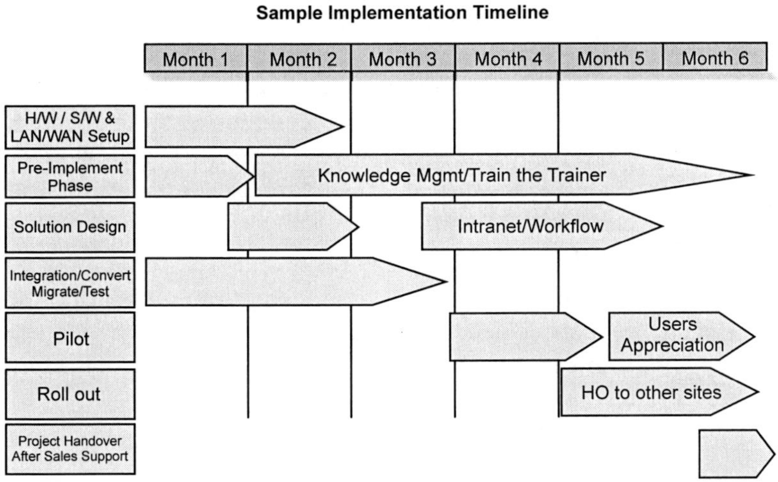

Fig. 4.2

The above timeline reflects the simple, phase based and priority based implementation plan for small and medium size company where an ERP system can be implemented successfully within six months period, provided necessary measures are taken as described in this chapter and earlier chapters. It is recommended to use project management program such as MS Project Manager to monitor and control the process, produce necessary Gantt chart, daily/weekly action plan and milestone charts.

Critical Path technique is essential in Composite project management planning. It is also recommended to use Program review and analysis technique (PERT). This enables you to assess and define the shortest possible timeline in which the project can be completed. PERT allows you to define a table chart indicating start-to-finish total project time and individual project milestone.

The PERT will be converted later into graphic form called Gantt chart normally used in project management.

Project Organization Plan

It is very important to develop a team and define the organization chart, roles and responsibilities of individual entities and the Project Management. The project team must be comprises of highly committed people and they should understand that the success of project implementation is fully depend on their dedication, commitment and teamwork.

Project Management team should be able to take the project ownership during the Project implementation and System ownership after the project handover. Necessary action plan, weekly review meetings, project update documentation and other aspects must be documented.

An Action plan assigning daily tasks and time table must be defined and action completed documentation also must be produced, indicating necessary milestone achieved as per the project plan and stating unachieved tasks and their reasoning and alternates.

It is recommended that a list of project stakeholders is made to know the entities that will be benefited from the project, people who can cause major impact on the project and to whom the project team is directly indirectly answerable for the success and the failure of the project.

A sample Project Organization chart is illustrated below which categorized the entire project organization into (a) Steering committee comprises of the executives, operational and business managers, (b) Project Manager and team, and (c) External consultants/trainers team. The key players in the project are the Project team, the location team and the consultant's team and each team has its team leader.

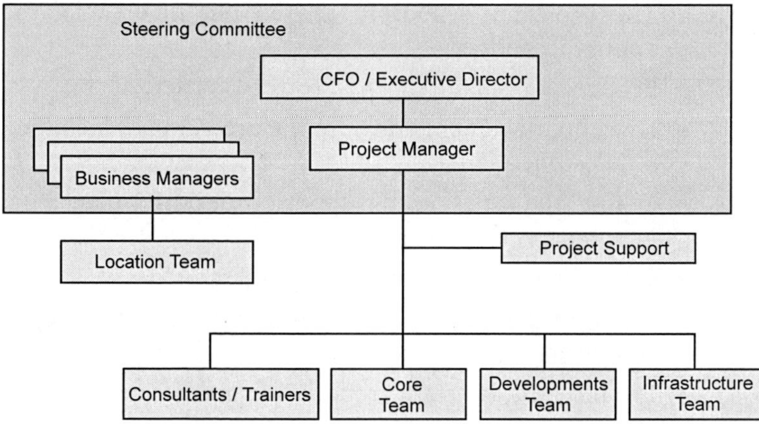

Fig. 4.3: Project Organization—Sample

A detail on the roles and responsibility of individual project entity is outlined below:

CFO/Executive Director (Project Sponsor): The Project Sponsor is responsible for the achievement of overall project objectives. He will:

- Define objectives and directives for the project in the framework of company's business philosophy.
  - Review and approve project plan.
  - Review and approve project related recommendations and expenses on timely basis.
- Ensure that the required resources are available.
  - Ensure that the business managers and key players are extending 100 per cent support and cooperation to project manager and his team members.
  - Encourage dedicated and committed project team members and announce necessary rewards/awards after successful completion of the project.

Project Manager: The Project Manager is responsible for overall project process and shall ensure that:

- The Project sponsor's objectives are met on time.
- Necessary milestone and deliverables are achieved as per the schedule.

- The project is smoothly carried out in view of the approved budget.
- Produce and maintain the Project Charter.
- Develop, document and own the project plan including a milestone plan.
- Define the roles and responsibilities of other team members in the project.
- Co-ordinate with Business Managers.
- Set up a project management system and set project standards.
- Produce regular status reports for management.
- Escalate issues when senior management action is required.
- Study and recommend necessary hardware, LAN/ WAN and communication requirements and ensure 100 per cent compatibilities and workability.

Team Leader

The Team Leader is responsible for managing the provision of agreed project deliverable to schedule, within budget and meet the quality specified.

- Participate in developing the project charter.
- Owner of the business process.
- Identify resources and skills required.
- Responsible for requirements identification, solution development, implementation, documentation, training and building controls.
- Build and manage an appropriate team, which will be responsible for completing the work defined.
- Develop and maintain the morale of the team members.
- Recommend contingency actions if slippage occurs.
- Escalate issues to Project Manager for resolution.
- Communicate progress and status to Project Manager.

Team Members

- Responsible for executing the project tasks assigned by the Team Leader as per the standards.
- Report the progress and issues to Team Leader.
- Provide continuity and support to the Team Leader/ Project Team.
- Be dedicated and committed to the project.

Consultant Team Leader

A detail on scope of consultant's works is discussed in previous chapters.

Structuring and Coding

Coding is the foundation work of ERP software implementation, therefore must be carried out astutely and efficiently. In most cases it is tedious work and all world-class ERP packages facilitate the users to design and define coding as per client's requirements. Coding must be user-friendly, consistent and intuitive.

Coding normally carried out during the Solution Designing of the Project Management base Implementation and mainly applies on the following elements:

- GL-COA (Chart of Accounts)
- Employee, Operation, Department
- Supplier, Shipment, Routing
- Work Center, Cost Center, Machines, Equipment
- Inventory-Stock, Warehouse, Product Class, Routing
- Sales-Branch, Geo, Customer, Sales Rep

Designing of codes need to be done efficiently taking into consideration the size of business and industry standard practices. Some ERP solutions generate automatic codes using in-built facility. Most of the time the coding is done out of the ERP solutions and then updated in ERP system. The fields where the code is keyed are of different field-size in different ERP solutions. Maximum 50-75 alpha or alphanumeric characters can be accommodated in one single field.

It is necessary to take into consideration the following aspects while designing the codes and updating in ERP system:

- Most of the code field in ERP system is a 'Primary Key' type, therefore cannot be changed or duplicated once entered or coded. Once a transaction is processed selecting element code the data integration and functional process is activated and storing process is executed on the basis of selected code as a 'primary key'.
- ERP system allows modifications of structuring or profile updated in the system but not the code as stated above. It allows you to delete the complete code only if there is no transaction value exists against the code or if the value is zero.
- Generally Numeric coding is recommended for all types of coding. This facilitates in producing queries and reports in different scales, ranges and parameters. However, it is not restricted as the requirement could vary from business to business.
- The GL Coding or COA should be simple. It should be categorized into different sets. It is recommended to place a prefix in the beginning and a suffix at the end. A nominal or activity code must be numeric. The prefix and suffix could either be Branch, Region, Geo or sub code. COA (Chart of Accounts): The chart of accounts is a list of ledger account names and account numbers. COA covers every single accounting activities of business operation assigned with a unique numeric or alphanumeric code.

L1	L2	L3	L4	EXPLANATION LEVEL – 1	EXPLANATION LEVEL – 2	EXPLANATION LEVEL – 3	EXPLANATION LEVEL – 4
11	9001			Company or Division	Element	----	----
A-	9001-	001		Division or Branch	Element	Element Group	----
WRJ	9001	700	100	Region + City	Element	Element Group	Sub Group
WRJ	9001	700	SERV	Region + City	Element	Element Group	Franchise

Fig. 4.4: Sample COA—General Ledger Coding

Sample Stock Coding

AP-TOY-HL-1130-R-R	FIRST 2 CHAR IS CATEGORY = AP = AUTOPARTS
AP-MER-HL-1130-B-F	SECOND 3 CHAR IS BRAND = MER = MERCEDES
AP-TOY-HL-1130-R-R	THIRD 2 CHAR IS PART = HL = HEAD LIGHT
	FOURTH 4 CHAR IS PART IDENTITY = 1130
	FIFTH 1 CHAR IS LOCATION = R = REAR
	SIXTH 1 CHAR IS COLOR = R = RED
TI-PIR-116570-CP	FIRST 2 CHAR IS CATEGORY = TI = TIRES
	SECOND 3 CHAR IS BRAND = PIR = PIRELLI
	THIRD 6 CHAR IS SIZE = 116570 = 11.6 × 570
	FOURTH 2 CHAR IS TYPE = CP = CROSS PLY

The above coding can also be defined in numeric as outlined below:

2010001113000 -	FIRST 2 CHAR IS CATEGORY = 20 = AUTOPARTS
2011001113000 -	SECOND 3 CHAR IS BRAND = 100 = TOYOTA
	THIRD 2 CHAR IS PART = 01 = HEAD LIGHT
	FOURTH 4 CHAR IS PART IDENTITY = 1130

– The stock code must be intuitive and instantly read, understand and communicable by the staff in different departments and also by the customers and other associates. The stock code must be descriptive and must also describe the brand, pattern and other necessary identification if possible.

- The customer code could be alphanumeric and must identify the initial of customers and master or sub relationship if exists. If possible it should also identify the concern branch and the geography the customer is related to.
- The supplier coding can be made in similar pattern of customer coding and must identify the category of products and if possible the type of supplier (local, overseas, parts, services, cash, credit, etc.).
- There are many other elements that require coding and any one of the above patterns can be applied for the same.

Like coding, structuring is also carried out during the Solution Designing Phase of the Project Management base Implementation and mainly required to update the profile described below:

- Group GL codes and assign/apply type of A/c (Asset or Capital etc.).
- Classify and categorize all the stock codes and assign a warehouse.
- Categorize customer and assign the branch and sales rep.
- Categorize supplier and assign or apply geography and terms.
- Apply different payment and discount terms codes against customer.
- Apply different payment and discount terms codes against supplier.
- Design and test different stationery forms and formats.

Transition, Data Migration and Historical Record Updates

This is the most critical phase of the project management based ERP implementation. It is necessary to determine the significance of historical Data update from old system to new ERP system. Different migration strategies can be set as per the available resources.

Electronic data update is one of the options and can be handled in following way:

- Firstly, it is necessary to set a cut-off date for old system and also to perform proper balancing and period-end closing in the old system and produce necessary reports for record reference and audit purpose.
- Secondly, using balance take-on option update the new ERP system. Balance take-on may be carried out for the following elements (in view of the RDS documents):
  - Closing value of individual GL Account or head.
  - Closing qty and cost of each stock item.
  - Closing AR balance of individual customer.
  - Closing balance payable against each supplier.
  - Current book value from individual Asset.
  - Current reconciled balance against each bank.
- It is recommended that the first financial year/period defined in ERP system must be identical to the closing period/year of the old system. For instance, the closing period in old system is December 2007 then the new ERP system should start from the same month and year. After taking necessary take-on and 100 per cent verifications, the period-end and year-end should be performed in the new ERP system (i.e. for Dec., 2007). Once you have done this successfully then your ERP system is ready to use from January, 2008 and the opening balances will be indicated against each GL accounts and each elements such as Customer, Supplier, Stock, Bank and so on.
- Most of the ERP solutions provide necessary tools and facilities to electronically update all above-mentioned take-on. It provides you a sample file structure, type and size of table, fields and records of each master table enabling you to map and design similar table in prescribed format. It guides you through how to import and transform database from old system into ERP RDBMS.
- It is recommended not to add historical data during the project implementation phase in live company and it should be updated only after the Pilot Run phase. Historical transactional data is normally required for

analytical reports and in some cases in SCM, CRM and BA system. Therefore, it is worth updating such large volume of database in a dummy/test company. A Report Writer program can be used to create the necessary links between the tables in RDBMS. If necessary one can use the ODBC (open database management system) or BA tools for such works.

- You have two options to have electronic update of historical data and they are: (1) Install a parallel ERP system on a dummy server and electronically update all the historical data in different phases. Obviously, this system will only be accessible for queries and report and all the transaction process will be locked or (2) Add a dummy company in live system using multi-company option of the ERP system and gradually update historical data. This system will also be available only for query and report purpose.
- Manual update of historical data is not recommended as it may not serve any major purpose. It is better to use Business Analytical tools to produce reports combining database of ERP system and database of old system.
- There should not be any transactional backlog from the running financial year and in view of the cut-off date all the pending transactions should be updated in live ERP system.
- Finally, it is recommended to continue with the old system in parallel with the new system for at least 3-4 months, and perform all daily routine transactions and verify it.

Prototype Testing

Prototype testing is always recommended in the ERP project implementation plan. Before data migration or transition and after the solution designing phase, it is necessary to have prototype testing. There are different approaches for prototype testing and a simple one is outlined below:

a. Install ERP system in dummy environment.
b. Follow the steps as described above in Transition and Data Migration.

c. Go through with the necessary setup and business definition process in the ERP system.

d. Go through with the RDBMS tables and system file structure provided by the ERP system and make necessary notes on the type of files, tables, linkages and their relationships.

e. Update codes (few codes) for the following elements. Many ERP systems provide in-built coding and allows to generate codes automatically:

   i. GL A/c codes (complete company chart of accounts)
   ii. Stock codes
   iii. Sales Branch codes
   iv. Warehouse codes
   v. Work centers in WIP
   vi. Supplier codes
   vii. Customer codes
   viii. Branch, Banks and salesmen

f. Ensure necessary financial periods are defined in each module and the counters are ON and ready for the accounting transactions.

g. Ensure the system integration is ON.

h. Copy the complete ERP system setup on another PC or take a backup of the database and structure files on some reliable medium such as CD or pen-drive.

i. Start simultaneous update of ERP system with the following tasks in LAN environment and make necessary notes and remarks on the gaps. One may refer the business mapping process table described in the previous chapter:

   i. User A to enter a PO and complete the cycle including goods receipt note (GRN).
   ii. User B to enter and update the structure and routings in BOM and definitions in WIP and MRP.
   iii. User A to make queries on the tasks he/she has updated while user B continue with his/her tasks as described above in ii.

iv. User C should make expense entries in GL and perform queries in GL, Inventory, Purchase and goods receipts and AP payment entries against the tasks carried out by A as described above in i.

v. Now user B should create and complete a job and the cycle of production and transfer the finish-goods into the inventory/warehouse.

vi. User A should enter a sales and complete the cycle and perform queries in sales and inventory.

vii. User C should perform AR payment against the task as described above in vi and should make necessary queries in Sales, Inventory, WIP, and AR. He/she should also produce necessary in-built reports available in the ERP system.

viii. Users A, B and C should make queries and print necessary reports from the in-built functions available in sub-ledger.

ix. User C should process balancing, period-end perform following tasks:
   - Printing and reviewing of transactional journals.
   - Distribution and balancing of each transaction in sub ledger and review the 'T' accounts.
   - Transaction posting in GL.
   - Produce Financial Report.

– IT Manager should make the WAN environment ready for the following testing:
   - Users A, B & C should test and repeat the above process 'i to ix' in WAN environment.

– I.T. Manager to perform following system testing in LAN & WAN environment:
   1. Communication Bandwidth
   2. Data Traffic bottleneck
   3. System response time
   4. Database failure and data Roll-back
   5. Data congestion

6. Internet Protocol testing
7. Users Security and accessibility in ERP system and in Operating System.

- I.T. Manager to perform following Data disaster recovery test (Detail discussion on disaster recovery on next pages):
  - Data Backup Software System testing
  - Periodic Daily, Weekly, Monthly Backup cycle
  - Backup & Restoring on dummy system
  - Backup in LAN/WAN online environment
  - Data backup tapes/CDS storage in different places

Most of the ERP software offers the utility to perform all kinds of system, LAN, WAN, backup, data and communication testing programs and it is recommended to use the same.

Training (issues, concerns and measures)

User's training is the most important and sensitive aspect of the ERP project implementation. It is necessary that the training is planned with the concept of 'train the trainer'. These trainers would be the key players of the company selected at the time of RDS and these trainers should be capable of taking the 'project ownership' during the project and 'system ownership' after the project implementation.

Training process can be categorized as follows:

- ***Training before Implementation:*** As discussed in previous chapter called 'RDS and project management planning', it would be worth taking some basic training in ERP software solutions prior to ERP purchase. The cost of such training is very nominal and the benefits at large will only be seen during and after the project. This reduces the dependencies on external supports such as 'business consultants' and/or ERP consultants. The critical part of this training is to find out long-term committed and dedicated key players (one or two) who can be sent for the training. The good part of such training is that the company can have a small scale prototype testing of their business automation requirements before spending large amounts of time and money on RDS, ERP selection and ERP implementation. Recently, I have recommended couple of companies in India and Middle East to send their key players for ERP training programs and the outcome was very positive.

- ***'System Owners' training with the concept of 'Train the Trainers':*** This is essential part of the training schedule and can be commenced from the day one of the project planning. It is recommended that, based on the size and operation of the company, one can select couple of key players (future 'project owners' and 'system owners') as described above in the first paragraph of this topic, and involved them from day one in the RDS and project implementation. This training will enable the trainers to develop necessary skills on selected ERP solution and in long run the trainers will develop more trainers or the users as and when required. These trainers are normally the operational managers and once they successfully develop a team of trainers and users, they can go back to their routine job responsibilities. In some cases I have noticed that the large companies, through the ERP vender, have employed couple of good trainers and involved them in the project from the day one and this could be one of the safe and long lasting methods in acquiring ERP skilled people.
- System Users' Training at pilot site: Users training at pilot site can be started in development phase. This training phase is very important and it is necessary to select, after necessary evaluation, couple of 'performers' from different operations such as F&A, Inventory, Procurements and Sales & marketing.

  In my personal experience it is necessary to select 'young performers' in compare to 'gray haired'. The reasons behind this approach is (a) youngsters are prone to adopt change and also to the modern technologies, (b) youngsters are enthusiastic to learn and grow career-wise and most importantly, (c) in view of the past ERP project experiences 'gray haired' employees may cause resistance to change and may not survive for long.

Above are positive sides of selecting the 'young performers' and the negative sides are (a) 'unqualified enthusiasm' has been seen in the past in the 'young performers' and this may lead to HRMS crises, (b) In this era of 'high speed culture' the frequency of changing jobs are very high and lack of long-term job commitments from the 'young performers' are common phenomena.

The above situations normally lead to human resources crises and ERP project failure even after successful implementation. 'Young performers' easily get attracted to new jobs and once the training program is over then they hunt for better opportunities. Nowadays these situations are very common in corporate world, however for ERP project implementation it may be very harmful. In view of these situations, it is recommended that the company planning for ERP should take into consideration necessary career growth planning, schemes for employee awards, rewards, incentives, bonus, salary hike, after the successful project implementation.

It is recommended that the users training conducted by the trainers or by the ERP consultants, obtains necessary user's appreciation and also that the company provides necessary certifications to the users with some incentives as described above. Providing training notes to the users are also recommended.

- ***System user's training at remote sites:*** It can be started during roll out and it will be conducted by the 'trainers' or system owners or other system users. It is recommended, for large size companies that they plan well in advance (a) the transfers of to-be-trainees from the remote sites or (b) the 'transfers' of trained users to the remote sites during the Roll out phase. Apart from transfers, the system owners and trainers will be required to initiate the Roll-out and make necessary arrangements of go-live at remote sites.

- ***Ongoing ERP training for 'System owners' or 'Trainers':*** Earlier, we have discussed the importance of system 'owners' and their long-term commitments. It is necessary that the post project task is planned well in advance during the System Development and Designing phases. These tasks include the training on forthcoming upgraded versions and ports of the ERP system. (ERP Upgrading and enhancements are discussed in earlier chapters.) Ongoing ERP trainings are normally provided by the venders through internet broadcasting services and necessary materials, information, literatures are provided by the venders in their online CRM based system. It is important to note that because of the user-friendly and intuitive nature of ERP solutions the 'Trainers' normally develop new skills and impart knowledge by self-study. This could also be achieved by providing a 'dummy system' where the enthusiastic users can learn.

In large size companies, it is worth forming a 'helpdesk' system from the team of well trained users and well trained trainers. After the project handover such 'helpdesk' system reduces the dependencies on venders or ERP consultants.

It is recommended that the helpdesk system maintain the knowledge management system developed and forwarded by the system 'owners' and the trainers. The significance of knowledge management is discussed next.

Knowledge Management

It is imperative that the knowledge and experience gained during and after the implementation is captured on an ongoing basis and made available to others. When a user or trainer encounters a problem, they can refer the knowledge base to see if such a problem has occurred before and when new problems are identified and solved, they should be updated in the knowledge base. Over a period the knowledge base will provide answers to most of the problems. In this way the knowledge base will remain with the company in most updated form even if a user or the trainer leaves the company.

The knowledge base also facilitates the users or helpdesk to communicate or inform the errors/problems to the venders who is in constant enhancements and developments of their ERP system and they can rectify such errors in forthcoming ports/versions.

Most of the ERP systems provide necessary features as to enable the users to make note of their errors and get online help from the venders and these information is accessible internally in LAN/WAN environment for the users.

Knowledge Management System can be comprises of the following documentation forms and can be stored electronically to provide access to the users:

- RDS documentation
- Business Process Mapping chart
- Gap Analysis documentation
- Operational procedures mapping documentation
- Documents designed during development phase
- Documents designed during coding and structuring phase
- Problems and errors reported during system designing and development phase
- Operational procedures defined during system development phase
- Users notes developed during training phases
- System architecture setup and planning documentation
- Post project adherence ('To do and not to do' tasks)
- Data disaster recover plan
- Issues discussed and documented from correspondences and 'internet chat' both internally and externally with the venders or implementers
- Many other necessary documentation

Disaster Recovery Plan

It is part of the risks analysis in ERP Project Management Planning to take necessary preventive measures and avoid unexpected disruption which may be caused by fluctuations in electricity and communication line, server breakdown and network failures. These elements may cause data corruption and to prevent it necessary gadgets, network switches, UPS system, standby computers and standby communication lines are deployed. Data rollback facility in RDBMS also plays vital role in preventing data corruption. (Detail on data rollback is discussed on next pages.)

Despite of taking necessary preventive measures, always there are possibilities of natural disaster and unavoidable accidental events that may cause total system shut down and consequently the business operation. It is, therefore, essential for the company to be prepared to take necessary action in such a situation. Most important aspect of such events is that the IT team must be aware of the crises management where they should bring back the system live in shortest possible time, meantime they should provide an alternate system so that the 'show must go on' in the business operation.

It is recommended that the IT team (or the system security department) must have a simulation of disaster recovery during the prototyping phase of ERP implementation.

System disaster may cause failure in (a) infrastructure, hardware and/or communication setup, (b) Software System files, and (c) Database/RDBMS files. For infrastructure failure it is recommended to always have standby computers and accessories. For software system it is recommended to keep separate backup of installation, setup, structure, users profile, system profile and other administration information of the ERP system. This backup is not periodic and will be carried out as and when the changes take place.

For database recovery plan, it is recommended to follow the periodic backup cycle based on daily, weekly, monthly and yearly backup cycle. Data disaster recovery plan in business automation is all about taking backup of necessary files in highly organized form so that it can easily be restored in emergency. Reliable storage medium must be used and multiple backup copies should be maintained. Essentially one copy of all types of backup should be kept in the safe away from the office premises, probably in a bank locker.

In order to have an organized backup of RDBMS it is very important to understand and document the file structure of RDBMS defined in the ERP system. For instance, how many data files are used in Inventory module and what are the names of the files and their relationship, likewise all other modules in ERP solution.

There are different techniques and methods used for data backup and they are either available in the Operating System or the ERP system itself. Server mirroring, remote backup system, tape backup, CD backup, etc. are few of them. However, it is recommended to follow the method defined by the ERP vender/ consultant. It is highly essential that the data backup is carried out without missing single day backup. In highly sophisticated setup and business environment, system runs for years without any failure and at some point in time the system security may ignore and miss any one backup cycle and this may cause an unrecoverable failure and enormous loss of business. Therefore, the backup cycle must be carried out religiously.

RDBMS

RDBMS stands for 'Relational Database Management System'. Some of the world-class RDBMS systems are Oracle, Microsoft SQL, SYBASE, DBII and INFORMIX database management systems.

Be it small or large, high-end or low-end, every financial and accounting software system works on certain back-end database management system. There are several types of back-end database systems and few of them are listed below:

- DBMS flat database system
- Index Sequential Access Method (ISAM)
- RDBMS 'Relational Database System'

The DBMS file works efficiently, however the problem with this system is it does not maintain the relationship, therefore performance-wise not appreciated. The ISAM files are very efficient when it comes to data communication, storage and retrieval. The disadvantage of ISAM files is that they do not support the 'rollback' facility or necessary levels of data integrity required for enterprise systems. If the server crashes, network problems occur, or the client PC fails, the data can be left in an incomplete state. For example: If the application is adding a Debit to one G/L account and then a Credit to another, the system could fail between these two parts of the transaction. This would mean that the General Ledger is out of balance.

The ability of the database to guarantee data integrity comes at a cost. This cost is performance security and integrity. This is achieved using Transaction Processing, which is the ability of an application to define a logical business function. For example: If the General Ledger system requires that both a Debit and Credit must be posted, then this may be defined as a transaction. The COMMIT/ROLLBACK logic ensures that either both the debit and credit part-transactions are applied, or (in the event of any problem, including system failure) that neither of these are applied to the database.

Some important aspects of the RDBMS files are defined below:

- A File is an organized collection of records or the storage device in which these records are kept. Each file is made up of a file structure. A file must identify its name and type. The name and type of the file is normally divided by a '.' dot and normally called the file extension.
- A Data File is a collection of related data records organized in a specific manner (e.g. one record for each inventory item showing product code, unit of measure, production costs, transactions, selling price, production lead time, etc.).
- A Data File Structure is the mode in which records are stored within a file, e.g. sequential, random, or index-sequential.
- A Metadata file comprises of the data or detail information of the database.
- Primary Key in RDBMS creates and maintains the link and relationship between tables, queries and other databases and also support maintaining, organizing, sorting and indexing the database(s).

- A FIELD (Column) is a cell to enter a text, string or value. Every FIELD has its own property i.e. 'type' 'size', etc.
- A RECORD (Row) is the collection and group of several fields and the data entries that have been processed and stored.
- A Data Table is an organized form of database a RDBMS systems allows users to update, view, store, maintain and print as and when needed.
- A Data QUERY is a process of extracting and saving different type of information stored in different tables in different databases.
- A Data FORM is a screen view that can be designed to suit ones requirement and it enables users to make data entries and also save in an organized and user-friendly manner.
- Data Integrity is a facility known as Transaction Processing. This facility ensures that a group of transactions is committed to the database.
- Data Warehousing and Mining is a process used to extract different types and sizes of databases, organize and maintain them in one or multiple forms, bookmark them, label them, transform them as per the requirements. As discussed earlier in this book, the data warehousing is part of BA and essential in modern business automation systems such as ERP, CRM, SCM, B2B and B2C.
- OLAP is a tool normally used for online analysis. It's a built-in facility in most of the RDBMS system.
- ODBC (Open Database Management Connectivity) is a tool utilized to extract, link, create and maintain different types of RDBMS or DBMS or other database managements in online and non-online environment. ODBC also enables a database to be converted or transformed into any application software such as Excel, Lotus and Access, etc.

Data Communication System

It is very important that you understand the requirement of data communication system for your business automation and must take this into consideration thoroughly while developing RDS. You must have a clear picture of your LAN & WAN environment in view of number of users and number of remote operational sites. You may have the following option to choose as your data communication system:

- *Non-online communication*: Where the ERP system/server is resided on each remote operational site and data replication takes place from multiple remote sites to central server on hourly or daily basis, using dialup lines or courier services who can carry the data physically on a CD or other medium. However, this is not an efficient ERP environment to work especially since the communication system is affordable.
- *Mixed environments of non-online and online*: This is recommended when it is not possible to have some remote sites online and communication system such as DDN, x.25, x.28, broadband, high bandwidth communication leased lines, Satellite or Microwave, etc. are not available or affordable. If so, then dialup system can be used in conjunction with the EDI system. As discussed in previous chapters, EDI is a cost effective solution to replicate data from remote operational sites to the central server however. EDI is recommended if the required online communication lines are not available at the remote operational sites, or it does not fit into the budget or the communication not justified.
- *Real time online*: This is an ideal ERP environment where all the remote sites are connected online through communication leased lines such as DDN-256 to 1MB KBPS, x.25, x.28, broadband or high bandwidth systems, with the central ERP server. All the world-class ERP solutions function meticulously in this environment. However, it is necessary that both the technical and functional team make necessary study in measuring/sizing the data-flow, data traffic, number of transactions per sites and approximate queries and reports processed/generated from per operational sites.

Apart from above, you may also use WAP, VPN and other such technologies to support real time online ERP-II environment. Please ensure that the data communication system is designed with the help of the consultants and the ERP vender must assure the compatibility of his ERP system with your required communication system and technologies.

Minimum Hardware Requirements for ERP Solution

It is recommended to follow the guidelines and specifications given by the ERP venders and the consultants to select appropriate hardware, operating system, RDBMS, Communication System, LAN/WAN setup and system architecture. It should be 100 per cent compatible with the selected ERP and specified by the vender or the consultants.

Minimum hardware requirement for an ERP system in PC environment in a SME is outlined below for the purpose of project estimation.

Main Server (OS/ERP/RDBMS/Business Logic):

1.8 GHz Server—Multi-Processor

800 MHZ processor

100 GB HD upgrade-ability to multiple storage

2 GB RAM with upgradeability

512 Cache

In-built Tape Backup and Mirroring if necessary.

Client PCs:	Min. Pentium I—preferably Pentium III or IV
LAN:	RJ45 Cabling for small LAN, Optic Fiber for large LAN >16P Hub.
WAN:	Cisco Router/Switch
Communication:	64K/128K DDN leased-line between HO and Remote site
	Dial-up/leased-line at Depots and remote sites
O/S:	Windows 2000 Server and Client/Unix/ Linex
Back-end:	MS SQL Server 2000 + Client 2000 or any other RDBMS

Sample System Architecture for ERP Environment

As discussed previously, the system architecture is normally recommended and designed by the Project Manager, Consultant and are based on the recommendations from the vender. The below sample will help you to understand how a system architecture can be planned for an ERP solution:

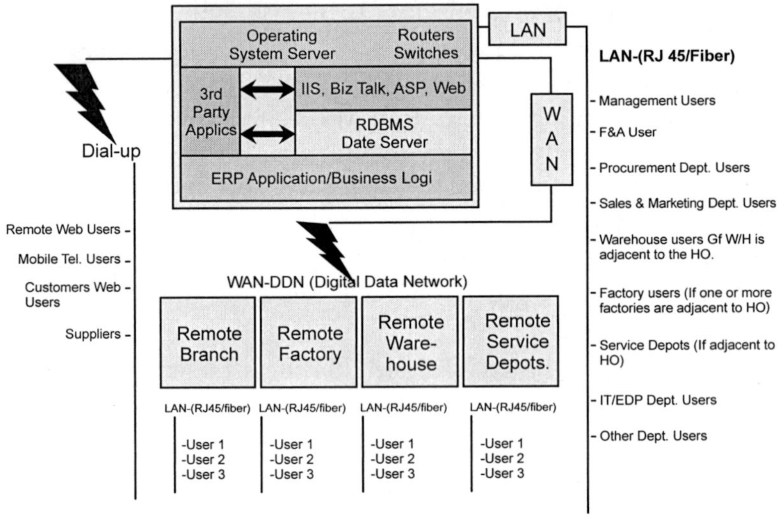

Fig. 4.5: Head Office

CONCLUSION

So far we have covered an overall study on the ERP and reached to the conclusion on the significance of ERP, pros and cons of ERP, the importance of optimum utilization of ERP, its role in business growth and finally the method of successful implementation of ERP solution.

This study will be incomplete if we are not aware about its past failures and the causes of the failures. Therefore, you will find that we have depicted different ERP failures from real life case studies in next chapter.

ERP Project Failures in the Past

5

Introduction

This chapter is all about the past ERP failures reported in different business domain. You will find that the failure stories are described in different patterns to enable you capture the reasons and the outcome of the failures. For study purpose, we have also discussed the solutions how the failure could have been avoided.

The objective of this chapter is to share some past ERP experiences and at the same time enable you to discover some unusual aspects of ERP solution which was not possible to discuss in the previous chapters.

In order not to hurt the sentiments of the concern persons/ companies, we have not stated the names.

At the early stage, there were many ERP project failures reported in different business segments and domains. There could be many reasons for ERP failures such as lack of awareness, lack of availability of infrastructure and communication system, user's resistance to change, scarcity of the professional ERP consultants, low level participation of ERP manufacturers, project delayed, project was not planned properly or project was not implemented professionally are few aspects due to which the ERP failure rate was high in the past. In some cases we have witnessed that although the ERP project was successfully implemented but later on due to non-adherence to the post project assignments a successfully implemented ERP reported failure.

Very few failures have been reported in the recent years. Study shows that primarily the ERP failures occurred due to the delay in ERP project implementation. However, successful implementation alone does not serve the purpose and it is imperative that the ERP solution is optimally utilized. An ERP failure could be a temporary failure and the success could have been achieved with little extra efforts from both the client and the vender. Such temporary failures are mainly caused due to the fact that the client got exhausted in spending on ERP solutions and this happened when the proper planning and budgeting is not done by the client. Instead acquiring a 'Hondas of ERP' or a 'Toyotas of ERP' the client has chosen the 'Rolls Royce of ERP' or the 'Mercedes of ERP' and ultimately the client (specially the SME) could not manage to afford it in long run.

There are other aspects that have been discussed earlier in this book. Let's review different scenarios created on ERP failures from live examples and they are epitomized below:

Case Example I

In this example we will learn how an ERP project temporarily failed even after it was professionally and successfully implemented. One of the largest tire distribution operations in Middle East planned to go for a world-class ERP solution in 1995. The tire operation was part of a very large group of companies who has been dealing in distribution of heavy machineries, equipments and automobiles. For business automation, the group has been using mainframe system for past several years. Total business automation system was comprises of several in-house customized software solutions and the off-the-shelf and accounting packages.

The in-house developed software was not suitable for the tire volume business or rather the tire operation was misfit into the complex business automation system developed in-house primarily for machineries and equipments, as it was said. Therefore, it was planned that the tire operation should be migrated from the existing mainframe environment to PC environment.

A World-class ERP solution was selected after going through rigorous selection process. Necessary RDS was developed and the ERP project implementation was successfully carried out in 9 months while the rapid business expansion also taken place during the implementation phase. Three months after the project handover it was reportedly complained by the users that the ERP system is unable to meet operational requirements and claimed that the selected ERP is failed to meet their requirements. The company invited the 'top cops' from the ERP venders for investigation.

The problems and solutions documented by the 'Top Cops' are outlined below. Based on the solutions corrective measures were taken and the same ERP solution successfully used.

Operational Problems and Solution

Problems

1. User's resistance to ERP system: The users were mainframe users and were accustomed to have their 'wish-list' fulfilled through frequently customized in-house software development team.
2. Physical stock count was not regularly practiced before the ERP implementation and during the implementation phase it was not possible to perform the massive stock count in given timeframe. Therefore, it was decided to continue implementation and let the physical count takes its course of action. Meanwhile, a unique feature available in the ERP system was utilized to meet the project deadline. The unique feature applied was 'Allow negative quantity on-hand'. This feature allows users to perform sales transactions selecting a warehouse where the quantity on-hand indicates zero and when the sales are processed this quantity on-hand becomes negative and indicates the value with minus sign.
   a. Implementation process went smoothly and meantime physical count was continued and accordingly the ERP system was getting updated. The ERP system meticulously handles the physical count and replaces the quantity on-hand physically counted and keyed in the system. The negative quantity is replaced by the

positive quantity during the course of counting and updating. The variance in stock value automatically appeared in the account head called 'stock adjustment'.

b. The problem occurred since the physical count carried out was not up to the mark and the stock was not physically sorted out and separated as good, bad, saleable, obsolescence or scrapped, etc. It was difficult to have accurate counting due to the massive stock and limited time, especially since the operation was running in full swing. So guess what happened next.

c. After couple of months it was found that (a) the stock quantity-on-hand started going negative once again. This means, the unique feature of 'Allows quantity-on-hand to go negative' was not switched off as it was planned to do so immediately after the physical count is over. (b) The final accounting treatment to the 'stock adjustment' through JVE was not carried out. (c) It was noticed by the management that the system was not monitored by the concerned authorities on regular basis.

3. There were >10,000 different types of tires movement taking place in a day from 12 different operational sites and this includes warehouses, storage, branches, depots, service centers. This required National Average Costing method to be applied and generally it was not possible in any ERP solution at that time.

Solutions

1. *User resistance:* This problem was solved by using following tactics:

   a. Users training re-conducted in Head office premises where different users from different operations were called. The idea was to give the users a change of working environment and a sort of importance to both the users and the training process.

   b. The analytical report writing was introduced using different tools such as ODBC.

c. Necessary certifications, incentives and awards was announced by the management for those who have successfully completed the training and shown their long-term job commitment.

2. ***Physical count:*** Although the whole scenario as explained above was taken into consideration during the project planning (in risk analysis, project constraints and contingency plan), however due to the budgetary constrain the bar coding technology was not part of the implementation plan. Later on, to solve this problem of massive counting the bar coding and labeling recommended for long run and meantime the rejected/obsolescence stock is removed to make proper and accurate saleable stock.
3. ***National average costing:*** This was considered as an operational problem and not the 'gap' in ERP system. The National Average Costing method is not a standard accounting practice. It is good to have sales and customer centric business but not at the cost of the inventory mismanagement. The operation workflow must be defined in a way that it gels very well with the concept of the business automation. The problem was resolved by changing operational workflow where the stock Issue and Stock Receipt function was adopted instead warehouse transfer function. This allows the receiving warehouse to key-in the required average stock cost at the time of stock receipt.

Infrastructural Problems and Solution

Problems

1. Remote operational sites were not working in online ERP environment, therefore the transactional database update was taking place through periodic data replication. This was causing missing transactions and duplication in transactional journal numbers.
2. ERP system was not running smoothly in WAN environment due to the low bandwidth. This was causing 'data traffic bottleneck' when producing online analytical reports.

Solutions

These problems were resolved by changing x.25 communication line to DNN online in major sites.

ERP Problems and Solution

Problem

- The ERP system was not compatible with the data roll-back. This coupled with the above-mentioned problem of low bandwidth was causing frequent data communication failure and data corruption.

Solution

- The problem was solved by upgrading x.25 communication lines to DDN (Digital Data Network) line. However, the vender also suggested that the client may migrate on to the latest ERP version which is compatible with the RDBMS and can have better performance in WAN and can also avoid data rollback.

Finally, necessary action was taken by the client and the ERP system was up and running smoothly.

Case Example II

During 2001 a mid-size pharmaceutical company in western India planned for ERP implementation project and selected a world-class, in fact the 'Rolls Royce' of the ERPs. The ERP solution was too big to be acquired, handle and utilized by the client. This client has been dealing in the manufacturing, contracting and distribution of large volume and vast nature of pharmaceutical products. The ERP vender approached to the client with the lists of successful ERP implementations to his credits in the Pharma industry. The client got fascinated by the stories how ERP solutions drastically reduced the production costs of his competitors. In this era of cut-throat competition it was quite natural for the client to get fascinated, especially since the client was planning radical business expansions and expecting high business growth. Hence, the client decided to go for the world-class ERP without taking into consideration the following crucial aspects, and at the end the ERP project was never completed and declared failed:

1. Carrying rapid business expansion together with the ERP implementation is critical. It is very difficult to synchronize the ERP implementation plan and rapid business expansion plan in the same period. This required a phase based and priority based ERP implementation plan and a gradual process. In this case example the client and the ERP vender did not consider these crucial aspects.
2. It is necessary to ensure that the business operation is ready for ERP solutions especially the complex operations such as manufacturing and production. The client's decision to implement ERP in manufacturing and Production Planning, when it was under the process of expansion, was not a wise decision. This caused major setback in achieving the objectives defined in ERP implementation plan. The client could have started with F&A and then S&D modules and finally the manufacturing modules as soon as the business expansions reached to some level of comfort.
3. It is imperative for the client that at the time of ERP selection he/she take into consideration and visit the successfully implemented ERP sites. However, it is equally imperative that the client should have its own RDS and should not just copy the RDS from such reference sites to start the implementation. The client in this case just did the same. Also the vender is equally responsible for such matters.
4. It is always possible to divert or slow down the ERP implementation process provided that necessary measures are taken during the RDS documentation under project risk analysis, assumptions and contingency planning. The client could have easily diverted the ERP project implementation plan or could have slowed down with the help of the vender or ERP consultants. This was the failure on part of project management team.
5. It is also necessary to properly schedule the timeline and estimate the project cost including post project

maintenance. It is common phenomena that the clients do not take into consideration the idle time in implementation and it is obvious that some ERP consultants keep silence on this aspect. Business expansion has always been the primary cause of incurring idle time in ERP project and it may lead to hundreds of idle man-days in rapid expansion.

In rapid business expansion process the project team and steering committee and all other project related staff get engaged in routine business and operational works and unable to dedicate time for ERP project implementation, whereas the ERP consultants and business consultants sit idle and wait for the project team to get free from their routine works. Initially it may start with few hours and then may reach to days and weeks. Consequently it hampers the project cost and the budget.

In above case example the client did consider some of the above-mentioned aspects in the RDS but gave up in view of the chaos caused by the rapid business expansion and the continuously incurring costs. At the end the ERP project was discontinued and declared failure and the company never ever tried, at least in recent years, to go back to any ERP solution.

Case Example III

During year 2000, a chemical manufacturing industry in Far East spent a large amount on an 'old timer' world-class ERP system and after using it for two years migrated to another.

In this scenario we will study how an ERP was failed as the vender was unable to enhance/upgrade the ERP system in view of the rapid technological development and change in business methodologies. It was the ERP solution that was failed and not the ERP project.

The ERP implementation was professionally planned by the client and a world-class ERP solution was selected comprised of F&A, S&D, manufacturing & PP modules. The RDS and the project planning was comprises of all types of risks and contingency planning. The infrastructure, communication line, system architecture, user's training, business and operational methodologies all astutely taken into consideration during the project planning and implementation. The ERP system was used optimally for two years until the time when the client found the need to go for the following advanced features that were essential in view of the development and change took place in the business and operational methodologies:

- **Co-products and by-products:** This was one of the requirements which ranked under low priority in the gap analysis developed at the earlier stage and the vender had promised to incorporate these functions in next release. During that time the chemical industry in general was not expecting larger benefits from such production methods, therefore these features were not considered highly productive.

  In recent years the chemical industry took 'leap-frog' in the production and start using innovated technologies and manufacturing methods where the co-products and by-products played major role in market penetration. There are hundreds different types of chemicals used in millions of products worldwide. This required chemical industries to efficiently apply the methods of producing co-products and utilizing the by-products. These methods drastically increase the productivity and profitability hence they become extraordinary requirement and many world-class ERP venders introduced them in their upgraded version.
- **APS:** The co-product and by-product methods are very complex by nature and required precise controls and monitoring of the whole process and timely decision-making in planning and scheduling. Therefore, Advance Planning and Scheduling was essential to be implemented along with the above features. The client was looking for a feature that allows him to make last minute adjustments in the production schedule, have an accurate forecasting and speed up order turnaround.
- **SCM:** Supply Chain Management System was required to control the supply of several different types of materials purchased from hundreds different local and overseas suppliers. 'Just in Time' inventory became essential for the

client to maintain inventory turnover. A system was required based on exceptional price/performance and functionality that assists client in furthering their Supply Chain control to achieve greater efficiency.

- **SFA:** Generally, the chemical industries are dependant on bulk sales orders and required continuous market exploration, therefore Sales Force Automation system, fully integrated with the S&D system, was essential in view of the business expansion took place at regional levels. The sales team required to travel across the borders in different directions therefore, group communication and centralize access system was essential which can automate the sales-force.
- **Web-enablement:** This feature was not part of the RDS. This requirement was realized in view of the development took place in internet technologies. The client decided to go for web-enabled services and this feature turned out to be equally significance along with the above requirements in view of the emergence of modern technologies and internet working environment. The client was looking for a feature in the ERP system that allows automatic process of the incoming orders by the sales-force from remote location, allows sales-force to query customer's balance and stock availability from their mobile phone.

In view of the above requirements it was essential that the vender provide these features in next versions but in vain. After declaring bankruptcy the vender was under the process of merging and tying-up and could not manage to offer the advanced features or ERP-II version. The associates and the VARS were ready to offer 3rd party customized solution to meet above requirements and it was rejected by the client as it was not a cost effective and efficient solution in mainframe environment.

It is worth noting that despite the setback from earlier ERP solution the client did not abandon the ERP solution. Altogether a new ERP solution was planned, purchased and implemented successfully while migrating from mainframe to PC environment.

The system users were familiar with the ERP environment therefore, it was easy for them to get trained on another world-class ERP solution. Since then the system has been utilized with advanced features and modern technologies and the client is using ERP-II.

Conclusion on ERP Failures

So far we have discussed at length on benefits of ERP, ERP-II, roadmap to select purchase and implement ERP, project management based implementation, ERP failures and many other related topics. All these topics discussed in this book evolve around (a) understanding the significance of ERP and (b) having successful implementation and utilization of ERP solution by avoiding risks of failures.

CONCLUSION

We have learnt different lessons from the past ERP failures described in previous chapters. Most importantly, we have understood that a successful ERP implementation is very much possible and what is required is 'a little extra effort'.

It would be an injustice to our study if we do not talk about a story on successful ERP implementation.

There are millions of successful ERP implementations carried out worldwide and hundreds of success stories are available through different sources. The author took the privilege to copy one of the recent case studies on successful ERP implementation developed by one of his management trainee and which was published in an IT convention organized by BMA (Bombay Management Association) and sponsored by L&T Infotech, Mumbai. It is incorporated in next chapter.

A Success Story of ERP Implementation

6

Introduction

This case study was published as a contest entry in an IT convention conducted by BMA (Bombay Management Association) and sponsored by Larsen & Toubro Infotech Ltd., Mumbai, India.

SABMiller

A Case Study in ERP Implementation

Ravindra Puri
Fr. Agnel's Business School

Foreword

This study has been developed by Ravinder Puri, the undersigned. I am a final year M.M.S. student of the Fr. C. Rodrigues Institute of Management Studies (Fr. Agnels' Business School). This study is based on the observation, evaluation and information collected during my training in eZeesoft (P) Ltd. The company names, persons names, brands and trade marks belong to the respective entity and shall not in any circumstances used/misused for any commercial or legal or any other matters.

During my MMS study I got in touch with eZeesoft (P) Ltd. which deals in ERP software consultation and have given patronage to Business Management students from various B-Schools including Fr. Agnels'. eZeesoft (P) Ltd. is based in Mumbai and is an authorized distributor of world-class ERP solution named SysproÔ, in India and ME. The CEO, Mr. Zubair H. Shaikh, has been in computer software business for past more than 20 years and served several international brands abroad. He has been associated with Syspro ERP software solution for past 12 years.

In eZeesoft, I was given an opportunity to learn ERP and also participate as a trainee in live project at a customer site in Jaipur called RBL (Rochee Breweries Ltd., a part of SABMiller India).

> SABMiller India Entered in India in October 2000. To Expand its business in India, soon alter its entry it embarked on a major effort to acquire a few Indian companies. It was the need of the company to adopt a state of the art system to integrate the data for the smooth functioning of the organization, in a highly competitive and global environment.
>
> The case highlights the process and challenges faced by SABMiller in its quest of a successful implementation of ERP (SYSPRO).

The Background of SABMiller PLC

SABMiller plc is one of the world's largest brewers with a brewing presence in over 40 countries across four continents and a portfolio of strong brands and leading market shares in many of the countries in which it has brewing operations. Outside the USA, SABMiller plc is one of the largest bottlers of Coca-Cola products in the world.

In June 2001, SABMiller acquired, through its subsidiary company, a controlling 76 per cent stake in Mysore Breweries Limited (MBL), a company listed on the Bangalore Stock Exchange. The MBL group operates two breweries situated at Bangalore and Aurangabad, employing 250 people. SABMiller also acquired, through its subsidiary company, SAB India Limited, a 53 per cent controlling stake in Rochees Breweries Limited (RBL) and in Narang Breweries, in Nawabganj, Uttar Pradesh, northeast of Delhi. Recently, SABMiller signed a joint venture with Shaw Wallace Group and acquired major beer market share in India and currently operating from more than 20 sites nationwide.

SABMiller India studied thoroughly their requirements and the how's and why's of ERP that are discussed below:

- Customized Software Solution leads to endless programming and developments. It is not a cost-effective solution. It does not allow business to follow Industry Standard Practices.
- Accounting Packages support limited functionalities. They do not provide seamless integration and therefore leads to duplication of works. It does not grow when the business grows.
- ERP software provides all those features that are not supported by Customized and Accounting solution as described above. In addition to this, scalability, future upgrading, user friendliness navigation, integrity and security are fundamental aspects of ERP solution. Modern business automation concepts such as CRM, SCM, PLM, E-commerce, web and internet compatibility, interoperability, platform and environment independency are built-in features of the world-class ERP solution.

In May 2002, after evaluating local and international ERP solutions and accounting packages SABMiller decided to go for IMPACTÔ / SysproÔ. The principal company, 'South African Breweries' in South Africa has been using Syspro's ERP solutions for past several years and this was one of the major factors that SABMiller decided to opt for SysproÔ. The other aspects SABMiller evaluated such as cost effectiveness, user friendliness and most importantly the system is able to grow as and when business grows in SABMiller.

SABMiller - ERP Evaluation

SABMiller has evaluated couple of local accounting packages as well as world-class ERP solutions. SAP R/3 and Oracle Financials were found to be too big and costly solutions. There were medium range ERP solutions such as IFS, SAGE, Great Plains and Syspro evaluated by SABMiller India. They have also evaluated the low-cost local accounting packages such as IBS and Tally (previously used in MBL) and found that they are unable to meet the criteria as discussed in above paragraphs.

Preliminary Planning

ERP implementation has certain risks, dependencies and challenges and SABMiller India too envisaged these challenges such as implementing ERP solution during rapid business expansion and change in corporate culture. Human behavior, users training cost, implementation timeframe, localization, infrastructure and data communication were few other challenges SABMiller took into consideration. The only relaxation SABMiller had at the time of decision-making was the past experience and confidence in Syspro ERP. Mr. Derek Kemp, then IT Manager SAB and Mr. David Kvalsavig the M.D. Mysore Breweries decided to call upon the directors of Syspro and eZeesoft to discuss the possibilities of implementing Syspro.

The key issues were discussed in the preliminary meeting are as follows:

(a) IT budget and investment plan.
(b) SABMiller's expansion plan.
(c) Immediate requirements and priorities.
(d) Phase based implementation plan.

Before SABMiller finalized the selection of ERP solution, they had contacted the principal company in South Africa. Syspro solution was implemented in SAB South Africa on the basis of RDS (Requirement Definition Study). SABMiller found that the existing ERP structure, setup and coding, chart of accounts and core business functionalities are more or less similar to what is required in SAB India. Seventy per cent of the core functionalities found to be the same. Finally it was decided to go for Syspro ERP solution.

IMPACT™ / Syspro™ ERP Solution

IMPACT™ and Syspro™ ERP solutions are designed and developed by Syspro Group. The foundation of Syspro ERP solutions were developed 25 years ago and traveled a long way of enhancements from Impact Award™ DOS based version to Encore™ GUI version and to the latest Syspro™ .Net version. Syspro ERP solutions are design on componentization basis and used by more than 5000 small, medium and large sizes of enterprises all over the world.

In order to maintain its presence and market share in the global ERP market, Syspro has been investing in development and enhancement that meet the modern business and technological concepts such as B2B, B2C, CRM, Engineering Change Controls, etc. Syspro comes under top 5-10 world-class ERP solutions. On several occasions Syspro ERP has been bench tested and applauded by prominent institutions such as Price Waterhouse, AMR, PC Magazines and many more.

Syspro solution offers all the necessary ingredients a world-class ERP solution must offers such as seamless integration, User-friendliness, adaptability, intuition, navigation, users security, platform independency, future upgradability.

Implementation Methodology

After several discussions with the Top Management team, it was decided that the following approach would be followed:

(a) Define phased based implementation plan to suit the rapid business expansion, management and cultural changes, study infrastructure, customization and localization.

(b) Implement F&A and S&D modules and go-live at existing 5 operation sites in Phase-1.

(c) Initialize the pilot project at MBL and follow the project management based implementation strategy and continue study on system architecture, manufacturing modulation, WAN and online data communication.

(d) Identify and eliminate the 'gaps', expand Syspro in WAN environment, adapt advanced technologies such as .Net, define centralized and de-centralized business process, implement consolidated management reporting system, and finally implement manufacturing and web-enabled modules, in Phase-2.

Modulation

Initially Finance & Accounting, Sales & Distribution solutions comprises of the following modules have been selected for pilot implementation at MBL.

Finance & Accounting	*Sales and Distribution Utility*
Accounts Payable	Sales Order
	Report Writer
Accounts Receivable	Sales Analysis
Cash and Bank	Purchase Order
General Ledger	Inventory Control
Fixed Assets	

It was recommended initially to purchase the license for small number of users and gradually increase the user licenses. This was a cost effective approach to save money in view of the future business expansion SABMiller planned.

Implementation Roadmap and Action plan phase-1 (Summary)

- Formation of 'System Owners' team and definitions of tasks.
- Discussion and presentation on the implementation process.
- Commence users training.
- Design and test a prototype based on the setup, definitions and coding from principal company in South Africa.
- Match COA GL codes of new system with old system.
- Installation, Setup and Testing of System Security in Client/Server environment.
- Document above, get management approval and file/ record.
- Modify necessary coding and Chart of Accounts and electronically update into GL Module.
- Manual update Supplier, Branch, Banks, Customers and other element codes.
- Define and link GL Interfaces.
- Design and define stationary formats / forms.
- Define the parameters for Opening Balances and update the system.

- Commence transaction backlog update.
- Produce sample built-in reports and circulate.
- Map the Financial reports of new system with old system.
- Map the opening and closing balances of Old system and new system.
- Define 'Daily Tasks' daily backup cycle and data security rules.
- Plan, document and test the data disaster recovery.
- Review and intensify Users security.
- Test Month-end and Year-end in Dummy environment.
- Go-live.
- Fine tune system, plan next phase, continue training at other sites.

Transition

During the prototype, the data transition was given utmost importance. It was decided to electronically transfer the data wherever possible and for this ODBC (Open DataBase Connectivity) tool was utilized. Syspro's built-in functionalities utilized to update customer, stock and suppliers history.

User Training

The major concern was users' training. The training was conducted with the concept of 'Train the Trainer'. 'System Owners' team was formed who takes up the project ownership during the implementation and system ownership after the project handover. Individual user appreciation is obtained and documented for record and reference. Small user notes and templates are designed in addition to the online help available in Syspro's software solution. A 'Helpdesk' system is planned for Phase-2 implementation. Syspro's built-in functionalities were utilized to customize the user's screen. This helps users to get trained better and faster.

Localization

Localization was the major concerns that were resolved with the help of eZeesoft consultants. Applying, calculating and updating the excise duties and taxes at the time of Sales Invoicing were resolved using the user-defined fields available in the system. Necessary interfaces defined and linked with the stock codes to automatically calculate and apply the excise duties. The GL interfaces in Syspro solutions are available at module / sub-ledger level and this makes the accounting implications and posting easy.

Problems and Solutions

There were several problems identified and foreseen at the time of development of the prototype. They were documented, resolved and eliminated and were as follows:

- *Users resistance to change.* This was resolved by ensuring that the key users own the system implemented and sustained the benchmark of 80 per cent satisfaction in training. Management also taken necessary measures to announce different rewards and certifications in long-term planning.
- *Rapid business growth and change in management.* This causes delay in implementation and lack of utilization. This was handled with the concept of 'Train the Trainer' in Phase-1 implementation plan and with the concept of 'NSO' (National System Owners) in Phase-2 implementation plan. By this approach the controls and optimum utilization were in place during and after the implementation.
- *Job insecurity to employees.* ERP for obvious reasons reduces the daily routine works, but only if they are unnecessary, duplicated or followed without industry standard practices and this causes sense of job insecurity among both good and bad employees. Initially it was encountered and the management has taken necessary measures to eliminate it by ensuring that ERP is meant for increase in productivity and efficiency and not to downsize the manpower structure. However, it was clarified that those who fail to contribute in achieving the objective may not survive on job.
- *Change in system functionalities, workflow and management.* Reporting cause distress. Migration from small accounting package to a powerful ERP solution

causes increase in functionalities and change in management reporting. The clear objectives of migration from accounting package to ERP were defined and documented at the early stage and awareness was created among every individual that these changes are going to play pivotal roles in increase in productivity, efficiency and ROI (Return on Investment).

ROI

SABMiller India at the early stage calculated the Return On Investment before deciding to opt for ERP. Within a year time they have started getting the results. Some of the areas highlighted below that reflect the astuteness of SABMiller's decision:

- The seamless integration of modules created the clear visibility of every individual transaction and eliminated duplication which resulted in speedy decision-making, especially to satisfy customer needs.
- Cost of Sales are determined at the time of transacting Sales Invoice, therefore the deal profitability and gross profit in general are instantaneously available and visible. This enabled the management to analyze the business on timely basis.
- Predefined selling pricing system helped in managing customers as per the classification.
- Predefined controls on Debtors and Creditors enabled F&A to have necessary ageing reports on timely basis and this consequently provided visible cash flow.
- Inventory movements became visible and instant. This supported the operation to control the purchases and deliveries and achieve better inventory turnover.
- Forecast, budget and actual figures are reported on timely basis and necessary analytical reports are directly accessible by top-levels.
- In view of all above, the Syspro ERP system in SABMiller increasing the efficiency, productivity and profitability.
- The Phase-2 plan is under process and SABMiller is planning to gradually enhance the system with

manufacturing, B2B, B2C and CRM modules available in Syspro. This seems how a world-class ERP grows when business grows and how it allow user to follow the phase-based implementation approach.

Author's Comments

My personal observation is that:

- An ERP should be selected as per the in-depth RDS.
- An ERP should be implemented with very well planned and organized approach and must be based on Project management based.
- An ERP implementation should be backed, supported and owned by all the management including the Big-Boss.
- The company must be ready to accept the corporate culture changes before deciding for ERP.
- Technologies and infrastructure plays major role in optimum utilization of an ERP solution.

Bibliography

The following web sites have also been referred in order to gather necessary information:

- www.ezeesoft.co.in.
- www.syspro.com
- www.technologyevaluation.com
- www.sabmiller.com

Market

7

Introduction

Writing on ERP market is a sensitive subject. There are rapid changes occurring in ERP market and one may not be able to do justice with the topics related to ERP marketing. Therefore, you will find some precise but highly useful information about ERP market which hopefully will be sufficed to supplement the topics discussed in this book.

Current and Future ERP Market

During past one decade the ERP market was growing at 3 to 5 per cent and during years 2003-2005 the market viewed as a matured market. According to Gartner, Inc. (NYSE: IT and ITB) in 2002, worldwide ERP new license software revenue totaled $5 billion, down from $5.5 billion in 2001. While 2002 was not a successful year for software providers, Gartner analysts said ERP application providers were able to reign in what could have been a potentially disastrous year. "A shift in buyer behavior, due in part to users' past experiences of software failing to meet expectations, has created a more cautious buyer that seeks smaller, less-expensive pieces of software to quickly drive positive bottom-line results", said Chad Eschinger, principal analyst for Gartner's worldwide software applications research group.

We have discussed the concept of ERPO in previous chapters and have also discussed in detail the problems, issues and concerns on ERP products, growth, costs, etc. Yet, ERP market is vibrant in view of the development in global economy, growth in corporate revenue and profitability, increase in sales and market penetration especially in China, India and different parts of Asia Pacific & Middle East region.

Key Players and Market Shares

ERP market divided into (a) high-end (b) mid-range and (c) low-end segments. Currently there are 3 key players in ERP market and they are SAP™, Oracle™ and Microsoft™. SAP (along with SAP™ R/3 & MySAP™) and Oracle™ (along with Oracle Financials and JDE) are categorized into high-end and Microsoft's Navision falls under mid-range. Earlier there were 15 key ERP venders worldwide as described in previous chapter and many of them vanished from the market due to their inability to cope up with the rapid technological developments and enhancements and change in business methodologies.

As part of their marketing strategies the above 3 players offer second brand ERP solutions for SME segment. SAP offers Business One™, Oracle offers JDE™ and Microsoft offer Great Plains™ for medium and small segment.

Approximately 50 per cent of the total ERP market shares are acquired by these 3 top ERP venders whereas SAP alone acquired 25 per cent. Oracle in view of its recent acquisitions/mergers acquired 15 per cent (this excludes Oracle's list of non-ERP products) and Microsoft with its business solution packages, such as Navision, Great Plains are holding approximately 10 per cent market shares.

Microsoft is vigorously marketing its enterprise solutions, targeting SME segment and capturing large market shares in South East Asia, Asia Pacific, Latin America and Middle East. Microsoft Navision enterprise solution is capturing market by competing with its contemporaries such as IFS, Syspro and Sage. Although Navision pricing is at higher side, however it is the Microsoft flagship that plays major role in the growth and market shares. Also Microsoft has been investing heavily in market penetration and opening business houses in different regions and appointing strategic partners worldwide.

Twenty-five per cent of the ERP market is occupied by mid-range ERP venders such as IFS, SYSPRO, Sage, etc. and the balance 25 per cent is occupied by those who targets low-end market segments and most of them are local ERP solution providers/venders.

Market Issues

A very large portion of untapped market is waiting to be explored. Most of the industries are not aware about the significance of ERP in their business. Some industries are studying the possibilities of acquiring ERP solution and some are mistakenly thinking that ERP is not required in their company or investment on ERP is not justified. ERP venders failed to create the required ERP awareness among these industries. Major portion of this 'neglected' market is medium and small industries which incorporates >75 per cent of the total market.

ERP venders somehow could not eliminate the 'myth' that ERP software is for corporate or large groups or it is a high-value commodity and so on. It seems that the medium and small industries are waiting for ERP venders to slash the cost and take some responsibilities of successful implementation. ERP venders are just waiting that somehow their channel partners will convince the clients to invest on ERP. The end result is slow growth in ERP market.

There is a fierce demand in the market that ERP venders should tailor their software to the needs of specific industry verticals. In view of technical and commercial viabilities it is not possible to design, redesign or rewrite the solution for several hundreds types of industries. However, to cope up this situation the ERP venders, to certain extent, have come up with a solution called SOA (Service Oriented Architecture) as discussed earlier in this book.

ERP venders are continuously inventing new functionalities and adding new features and modules to attract the customers and this is inflating the size and the cost of the total solution. On one hand this has been giving leverage to large corporate houses to increase productivity and on the other hand this inflation in ERP cost and size is causing difficulties for SME segment to decide on ERP.

Although it's a fact that additional features and innovative functionalities are very much required by the high-end segment and they can invest heavily on ERP and can have good ROI too. However, it is also a fact that such a trend is sending wrong signals to the SME segments in the market and as discussed earlier SME segment thinks that ERP is not for them and is for big corporate groups only.

It is worth noting that >75 per cent of the global SME market is untapped market for ERP and most of them are small manufacturing industries highly potential for ERP. 'Global Fortune 25,000' companies have already embraced the 'Rolls Royce of ERP' solutions. However, clients in SME segment have not got convinced so far despite continuous efforts exerted by the ERP venders and their channel partners. As discussed in previous chapter, if the bone of contention is the cost for SME then the ERP vender should come out with an alternate solution. ERP on rent and ERPO could be an alternate solution, as discussed in previous chapter. The subject matter needs to be studied in detail and the commercial and legal viabilities need to be determined by the venders. The author will be discussing this subject in detail in next edition.

It is pathetic that the 40 Billion dollars ERP market has been estimated and there are very little to see, read and know about it. ERP ads rarely appear in the newspapers and business magazines for such matter in electronic media.

Some world-class ERP venders have already taken necessary actions in creating ERP awareness among SME segment and small size (small in operational but big in turnover) industries. As part of their marketing strategies these venders are conducting seminars and training for SME segments and offering second brand and low cost ERP solution with guarantee on successful implementation. Many world-class ERP brands have become the part of the syllabus of management studies and this will create more 'ERP-man' in the future which is an essential aspect in growth and long lasting of ERP market.

As per the market reports, ERP market is increasing from 20 Billion to 40 Billions by year 2012 and this is the clear indication of the significance of ERP as product and solution and also as a market.

CONCLUSION

This book ends here but not the subject matter. It will go on because the future of the business automation is ERP!

I am thankful for your patience while reading this book and am sure that this book will not be a decorative object in your shelf.

Bibliography

Following websites have been referred for necessary information on ERP products, brands and marketing.

www.technologyevaluation.com

www.gartner.com

www.sap.com

www.syspro.com

www.oracle.com

www.automationworld.com

www.arc.com

www.amr.com

Following books, articles and documents have been referred by the author:

- *ERP Demystified*

  By Alexis Leon,
  Tata McGraw-Hill, 2000.
- *Management 21C,*
  Author Subir Chowdhury
  Prentice Hall,
  Pearson Education.
- *Financial Management, Theory & Practice*
  Author, Prasanna Chandar,
  Tata McGraw-Hill.
- *Project Management for Business and Technology,*
  Second Edition
  Author John M. Nicholas
  Prentice Hall India.

- *Management Information System* Second Edition Authors Gordon B. Davis & Margrethe H. Olson, McGraw-Hill International Editions, Management Series.
- Different articles from *Harvard Business Review*, especially articles related to Business Management, Marketing, Operations and case studies, have helped the author in writing this book.

Glossary

AP (A/P)	= Accounts Payable Module.
AR (A/R)	= Accounts Receivable Module.
ASP	= Active Server Pages. Microsoft technology that allows developers to create dynamic web pages that execute on the web Server.
BizTalk	= Microsoft Server Operating System. Interprets between different Applications and components.
BOM	= Bill Materials.
CAT RJ45	= Category and type of cabling used in Local Area Networking.
COM	= Component Object Model. Microsoft's model for creating and using reusable components that allows applications to link in Windows environment.
Componentization	= Concept of modulation in Integrated software package solutions that allows the customers to choose specific module(s).
COS	= Cost of goods sold, normally achieved from the production cost calculation or net landed cost calculation and used as a factor to calculate the Gross Profit.

CRM = Customer Relationship Management software. Online information support system that enables users to manage customer interactions.

Data disaster failure = Data failure that may occur due to the fluctuation or collision in electricity and/or telephone lines despite preventive measures and may distort data integrity.

Data Roll back = Controls defined in the software programming to prevent partial transaction update in the event of data disaster failure.

DDN = Digital Data Networking. Communication leased-line normally subscribed by the users to have WAN connectivity.

EDI = Electronic Data Interface (Electronic Data Interchange). An interface that enable users to Export and Import data.

EDP = Electronic Data Processing Department.

ERP = Enterprise Resources Planning. Integrated Software Package solution that meets the complete business requirements adhering to the Industry Standard Practices, will normally cover Sales, Distribution, Inventory, Purchase order processing and Financial Accounting.

ESCROW = A clause in the software license contract that guarantees access to the Software Source Codes if the software manufacturer is declared bankrupt or goes into liquidation.

F&A	=	Finance & Accounting.
Fiber Optic	=	Type of cabling used for speedy long distance data communication. The fastest and most secure method of computer connectivity.
GL	=	General Ledger Module.
GSM	=	Global System for Mobile Communications. GSM is an open, non-proprietary system that is constantly evolving. One of its great strengths is the international roaming capability. This gives consumers seamless and same standardized same number contactability in more than 170 countries. GSM satellite roaming has extended service access to areas where terrestrial coverage is not available.
Hub	=	Device that links computers via internal cabling in local area network and also performs distribution and control over data traffic.
IIS	=	Internet Information Server. Microsoft's Server Operating System designed to work in Web environment.
ISDN	=	Integrated Services Digital Network. Fast digital data communication services.
JVE	=	Journal Voucher Entries normally carries out in General Ledger to book operational expenses and adjustments.
LAN	=	Groups of computers connected on local site.
MCC	=	Modern Computers & Communication Co. Ltd.
Modem	=	Device that interprets the data in telecommunication.
NETBIEU	=	Communication protocols used to create links between computers or group of computers.

NLC = Net Landed Cost calculated in distribution operation and which comprises of Cost + Freight + Insurance + custom clearance + import duties, mooring & mooring and inland haulage.

ODBC = Open Database Connectivity. Software tool that enable user to create data connectivity and relationship.

POD = Proof of Delivery.

RDBMS = Relationship Database Management System.

Routers & Switches = Devices that link computers via modems and communication lines in wide area networking and also distribute and control the data traffic.

SCM = Supply Chain Management software. Online information support system that enables users (suppliers and distributors) to access, view, communicate and exchange information on products, stocks production, supply & delivery and financial accounting.

SDK = Software Development Kit offered by ERP venders which enables the client to do customization and/or 3rd party integration.

SOAP = Simple Object Access Protocols. Microsoft enhanced technology.

TCP/IP = Transmission Control Protocol/Internet Protocol.

IP - is responsible for moving packet of data from node to node. IP forwards each packet based on a four byte destination address (the IP number). The Internet authorities assign ranges of numbers to different organizations. The organizations assign groups of their numbers to departments. IP operates on gateway machines that move data from department to organization to region and then around the world.

TCP - is responsible for verifying the correct delivery of data from client to server. Data can be lost in the intermediate network. TCP adds support to detect errors or lost data and to trigger retransmission until the data is correctly and completely received.

WAN	=	Wide Area Network. Group of computer-sites that communicate over a wide geographical area.
WIP	=	Work-in-Progress Module.
WAP	=	Wireless Application Protocol.
XBRL	=	Extensible Business Report Language. Translate and link two different reports in Web Browser.
XML	=	Extensible Markup Language. Universally adopted data exchange format. The format refers to the data content.
XSL	=	Extensible Style-sheet Language. Allows transformation of the raw XML data into readable content in a Web Browser.
Y2K Compliance	=	Year 2000 Date Compliance.

Success in Selling

Thirty Valuable *Mantras*

A. Nag

ATLANTIC
PUBLISHERS & DISTRIBUTORS (P) LTD

Published by
ATLANTIC
PUBLISHERS & DISTRIBUTORS (P) LTD
7/22, Ansari Road, Darya Ganj, New Delhi-110002
Phones : +91-11-40775252, 40775214, 23273880, 23275880
Fax: +91-11-23285873
Web: www.atlanticbooks.com
E-mail: orders@atlanticbooks.com

Printed & bound in India by Atlantic Print Services

Dedicated to
All Persons Who Aspire
to Make a Career in Selling

Preface

Selling is a fascinating profession. To many, selling appears simple; and, they get into the selling profession as a sales representative or salesperson hoping to have an easy time, and lots of money. But, they soon realise that it is not so. But, it is not so difficult also. If they have the intent, learn the tools and techniques and develop the skill for professional selling, they can achieve success.

Many books, including textbooks, are available on sales management. Text books are primarily meant for MBA, PGDM students. These are essentially foundation courses.

Not many books are available which give more real world, practical lessons or guides for success in selling. The present book intends to provide that.

We may call this book a "Workbook" or a "Toolbook" or a "Guidebook". The book prescribes thirty *Mantras* for success—thirty different ways to orient, improve and reach perfection in selling.

The book is meant for persons who wish to start/make a career in selling, those who are already in selling, and also those who dream of becoming star performers or sales superstars.

A. NAG

anag_123@rediffmail.com

Contents

Mantra 1

Feel Proud to be a Salesperson

Production minus sales is equal to scrap....

Selling is like a "Locomotive"; it pulls all other departmental carriages (of a company) together to the marketplace....

First, and, foremost, feel proud that you are a salesperson. You are delivering (selling), something (product) to somebody (customer) to satisfy his/her need. So, take pride in this.

Do not treat selling just as a job. A plumber, carpenter, mason—they all do a job. A job can be casual. Treat selling as a *profession*. A profession is more regular and serious; **it has more commitment, discipline and ethics.** That is selling.

WHY YOU SHOULD BE PROUD OF SELLING

There are many reasons why you should take pride in selling. Fifteen good reasons are given below. These are derived from the experience of some successful salespersons I know and my own experience.

1. Selling is a Professional Job: The salesperson follows principles, methods, and discipline to develop the virtues of a professional—the virtues of commitment and dependability of the company and the customers. The salesperson enjoys the results and achievements like a professional.

2. Selling means giving People the Product(s) they Want: Selling is not just a transaction—supplying a product and receiving a payment. It is more than that. It means meeting their need and giving them satisfaction. The salesperson feels proud to do so.

3. Selling gives Good Compensation for Performance: The compensation package in selling is attractive. It is not only the monthly wage or salary. It also contains other financial and non-financial benefits. These make the compensation package attractive.

4. Selling gives Freedom to Work: The salesperson is almost left to himself (herself) to work or perform. Of course, guidelines or instructions may be given by the company or the sales manager. But, given those guiding factors, the salesperson has the freedom to work the way he (she) likes. Freedom gives responsibility, but, it also gives satisfaction.

5. Selling means Enjoying Work with Sales Aids, etc.: The salesperson has, at his (her) disposal, many sales aids, props, samples and even gimmicks to play with. These give him (her) vintage. He (she) can use all these and enjoy his (her) salesmanship.

6. Selling gives an Opportunity for Learning: Selling gives an opportunity to the salesperson to enjoy working with other salespeople often as a team. The salesperson can share experiences, success stories, mistakes, failures, etc. This is a big opportunity for learning and improvement. This helps (him or her) to become a more mature and, a more complete salesperson.

7. Selling gives an Opportunity to Help Other People: Selling is a profession in which salespersons, with skill and experience, can help and guide others who want to make a career in sales. This way, the salespersons can change the course of lives of many unemployed and aspiring people.

8. Selling gives Challenge to Sell new Products of the Company: Companies make product modifications, develop new products or brands and those are offered for sale. Salespeople have a challenge in selling the modified or new products or brands. This breaks the monotony of selling the same old products/brands. Selling new products/brands becomes a new challenge which can be exciting and also rewarding.

9. Selling gives Recognition for Accomplishment: Every individual likes recognition of effort or accomplishment. This is true of salespersons also. Most companies recognise performance in their own ways. The recognition is important. This encourages salespersons to strive for more recognition.

10. Selling gives Opportunity to Advance Professionally: Recognition for performance inspires salespeople to advance professionally. You are proving yourself through your own effort. The company does not see what is your qualification or experience; the company watches how you are performing. So, in one sense, the salespersons progress or promote themselves through their own efforts.

11. In Selling, the Company Motivates Salespersons to Perform Better: In selling, one of the major objectives of companies is to motivate salespersons to increase their productivity and perform better. Different companies use different motivational methods or tools to motivate salespersons. These give the salespersons necessary inducement or inspiration to perform better.

12. In Selling, the Company Imparts Training for Improving Skill and Capability of Salespersons: Like motivation, training is also regularly organised to improve skills and capability of salespersons. Need-based training programmes are organised from time to time for improvement of skills and capability of individual salespersons. Many salespersons have greatly benefited from such programmes for enhancing their skills and capabilities to sell.

13. In Selling, Special or Outstanding Performance is Rewarded: Every company in selling invariably rewards special or outstanding performance. The rewards can be in the form of cash incentives, paid holidays, special gifts depending on the company and the nature or type of performance. This is the characteristic of the selling profession. These rewards are great motivators.

14. In Selling, you Enjoy an Exciting Life: Selling means challenge and excitement. So, if you are in selling, you can enjoy the life a professional lives. If you are active in selling, there may not be any dull moment in your career. That is something to be proud of.

15. In Selling, you may Enjoy Competing with Champion Salespeople: In selling, you have to compete with other salespeople. If you like or love competition, you may enjoy competing with world class champion salespeople. You may not run like Johnson, swim like Spitz or fight like Tyson. But, you can sell like anyone in the world. So, you can take great pride in your selling.

PREPARE YOURSELF TO BE PROUD OF SELLING

After going through these fifteen reasons or points, do you think you should be proud to be a salesperson?

If your answer is 'Yes', you have got it right. You have understood why you should feel proud of selling.

If your answer is 'No', go through these fifteen points again, ponder over them till you feel proud to be a salesperson.

Start your sales career with this mindset.

Taking pride in what you are doing implies a more fundamental mindset. Develop this mindset. This is important in every profession. More so in selling.

Selling is exciting if you enjoy it and take pride in it. Selling is dull if you don't enjoy it and feel proud of it.

So, prepare yourself to be proud of selling. If you are already proud, you are in the right profession.

Just take off!

Mantra 2

Know Your Sales Orientation

Sales orientation is the base; Salespersons have to develop or build their career on this....

You may take pride in your profession of selling, but it is useful, and, also important, to know your sales orientation. This is like a starter. This will help you to prepare yourself better for selling.

YOUR SALES ORIENTATION

The best way to determine sales orientation is to use some quantitative indicator or measure.

Twelve simple exploratory questions are given below. Answer these in 'Yes' or 'No'. The answers will indicate your sales orientation.

Tick(√) 'Yes' or 'No'

	Yes	No
1. Is selling widely accepted as a key business philosophy in your company?	☐	☐
2. Have you taken to selling because of pressure or circumstances?	☐	☐
3. Have you chosen selling by your own choice?	☐	☐
4. Do you think you have the necessary skill for selling?	☐	☐
5. Do you have previous experience in selling?	☐	☐
6. Do you think you need some training to be a better salesperson?	☐	☐
7. Do you know the product well that you are selling?	☐	☐
8. Have you studied the market or territory allotted to you?	☐	☐

Tick(√) 'Yes' or 'No'

		Yes	No
9.	Are you clear about the price and discount policy of your company?	☐	☐
10.	Do you know well your nearest competitor(s)?	☐	☐
11.	Are you happy with the present compensation package offered to you?	☐	☐
12.	Do you want to make a career in selling?	☐	☐

The answers to these questions are analysed as below:

Score (Total 'Yes')	Selling Orientation
10 or more	Excellent
8 to less than 10	Very good
7 to less than 8	Good
6	Average
Less than 6	Poor

If your score is '6' or less, your sales orientation definitely needs correction or improvement. If the score is between '7' and '9', you should work towards making your sales orientation 'Excellent'.

DEVELOP THE RIGHT ORIENTATION

Based on the score level, your sales orientation should be developed or improved.

Score 8 or More: If your score is '8 or more', don't get complacent. You have to remember that you need to sustain your performance. **To sustain excellent performance, you have to continue to put excellent efforts.**

Score 7 to Less than 8: Your sales orientation is 'Good', but, it requires further improvement. The benchmark should be 'Very Good'. You should analyse or review the answers, and, work on converting more 'Nos' into 'Yes'.

Score 6 or Less: This is a very disappointing situation. 'Less than 6' is more disappointing and, requires major or drastic corrections. You should sit down and try to identify the missing links. Check your motivational level. Also, check if you have the necessary skill to perform well. Do you need some job-specific training?

Based on your identification of the orientation gaps, you should work on them and improve your orientation level. During this process, you should consult your senior colleagues and seek counselling and advice from the sales manager.

Remember: Orientation and improvement is a continuous process.

Mantra 3

Remember: Attitude Determines Half Success

Attitude, Ambition and Action are the three 'A's for success in selling....

A positive attitude is a winning attitude....

In any sphere of life, the attitude of a person is vital in whatever he(she) does. One can be an entrepreneur or businessman (business woman), a corporate manager or a salesperson. The attitude determines, to large extent, the success or failure.

POSITIVE ATTITUDE AND NEGATIVE ATTITUDE

When we talk of attitude, it is essentially the difference between positive attitude and negative attitude. Positive attitude means positive thinking and approach towards things; negative attitude implies negative thinking and approach. Positive attitude means happiness, optimism and success. Negative attitude implies sadness, frustration and defeatism.

I give here a classic example of the difference between positive attitude and negative attitude. This is the water story. The water story is a classic example of how the same object can become positive or negative depending on how it is perceived or described. A glass half filled with water can be described in two ways: we can say the glass is half full or the glass is half empty. If we say 'half-full', we have shown positive attitude, and, we have achieved half a glass of water. If we say 'half-empty', we have shown negative attitude, and, we have lost half a glass of water. Water is only symbolic. It can easily be gaining half a business or sale or losing half a business or sale.

Every morning, the optimist says: "O God! One more good morning!" and begins the day with this.

The pessimist says: "Good God! One more morning!" and, begins the day in pessimistic way.

Start everyday by saying "Good morning!" Your day will be good. Also remember the five finger principle.

THE FIVE FINGER PRINCIPLE

To build positiveness, you may resort to the Five Finger principle. There are five fingers in the hand, and each represents a basic principle. These principles were developed by Dr. Edward De Bono to inspire a positive revolution.

1. **Effectiveness:** Effectiveness is represented by the *thumb* on the hand, because without the thumb the hand is useless. Without effectiveness, efforts are only dreams.

2. **Constructiveness:** This is presented by the *index finger* because that is the finger one uses to point out the direction and the way to go. The direction should be positive not negative, constructive not destructive.

3. **Respect***:* This is represented by the *second finger* which is the longer finger in the hand and respect is the most important principle of all. Interpersonal relations are built on mutual respects—both as individuals and as professionals.

4. **Self-Improvement:** This principle is projected by the *third finger*. We do not notice this finger much but it is there all the time. So self-improvement must be a silent, but a continual process.

5. **Contribution:** Contribution is symbolised by the *little finger* to remind us that we can contribute even if the contribution is very small. Small contributions eventually add up to big efforts.

So look at the five fingers of your hand. Act on the five principles to become positive and develop pride in selling.

ATTITUDE AND SELLING

Always start with the attitude to succeed. I give here two examples of what difference in attitude makes to selling.

In remote villages, most of the people do not wear shoes. A company wanted to sell shoes in distant villages. They sent two salespersons to explore the market in those areas.

The first salesperson had a negative attitude. He went to those areas and saw that most of the people were not wearing shoes. He replied to the sales manager/headquarter that there is no market or potential for selling shoes in those villages because most of the people there do not wear shoes.

The second salesperson, with positive attitude, surveyed those villages and discovered that there is a big potential market for selling shoes there because most of the people were going without shoes. They can be told about the benefits or advantages of wearing shoes and persuaded to buy shoes. He sent a message to the headquarters accordingly.

In another example, we consider a crowded urban market. The first salesperson, with negative attitude, feels that there is no potential or possibility of selling shoes there because the market is already overcrowded with shoe sellers. The second salesperson, with positive attitude, finds that the market is very big, and, his company can capture part of the market. His reply to the headquarters was: "If others can sell, we can also sell".

This is what the difference in attitude makes to selling.

So, if you have the right attitude, you have gone almost half way. The rest half you have to fill with the company's product, price, your skill, capability, approach, persistence and dedication. Your attitude and these together will make the glass full of water.

Mantra 4

Follow the Basics

A career in sales is like swimming: you jump into the sea and either sink or swim; or, you learn the basics and swim steadily....

Basics says: create sales opportunities, and, don't wait for them....

In any art, discipline or profession, the basics are very important. But, we often neglect this. And, this leads to many failures.

I narrate here a story of how forgetting the basics can result in a disaster. A newly married young lady wanted to cook a dish in her in-law's house. She bought a recipe book. She ceremoniously followed all the steps or instructions given in the recipe book. After she completed the cooking, she discovered that nothing was cooked. She wondered why. Then she found that she did not light the gas burner because, it was not mentioned in the recipe book.

This may sound silly. But, it makes sense. This is a reminder of the bare basics.

So, follow the basics in selling.

FOLLOW THE BASICS

Get Started

Many people who decide to become salespeople may not know anything about selling to start with. Some may not even know how to find a job in sales. But many of them become successful salespeople. Of course, there are sloggers and there are failures. But this is true of every profession. Nothing peculiar to sales! So, if you want to make a career in sales, get started.

But just do not jump into the fray like people jump into the sea for swimming. You may get lost. Plan before you jump. Planning gives success. Prepare yourself. Preparation gives confidence. Follow certain steps. You may call these the stepping stones. Here are six such steps:

Step 1: ***Convince yourself; Start Determined***

Do not take a wavering attitude before starting. Wavering people always lose directions. Think and decide. But once decided, get determined and take the plunge. You have to give it full try. **Success never comes the easy way.**

Many people come to sales not because they want to make a career in sales but just because they wanted a job. And they wanted fast rewards. Needless to say, many of them left the sales job not because they were not fit for it but because they were not prepared for it. We must remember that even if we take sales as a job (and not as a long-term career to start with), we have to take it seriously if we wish to be rewarded and become successful.

We may then find that **the job is becoming a career.**

Step 2: ***Enlist the Support of your Family as you Enter into a Sales Career***

Choice of your career—whether sales or any other—should always be your own. It should depend on your perception about your career, your aptitude and your capabilities as you perceive them. But, you must enjoy the support of your family—parents, wife or any other family members. It may be choice of profession by family consensus or you convince them. The support of your family always becomes a good motivator. It also gives you more courage and strength.

Step 3: ***Dress Well and Appear Self-confident***

Selling cannot only be a fantastic career, but also an art if it is handled properly. A key feature of true salesmanship is that everyone involved in a sale should benefit from it. This is the ideal situation. Realities can be different. But the salesperson should always endeavour to achieve the ideal.

Some even feel that if everyone concerned does not benefit from the sales you make, you cannot properly call yourself a salesperson. In fact, you may even be called a con man or a crook. A crook can always pretend to be a salesperson, but no salesperson should ever be a crook. Ethics is important in every profession.

Externalities are also important. So, dress well and pose well. Your outfit, posture and personality make the first impression. This is very vital in personal selling. This makes the first impact;

this might also make the final impact. Of course, substance in salesmanship is equally important.

Step 4: ***Investigate before Investing your Efforts***

This is about choice of the right sales job. We know that, in most of the cases, you may not have any choice in your first job. You are just beginning with no experience or performance record or verdict behind you. But once you are in the sales stream, you can always do some job-hopping. This definitely lends variety or versatility to your sales career. This also helps in career building.

Step 5: ***Be Prepared for the Initial Struggle***

Sales jobs, like all other jobs, are demanding. It is a new trade or profession for you and you have to develop the right traits for this. This means learning. And learning may sometimes mean some initial struggle. You may also call this the basic training or orientation. Many professional training programmes may follow later.

Joe Girard is the world's best salesman according to the Guinness Book of World Records. But he did not become the world's best salesman automatically or overnight. If you look into his career growth, you will see many phases of struggle including the initial ones.

So, be prepared for some initial struggle. And there is nothing to lose heart in this. Observe others. Take example from them. Initial struggle does not mean that struggles are going to be a regular feature in your career. History does not say this. In fact, initial struggle may mean a smooth sailing later, because it helps to remove the bottlenecks. It also infuses in you fighting qualities so essential in career building and career progression.

Sometimes, you may do well in a sales job, but the earnings or rewards may be low. The reason is simple: whenever something is easy to sell, no company is going to pay you a lot for selling it. **If something is difficult to sell, the rewards also would be proportionally high.** This is a natural law of sales. Some salesmen say that this is as true as the law of gravity.

Study salesmanship closely. Watch others and learn from them. As you discover and study the basic principles of selling, try to apply them on every call you make. Try to develop mastery over them. The sooner you do that, the faster you will tide over the initial faltering days, and it will not be long before you become successful in selling. But make the principles your constant companion.

Step 6: ***Set High Standards for yourself, but Work within your Limitations***

Most of us may be knowing the old proverbial saying, "be ambitious; sky should be the limit. But when you are walking, look for the ground and walk firmly on the ground." If you do not keep your feet on the ground, you may slip and may even perish. So, you should set high standards for yourself, but be realistic in your approach towards goal achievement. This is what brings out the best in you.

If you only think in terms of how much money you can make, you may soon reach a plateau and you may even lose directions. We all know that money or financial gain is the ultimate driving force behind everything. We work because we want to earn money and live well. But, most of the time, earning is proportional to your performance and capability. And you cannot overstress yourself too often. This can be counterproductive.

You should try to be a dreamer who does. You should dream to be big, and, at the same time, keep up your performance level. And do not forget your limitations. All of us have limitations. Even the best salesman in the world has his limitations. The best approach is to work within your limitations. This is the best way to achieve the goal.

Of course, we can always try to overcome our limitations through counselling, training and hard work. We must constantly endeavour to do that with self-respect and pride.

Once we enter the real world of selling, a new factor emerges. For the first time, our powers of persuasion, and our sales abilities, are being judged. This can be intimidating; and so we respond by convincing ourselves that we cannot sell, we do not know how to sell or do not want to sell. We then use these mental roadblocks to justify our lack of sales potential. If you wish to become a salesperson, do not fall into this trap.

This is what the basics teaches us.

Mantra 5

Go through the Selling Process

The selling process is, in essence, a matching game: matching the buyer and, the seller....

Go through the selling process. You may be going through it every day. Go through it again. Even if it means another refresher course, take the course or steps. These will be useful inputs or guides in selling.

THE SELLING PROCESS

Anatomy of a Sale

If we make a step by step analysis of a copy book sale, we can perceive the complete anatomy of a sale. Very few salespeople take the time to carefully dissect a sale or the selling process to find out what are the elements that it is really made up of. Such a step by step analysis acts both as a guide and a checklist for actual selling.

Major identifiable steps are:

1. *Opening the sales call*
   - √ Introducing yourself
   - √ Introducing your company (if it is the first call)
2. *Sales proposition*
   - √ Understanding the buyer
   - √ Probing
3. *Presentation*
   - √ Explanation
   - √ Demonstration
4. *Motivating the customer*
   - √ Managing objections
   - √ Creating urgency
5. *Closing the sale*

Anatomy of Buying

If the buying process and its correspondence with the selling process are clearly understood, the salesperson's job becomes much easier and the success rate increases.

The buying process can be broken down into several stages through which the buyer's mind passes to come to a decision. The major stages are:

- I am important.
- Consider my needs, not yours.
- How will your offer help me?
- What are the facts?
- What are the snags?
- Should I buy?
- I buy/I don't buy.

The Matching Game

Any sales effort that ignores the above stages is unlikely to result in an order. The buying mind has to be satisfied at each stage before moving on to next; the sales presentation sequence must match the buying sequence and run parallel to it. The two keys to success are the process of matching the buyer's expectations and presenting the product in a way that relates to the buyer's needs. This is the matching game: matching the buying process and the selling process. Table shows the matching game.

The Matching Game in Sales

Buying	Selling process	
	Sales Objective	How to Sell
Consider my needs	To identify the customer's needs	Opening the sales call
How will you help me? What are the facts? What are the snags?	To present benefits that satisfy the customer's needs	The sales proposition The sales presentation

Should I buy? I buy	To obtain a buying decision or a commitment	Handling sales objections Closing the sale

In all successful sales, the buyer and the seller would generally go through this sequence, stage by stage. Some of these steps are not always clearly visible or distinct, but the mind passes through these steps or stages in certain order. This is a mind game.

One should try to master the matching game in sales. That is the best way to perform the selling job.

MODERN SELLING

The above shows the conventional selling process. Over time, the selling process has changed in terms of focus on different factors or steps. Like any other business, evolution takes place in selling also. The roles of major factors or steps have undergone some change. The changed process, in terms of the major steps are shown below:

Selling Process	Past	Present
Need	30%	30%
Rapport	10%	20%
Presentation	20%	30%
Solution	20%	10%
Close	20%	10%
All	100%	100%

Sixteen detailed steps in modern selling are mentioned below:

Step 1: Planning for a sale

Step 2: Preparation

Step 3: Prospecting

Step 4: Pre-approach

Step 5: Approaching the customer

Step 6: Receiving attention

Step 7: Establishing rapport

Step 8: Sales presentation

Step 9: Fact finding

Step 10: Presenting a solution

Step 11: Trial close

Step 12: Handling objections (if any)

Step 13: Closing the sale

- -

Step 14: After sales service/commitments

Step 15: Getting referrals and new business

Step 16: Relationship building for future

These steps show that the selling process today does not end with closing. It goes beyond that. After closing, all after sales services or commitments—call them customer service—have to be fulfilled.

Modern professional selling process ends with relationship building for future sales. This is the long-term selling process. Every salesperson should follow this process. This is the way for long-term success.

Mantra 6

Remember: Prospecting is as Important as Selling

Prospecting is like sowing seeds; these will grow into trees to bear fruits, i.e., selling.....

Every salesperson wants to focus on selling. He (she) tends to overlook, or, does not pay enough attention to two important stages before selling—prospecting and handling objections.

Prospecting is the starting point of selling or personal selling. ***If there is no prospecting, there is no selling.*** This shows the importance of prospecting.

Just to refresh you, *prospecting* is *finding or identifying a potential buyer* or a prospect. A prospect is an individual or a family or a business organisation who requires the product (includes service product) a company or a salesperson wants to sell.

PROSPECTING: STEPS OR STAGES

Prospecting is done or completed in four steps or stages one leading to the other. The four steps, in sequential order, are:

Lead generation
↓
Qualifying
↓
Pre-approach
↓
Approach

Lead Generation: This is the first step in prospecting. A *sales lead* indicates the names of a person or a family or a business organisation who is likely to be a prospect. Names generated through sales leads are just indicative or tentative. These names have to be processed further.

Qualifying: Qualifying means screening or short-listing the long list of lead names for finding out probable prospects. This also means laying down the conditions or criteria for short-listing. Two conditions or criteria are important for proper/effective qualifying.

These are:

(a) The probables have a need for the product to be sold.

(b) The probables also have the ability (financial) to buy the product.

Qualified prospects are usually classified into three categories: hot prospects, warm prospects and cool prospects. The classification is based on two dimensions or criteria: requirement and ability to pay. Based on these two criteria, the classification is shown below.

Hot Prospects, Warm Prospects and Cool Prospects

Prospect	Requirement	Ability to pay
Hot prospect	Strong	Strong
Warm prospect	Average/Medium	Strong
Cool prospect	Low	Weak

Hot prospects are strong candidates for conversion into the company's customers and all efforts should be made to do so. *Warm prospects* require follow-up or further probing as probables or prospects. *Cool prospects* are usually kept in the pending list for further follow-up.

Hot prospects are clearly the most important category for follow-up for generating enquiries. A study has found that salespersons, in general, get 80 per cent of their customers' order or business if they systematically follow-up a sales enquiry, and only 40 per cent if there is no follow-up. It has also been observed that it usually takes three to four calls on an organisational or business prospect to convert an initial enquiry into sales.

Pre-approach: Pre-approach is preparatory to approaching the customer. The preparatory step consists of two tasks: information collection about the prospect and planning the sales call.

The nature of information to be collected depends on the type of prospect or customer, that is, whether an individual or family or a business organisation. If it is an individual or family, information gathering is always difficult; it can be done either through word of mouth from neighbours or existing customers or through telephonic talk or call centres. If the prospect is a business organisation, information is more structured, and the collection of the same is easier.

Proper or adequate information helps planning the sales call on the prospect. Planning includes finding out appropriate date and time to meet the prospect/customer, opening of the talk, basic details about the company, product, etc. Planning a sales call on a business organisation requires more detailed preparation.

Approaching the Customer: Approach or approaching the customer means meeting the prospect for the first time, and the way to do it. It is almost obvious that the salesperson will take an appointment with the prospect, and then meet him. The first meeting may take a few minutes, but it is vital—it can make or break a sale. The first impression should be good or favourable; only then, future meetings or calls or sales presentations are likely to have positive impact or result. This implies that the salesperson should present himself (herself) in an appealing way (includes dress or attire), show the right attitude, and start with a carefully phrased statement.

SOURCES FOR PROSPECTS

Information about prospects has to be collected from different sources. Many sources are available for this. The salesperson or the sales team should carefully scan various sources. After scanning, the right sources should be chosen.

Fifteen probable sources for prospects are:

1. Referrals from relatives/friends
2. Referrals from customers

3. Referrals from external stakeholders (suppliers/vendors, intermediates)
4. Telemarketing
5. Industry sources (industry associations, directories)
6. News media (newspapers, magazines, etc.)
7. Social media
8. Trade shows (exhibitions, trade fairs)
9. Advertisements
10. Company networking
11. Direct mailing
12. Cold calling/canvassing
13. Signature contact/presentation
14. Networking by salespersons (salespersons becoming members of organisation like Lions Club, Rotary Club)
15. Competitors

'Cold calling/canvassing' needs some clarification or elaboration and 'signature contact/presentation' requires some explanation; also 'competitors'.

Cold calling/canvassing can take place around your appointment areas/neighbourhood. As you go for your appointment, you can also make few calls around that area which are not scheduled. Some of these calls may lead to prospects.

Signature contact/presentation takes place in a get-together or party. As you meet different people in a get-together, some might ask: "What do you do?" You reply very shortly, may be in one or two sentences. He (she) may show interest in you. Explore this further for a prospect.

Competitors can be a source for prospects through their advertisements for their own business, plans and product offering. These gives some clues.

Scan through different sources for prospects. Try to choose the right sources. *This is like a trial and error method.* Build a good base of prospects. This will pave the way for selling.

Try to do prospecting regularly or daily. Doing prospecting is like sowing seeds everyday. This ensures that you can harvest continuously, i.e., sell daily or regularly.

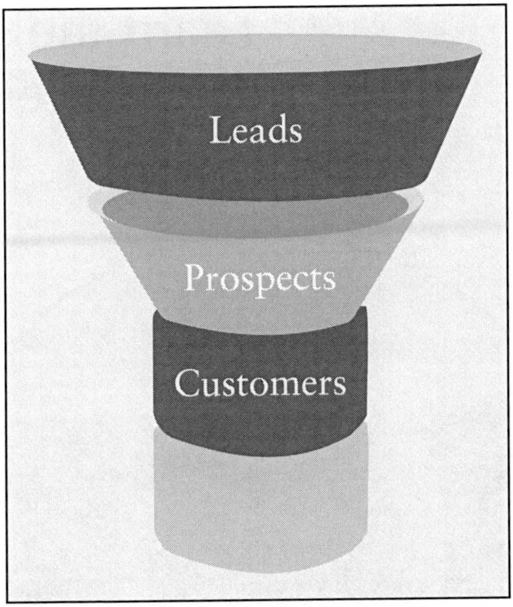

Mantra 7

Learn the Art of Handling Objections

An objection is not a setback: it is a milestone to be crossed....
An objection is indirectly an opportunity for closing a sale....

During the sales presentation process, objections from the prospect or potential buyer are a common factor or phenomenon. Objections do not mean that the prospect is disliking the sales presentation or is not interested in the purchase. So, objections should not be taken in the negative sense. Objections mostly mean that the prospect wants to have more clarity or information or details about the company, offer or product's features and performance.

TYPES OF OBJECTIONS

Objections can generally be one or more of the eight types:

1. I do not require the product now/
   I am not sure whether I require the product;
2. I am happy with my present supplier;
3. I have no incentive to buy your product/
   buy from your company;
4. Your product is expensive;
5. I want to think it over; I need some time;
6. I have another alternative (substitute) to try;
7. I had a bad experience with your company—product or transactional problem;
8. I am busy now—contact me later.

HANDLING OBJECTIONS

Objections are sensitive and can sometimes be awkward. Therefore, objections should be dealt with patience, carefully and skilfully. Salespeople can use different ways to deal with objections. Lancaster and Jobber have suggested seven ways for handling objections. These are:

1. Listen without interruption
2. Agree and counter
3. Forestall the objection
4. Question the objection
5. Straight denial
6. Hidden objections
7. Trial close

Also see the diagrammatic presentation below:

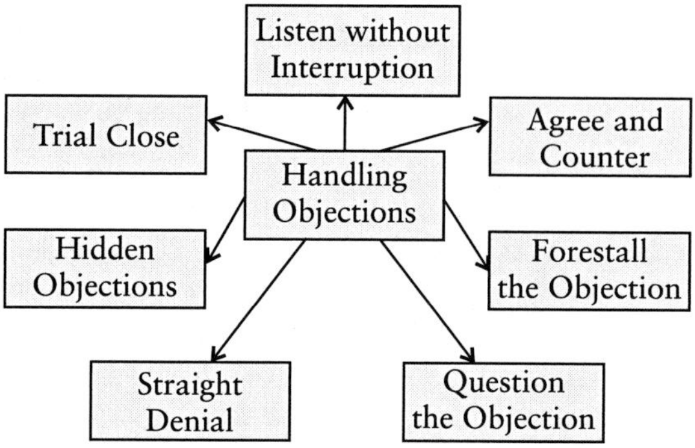

To Listen without Interruption is to give respect to the point or view or contention of the buyer. Interruption always means break or disturbance and most prospects do not like it. The point or objection made by the prospect may be trivial or even wrong. Listening patiently and respectfully shows that the salesperson is keen to clearly understand whatever the prospect wants to say. This may sometimes reveal or reflect the feeling or emotion of the prospect which is also important for the salesperson to know.

To Agree and Counter is to first listen carefully and then make a point or counterpoint to put the issue in the right perspective or to correct the factual position. The objective here is to listen to each other with respect so that the presentation or discussion proceeds on the right course and with more objectivity. For example, the prospect may say: "Your equipment does not give a very elegant look." The salesperson listens to this and then replies: "I fully agree with you, sir, but, for an electrical equipment, you may be more interested in its performance than the appearance."

Forestalling the Objection is a pre-emptive technique. Because of his experience in making sales presentations and dealing with customers, and also because he knows his company's product and its features well, an intelligent salesperson can often anticipate certain likely questions or objections. Instead of waiting for the prospect to raise the objection, the salesperson can mention it at the appropriate time in course of the sales presentation. It shows that the salesperson is aware of all the relevant points or issues and does not hesitate to mention them even if it concerns his company's product, its features, pricing and competition.

Questioning the Objection is a rather sensitive way of handling objections and it should be done with care. 'Questioning the objection' should not be interpreted or understood too literally. In sales presentation, this should actually mean seeking more clarity about the objection so that it can be understood precisely and answered or dealt with accordingly. For example, a prospect might say about a bathing soap: "The quality is not good." By this he/she may mean that it does not generate enough foam, or its fragrance is not every soothing, or it does not cleanse well, or he/she may even mean that the colour of the soap is rather dull. A question is necessary or appropriate to ascertain which one or ones the prospect actually means. Once that is clear, the salesperson can deal with it accordingly.

Straight denial is more sensitive and delicate than questioning an objection and has to be used with enough caution, but it sometimes becomes necessary either to correct a factual position or put a particular point or issue in the right perspective. For example, the buyer says: "I like the curtain cloth, but it may be difficult to wash." The denial should be soft so that the atmosphere continues to remain cordial.

Hidden objections are not uncommon in personal selling. Sometimes, a buyer may have some points or issues related to the product offering, but he/she may not come out openly. One common reason is that the prospect may not like the presentation to go for long (may be because he/she is not keen on buying or has some other engagement). Whatever is the reason, the salesperson's job remains incomplete. The salesperson, therefore, has to make a good guess when the prospect is maintaining silence for sometime and induce him/her to come out with any point or issue he/she has in mind. Sometimes, it may require mild prompting or provocation.

Trial close is not, strictly speaking, a way of handling objections, but an effort to close or conclude a sale without continuing with the sales presentation or the selling process any further so that the prospect does not raise any more objection. This is usually done towards the end of a sales presentation, and after some objections have already been dealt with. But the timing of this is very important and the salesperson has to use good judgement for this.

PRE-EMPTING THE OBJECTION

Often, it is a good strategy to pre-empt an objection. Common objections are on price and quality or product features. A smart salesperson, based on his (her) experience, and, initial dialogue with the prospect, may try to anticipate an objection. Then, he (she) can try pre-empting. If it is price, he (she) may explain in terms of quality. It may be a niche product or of premium quality. Otherwise, he (she) may offer an appropriate discount. If it is quality, price offered may be low or lower than that of competitors. He (she) may also explain that it is the price-product combination that the prospect should consider, and, not quality in isolation. It should be always linked to price.

Other kinds or forms of objections can also be anticipated and pre-empted.

By intelligent pre-empting, you may be able to shorten the presentation period or cycle, and, lead the prospect faster to the close of the sale.

In practical situations, rarely a sale takes place without objection(s). Objection actually shows the direction in which the prospect's/buyer's mind is moving. Follow that direction. It will be easy to handle the objection.

An objection appears to be a setback in the selling process. Handle the objection carefully and turn the setback into a comeback; and, come back strongly and close the sale.

Mantra 8

Master the Art of Closing

Closing a sale is same as selling success; not able to close the sale is same as selling failure....

Closing a sale is the last step or stage (except after-sales service) in the selling or personal selling process. But, this is the most important stage. All efforts (sales presentations, etc.) made during the selling process should culminate in closing the sale; otherwise, these efforts, howsoever sincere, may go in vain. This shows the significance of the **close**.

FUNDAMENTAL RULES FOR CLOSING

Many Ways to Close a Sale

Because buyers are diverse and their minds keep fluctuating, there can be many ways to close a sale. There are also many opinions on how to close a sale. If we analyse these various ways of or opinions on closing a sale, these would boil down to three basic questions the salesperson should ask himself:

(a) Is this the most effective way to present my product/service and close the sale?

(b) Is this the way my company has taught me to present and close?

(c) Is this the way the customer would like it (most) to be closed?

If answers to all these questions are 'yes', you have chosen the ideal way to close, and it may work like magic. If all the answers are 'no', you have chosen a wrong way and you have to rework. If the answer is 'yes' to one or more questions and 'no' to other(s), you have to modify or refine your approach for successful closing. Such modification or refinement would depend on the sales manager's counselling, the situation and the customer.

Ten Rules for Closing

Many ways of closing a sale do not mean that there are no ground rules or fundamental principles of closing. Fundamentals are important in every profession and so also in selling and closing a sale. Here are ten fundamentals:

1. Standardisation
2. Three Basic Elements
3. Value
4. Clarity
5. Urgency
6. Display of Confidence
7. Paperwork
8. Shaking Hands
9. Thank Everyone
10. Sales manager's Evaluation

Standardisation: Every salesperson should master the standard sale presentation and closing developed and taught by the organisation. Every time you walk into a modern fast food chain like McDonald's, you can see the value of standardisation. *Standardisation does not mean rigidity; it means harmonisation.*

Three Basic Elements: To make fire, three basic elements have to be present. They are heat, fuel and oxygen. Like fire, every successful sale must also have three basic elements: *value, clarity* and *urgency*.

Value: Value is critical to any sale because it is the only reason anybody buys anything for. Building value must be made an integral part of your introduction or explanation and close. Close will become easier and smoother when you build enough value throughout your sales progression—value of your offering to the customer.

Clarity: Clarity means making a presentation appear simple and focused. All ambiguities should be avoided. Many potential sales do not materialise because the customers do not clearly understand the offering being made by the salesperson. Sometimes, it is ambiguous, sometimes even clumsy.

Urgency: Urgency means giving customers sound and logical reasons for buying now. If salespeople work properly, it is possible to build urgency into almost any selling situation. But urgency does not mean rushing. That is suicidal.

Display of Confidence: Always make the presentation and close as confidently as you can. Practise your presentation again and again—rehearse till you have perfected the words you say, movements you make, the way you deliver and timing. This gives you necessary confidence. But, don't show overconfidence. Most customers do not like it.

Paperwork: During the presentation, make sure to write figures boldly and neatly. If you use a work sheet, write your figures the same way every time. Paperwork should be simple and short. Paperwork can also be an art for building values and closing a sale.

Shaking Hands: One of the basic parts of a close is also the simplest. After you have completed the presentation (this includes handling objections also) and closed the sale, reach out to the customer and say: "Thank you." You may, most of the time, expect your customer to say 'OK' and also shake hands.

Thank Everyone: After the close, make sure to thank everyone involved in the sale whether it is a business sale or a consumer sale. **Thanking is a "free investment" for your future sale.**

Sales Manager's Evaluation: Every salesperson should have his (her) presentation and close evaluated by the sales manager on a regular basis and make changes (whenever required) to make the close convincing and successful. This is also an investment for the future.

METHOD OF CLOSING A SALE

Ideally, or in theory, every sale should be closed at the peak. But, in practice, it may often be difficult to determine the peak. In fact, during the whole process of a sales presentation, a number of peaks may appear to occur. Then the question arises: Which is the right peak? The answer may not be easy.

Because of this, and as mentioned above, there are many methods of closing a sale. The applicability of these methods depends on the sales situation—the nature and content of the sales presentation and the prospect's behaviour or attitude towards buying. For closing a sale, a salesperson needs to use the most appropriate method.

The adoption of a particular method or the most appropriate method depends on various factors like the product—quality, features—price competitiveness, etc., characteristics of the buyers and the environmental or circumstances of the sale. In course of the sales presentation, the way the prospect's mind moves or acts or reacts also becomes a critical factor and has an important bearing on the methods of close.

Depending on these various factors, one of the ten different methods may be adopted for closing a particular sale. These ten methods are:

1. Simple ask for the order
2. Summarise and ask for the order
3. Narrowing the choice
4. Action agreement
5. Objection close
6. Trial close
7. Concession close
8. Suggestive close
9. Side close
10. Alternative close

Simply Ask for the Order: This is the simplest method and the most straightforward. After the sales presentation, the salesperson straight way asks for the order, but not by saying: "Please, give me the order." Instead, he/she puts a closed question like:

"Should I understand that you are buying one?"

The question requires or prompts a 'yes' or 'no' answer. The question leads the buyer to a decision. If the sales presentation is good and effective, the answer may often be positive.

Summarise the Presentation and Ask for the Order: Some situations may demand/warrant (depending on the buyer's posture/behaviour and the salesperson's assessment of the situation) that the salesperson does not ask for the order immediately after the presentation. Maybe some time should be given, and one of the ways to do it is to go through or highlight the main selling points of the presentation in a convincing way, and then ask for the order like this: "Maybe we are now in a position to transact the business."

Narrowing Down the Choice: Sometimes, a salesperson may observe during his/her sales presentation that the prospect is suffering from a general indecision problem. The observed indecision can also be because of the variety of choices offered to him/her. In such situations, a skillful salesperson may have to gradually reduce the options to lead to the close. This method is also known as 'option elimination technique'.

The salesperson may initially start by offering a range of varieties because of the nature of the product. The product may be sarees, dress materials, gents' suitings/shirtings, bed linen, curtain cloth, etc. As the presentation progresses, the salesperson may observe a situation of indecision, i.e., the problem of decision making is showing up. Judging the thinking or mind of the prospect, the salesperson may skillfully eliminate certain choices by saying: "Sir/Madam, this may not match you or this may not be of your liking".

Elimination of certain choices helps/guides the prospect to focus on fewer options and would be in a much better position to make the final choice or decision.

Action Agreement: In some situations, the salesperson cannot simply ask for the order nor he can summarise and ask for it. Narrowing down the choice also does not apply because the range of products is not large. The nature of products is such that a sale cannot be quickly closed nor it is appropriate to close it in the first interview or presentation. In such cases, an 'action agreement' is entered into which can later mature or culminate into a close.

Action agreement is appropriate for many industrial and pharmaceutical products. The purchase of industrial products involves a large amount of money or funds, and because of this, decision by the buyer may not be taken in the first presentation itself. There are many issues involved and are to be sorted out. The salesperson also may not like to close the sale in a hurry. Instead, the salesperson or the sales team tries to enter into an 'action agreement' through which both sides agree to do certain things or take some steps before their next meeting. Similar is the case with many pharmaceutical products. In the case of pharmaceutical products, the salesperson attempts to enter into an 'action agreement' with the doctor who prescribes drugs which are bought and sold by retailers.

The final close in such cases depends on timely follow-up, abilities to pursue and persistence. The salesperson/sales team should try to score on as many evaluative criteria as possible and close the sale at the most appropriate time.

The Objection Close: In this method, the salesperson uses an objection by a prospect, or, rather, an answer to an objection to conclude a sale. The answer to the objection is utilised as a stimulus for decision-making or to buy. If the sale presentation is progressing smoothly but an objection raised by the buyer appears to be a major hindrance, the salesperson may handle it like this:

Buyer: The model of the car you are proposing is rather expensive.

Salesperson: If I can satisfy you that this particular model is the most price competitive in its category, I hope you will buy it.

Such statement by the salesperson may be backed by a statistical comparison of features and prices of similar models. With this, a positive answer from the buyer is most likely, and the sale may be closed.

Sometimes, a prospect may raise an objection which may be very general. In such situation, the salesperson should ask the prospect to be more specific and mention the exact nature of the problem. The salesperson can then answer the query and that may lead to closing of the sale. Taking again the car example, the objection and the answer may be like this:

Prospect: I don't like the look of the car.

Salesperson: What exactly in the look you don't like?

Prospect: I don't like the colour.

Salesperson: We have a big range of choices in colour. We will paint your car with the colour you like.

This will help to close the sale.

Trial Close: As the name indicates, a trial close is not the final close; it actually means 'trying to close' a sale even before the sales presentation is complete. This is a kind of pre-emptive closure, i.e., an effort to close the sale when the presentation has made good progress so that the prospect may not raise any further objection. The advantage of this method is that if the prospect raises further objection, the presentation can still continue with the intention to close the sale.

The objective of a trial close is to try to get a clear signal from the prospect at an appropriate time and not to prolong the presentation. A trial close may happen like this:

Salesperson: Would you like the refrigerator to be delivered at your house and also set it in operation?

Prospect: Yes, I would like that.

The sale is almost closed. If some more queries still remain, those can be quickly answered to lead to the final close.

Concession Close: This is one of the more straightforward and commonly used methods of closing a sale—giving a final concession to seal a deal. A concession is actually an inducement to the buyer to buy. Therefore, this method of closing is also known as the 'inducement close.'

A more common way of giving a concession is price discount. After the sales presentation is over and most of the relevant issues have been discussed and the prospect has shown some willingness to buy, but there is also some wavering, the salesperson may try to clinch the deal by saying: "If I give a 3 per cent discount in price, would you place the order now?" The prospect may be induced to say 'yes'.

Concession or inducement need not be only in terms of price; it can be in various other forms as well. It can be in the form of deferred payment or credit with attractive interest rate, free home delivery, extended warranty or guarantee, etc. Depending on the nature of the product, the form of concession or inducement may vary.

Suggestive Close: Sometimes, a salesperson may not give a direct concession, but indirectly offer inducements in the form of suggestions which may appeal to the buyer and induce him/her to place an order. This is an innovative approach because the suggestions should be appealing enough.

For example, a consumer may be interested in purchasing a room/window air conditioner. The skillful salesperson may suggest that the prospect may rather buy a split air conditioner than a window air conditioner. There are many benefits. First, it will be absolutely noiseless; second, it will not block any window; and third, installation and any maintenance/repair work will be done from outside and room privacy will not be disturbed.

Suggestive close can also be used for selling paints (interior or exterior), carpets, decorative items, etc.

Side Close: Often, it happens that even after the sales presentation, the seller and the buyer fail to agree on many points. This may include the basic product itself and side issues or points like features, colour, size, delivery, payment schedule, etc. These apply to FMCGs, consumer durables and finished industrial products or office equipment.

The salesperson realises that the differences on the side points are overshadowing the decision on purchase of the product. He, therefore, concentrates on those points. If it is a shampoo, he may say: "Would you like the 50 gm pack or a 100 gm pack?"; for a soap, he may ask: "Would you like the white or pink or yellow colour?" If it is a consumer durable or an industrial product, he may ask, "Would you like to pay cash or avail of credit facility?" Through such inviting questions, when the side points or issues are settled or closed, the sale may also be closed. The salesperson should always focus on those side points which may convince or satisfy the buyer sooner.

Alternative Close: The alternative close is similar to, and can also be called an extension of, the side close. This method is used when the prospect is willing to buy the product but is indecisive about a few related points or issues—quality, features, delivery, etc. To lead to decisions on these points, the salesperson suggests two alternatives to choose from. Suggesting too many alternatives may confuse the prospect and again push him/her into indecision.

Closing only Three Times

Lloyd Allard, a professional salesperson—and a successful one—has some important things to say on closing based on his personal selling experience. Allard contends that he had "memorised and perfected eight-eight separate closes. Like each of the eighty-eight keys on a piano keyboard, these different closes were available for use in certain situations, at certain times, and in certain places." But, as a matter of policy/strategy, he would use no more than three closes with any one customer. "If the customer wasn't sold after I tried three different closes, I would simply leave".

Here is a lesson for all salespeople. Instead of spending hours on abortive attempts to close a sale with a wavering or reluctant prospect, leave him (her). Go to some other place, to some other prospect, and try to close some other sale. ***Grinding is never advisable in selling.***

This, however, does not mean that persuasion and persistence have no role in selling. **It should be persistence, not insistence.** You should decide according to the situation. **Judgement is always important. Judgement is entirely your personal or private tool. Use it judiciously.**

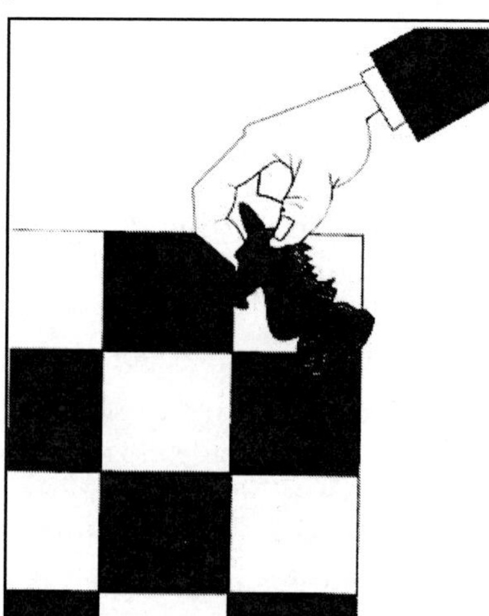

Use the Right Strategy

Mantra 9

Remind Yourself of ABC of Closing

ABC (Always Be Closing) is a dream; every salesperson should dream ABC....

Successful salespersons convert ABC into Reality....

ABC in selling means *Always Be Closing*. This should be the target or goal or dream of every salesperson. And, every salesperson should work towards achieving this goal.

For achieving this, you can follow a number of principles or methods.

AIDAS PRINCIPLE FOR CLOSING

AIDAS principle focuses on sales presentation and is based on the assumption that, during a sales presentation, a prospective customer goes through five stages of reaction, response or preparedness to buy. The five stages are: Attention, Interest, Desire, Action, Satisfaction (AIDAS). These are the stages through which a buyer's mind usually goes through during the selling process or sales presentation. These five stages are quite logical and are almost in sequential order:

Attention → Interest → Desire → Action → Satisfaction

Attention: This is the first important step or stage. During the process of personal selling or presentation, the salesperson should be able to attract the attention of the prospect. This depends partly on the approach of the salesperson and the timing of the sales meeting. Both are equally important for attracting the attention of the buyers.

Interest: Once the prospect has paid attention to the presentation, all efforts should be made by the salesperson to arouse interest in him/her about the product, its quality and features. During the process of creating interest, it is necessary for the salesperson to know about the attitude, likes, dislikes, lifestyle, preferences, etc. of the prospect. The presentation and the process of generating interest should be geared accordingly.

Desire: Interest in the product or presentation leads to the desire to buy. As the buyer shows interest in the product, the salesperson should focus more on inducing the prospect to express the desire to buy. The prospect may have some questions; those have to be dealt with carefully. The salesperson should keep in mind that the desire to buy should be treated as an extension of the interest in the product and presentation.

Action: This is the most critical step or stage—the stage to convert the desire to buy into an actual purchase decision. This is the stage when some difficult queries may be made or objections may be raised. This may include testing the knowledge of the salesperson about the product, any financing scheme or any discount which may be available. These may apply typically to consumer durables such as water purifiers, household electrical equipment, consumer electronics, etc. For FMCGs, cash or price discount may apply.

Even after the queries have been answered and objections handled, the prospect may still be in a state of wavering or indecision. This often happens, and is the most tricky or delicate stage in the buying or selling process. For converting the desire into action or decision, the salesperson may have to lead the way either through push, persuasion or inducement. This is the art of closing the sale.

Satisfaction: Satisfaction flows from right action or decision, although real satisfaction comes through use of the product. But, at the moment, the feeling of right decision should give the buyer immediate satisfaction. The salesperson can also play a part in this by trying to give the impression to the buyer that he/she has taken the right decision. If delivery of the product at a later date is involved, the salesperson can promise delivery at the right time and also prompt after-sales services (wherever required).

METHODS OF SUCCESSFUL CLOSING

Success Rate in Closing of Sale

On an average, a professional salesperson closes one sale out of every five sales presentations (not calls). This is the observed average success rate in closing.

If a salesperson can close the sale in every presentation, he (she) is a *sales superstar*; if he (she) closes one sale out of every two presentations, he (she) is a *sales star*; if one sale is closed out of every three presentations, the salesperson is a *good closer*; if the salesperson closes one sale out of every five presentations, he or she is an *average closer*; if the rate of closing is one in more than five presentations, the salesperson is a *poor closer*.

Use Closing Ratio as Guide

Closing ratio is defined and measured as the ratio of customers who *actually buy* and customers who *can buy*, i.e., potential customers. In other words, the closing ratio shows the gap between actual sale and potential sale. This indicates the role of salesmembership.

The closing ratio should be ideally 1 or 1:1, i.e., every potential customer should be converted into an actual customer, or, every potential sale should be converted into an actual sale.

The ideal situation of 1:1 hardly happens in reality. In fact, some sales analysts and trainers feel that, if for a salesperson, the ratio is 1:1, he (she) is not a salesperson, but, an order taker, i.e., he (she) is just collecting an order from a customer of a pretested and used product (repeat order). No selling is really involved.

The closing ratio in practice usually varies from product to product or industry to industry. It will be one ratio if you are selling a toothpaste or a toilet soap or detergent. It will be different if one is selling an automobile or a refrigerator or an washing machine or an industrial product. The ratio may also vary from time to time depending on changes in market conditions and the level of competition.

Seven Requisites for Successful Closing

Successful closing of sale requires many attitudes or qualities or techniques of a salesperson. Seven more important requisites are:

(a) Positive attitude

(b) Effective presentation and demonstration

(c) Allowing questions

(d) Holding the prospect's attention
(e) Use of reserve selling points
(f) Striking at the right time
(g) Letting the prospect decide

Everybody in business should have a *positive attitude*, particularly salespersons. **Negativity kills propositions.** A salesperson is in a sensitive job because he is dealing directly with people—families and individual consumers. Therefore, he should maintain a positive attitude or approach throughout the sales presentation till the close of the sale. This also induces or inspires the prospect to adopt a positive approach and show a more favourable attitude.

Effective presentation and demonstration is at the root/ essence of any sales success. Every salesperson should prepare well and master his presentation and effectively use product demonstrations wherever necessary (or applicable) to convince the prospect about the quality, features and performance of a product. A good presentation uses pauses and occasional breaks, but the salesperson has to ensure that continuity and eloquency is maintained and the prospect's interest is sustained and the presentation gradually but logically leads to the close.

In fact, pauses and breaks are necessary for *allowing questions* by the prospect or seeking clarifications. The salesperson should never think that his (her) presentation is very convincing or perfect and no questions need to be asked or allowed. A successful presentation and closing requires that after a certain stage has been reached in the presentation, the salesperson should invite the prospect for any question like this: "Sir/madam, do you have any query at this stage or I should proceed with the presentation?" Before a salesperson attempts to close a sale, he (she) should ensure that all questions of the prospect have been entertained and satisfactorily answered.

Inviting or allowing questions is one of the ways of *holding the prospect's attention*. For success, the salesperson has to ensure that the prospect remains attentive to his presentation. It may happen sometimes that, initially, the prospect may not show enough interest or pay sufficient attention to the sales talk or presentation. In such situation, the salesperson may say: "Sir/madam, if you are busy, should I come at some other time/day?" This is likely to quickly draw the attention of the prospect. During the presentation also, the salesperson may have to do certain things to ensue continuing attention of the prospect. These may include repeating some selling points, part of presentation, demonstration, etc.

One of the effective ways to attract or hold the attention of the prospect is to use *reserve selling points*. As a matter of strategy, every salesperson should reserve some special selling points to be used at an appropriate or opportune moment to expedite or ensure closing of a sale. These may include a special feature of the product not disclosed so far, an additional price discount, a special incentive, a package offer, etc. Such special selling points or propositions, if intelligently used, often become very effective in clinching a deal.

The use of reserve selling points also indirectly means *striking at the right time*. As the sales talk or presentation progresses, the salesperson should be looking for an opportune moment to close the sale. Timing or time of use of reserve selling points is one such moment. Even otherwise, closing moments may come. Using his skill and experience, the salesperson should be able to 'smell' indications or signals of agreement or acceptance of the offer. This is the time to strike. The ideal moment to strike is when the prospect's mind and the salesperson's mind are in harmony with each other. This is not easy, but the experienced salespeople may use their judgements to decide the most harmonious moment.

Striking at the right moment does not mean that the salesperson should say: "OK, then, the sale is done." The fundamental principle of closing is: *Let the prospect decide*, i.e., he/she should be the final person to say: "OK, the deal is done", or "let us conclude the sale", or "I have decided to buy." The prospect should not feel that the sale is forced on him. The salesperson will do everything to guide or lead the prospect to the closing, but the prospect would always complete the final formality of closing.

USE CROSS-SELLING

Cross-selling means selling other products/brands from your company after the sale of one product/brand has been concluded.

An example of cross-selling: you have gone to a bank for opening a savings account. After opening of the savings account is over, the bank official, a smart salesperson, gets into action. He (she) tries to induce you to avail of other services of the bank like recurring deposit, term deposit, safety locker, etc.; and, he (she) successfully sells one or more of these services or products. This is cross-selling.

Every cross-selling generates additional sales or revenue.

USE UP-SELLING

Up-selling means selling a product or model or brand to the same customer which is superior to the product/model/brand originally offered for sale.

Example of up-selling: you have finalised the sale of a consumer durable like a car or motorcycle or a washing machine. Then, you tell the customer that he (she) can have extra features or a superior model by spending a small additional amount. You say: "Sir/madam, you don't make an investment on such products often. By spending a small extra amount, you can get more utility and satisfaction." This is up-selling.

Like cross-selling, every up-selling generates additional sales or revenue.

USE COMBINATION SELLING

In certain situations, depending on the nature of response or body language of the prospect/customer, you can use a combination of cross-selling and up-selling.

Example of combination selling: As you are selling a colour TV, you can offer a CTV with HD property or feature (up-selling). Once you have sold this, you can also offer a microwave from your company (cross-selling). If you can achieve both, you have done combination selling. This gives you more than additional sales or revenue. *It is like hitting a sixer.*

SALESPERSON'S SAFEGUARDS OR CAUTIONS

However, whether it is cross-selling, up-selling or combination selling, the salesperson should keep some safeguards or cautions in mind. Five such safeguards or cautions are:

1. You should be fully conversant with all the products of your company—their features, benefits and prices;
2. Relationship between different products of the company—how much related or close those are;
3. If the customer has immediate requirement for one product, which other product(s) he (she) may be interested in buying soon?
4. Make sure the customer knows about all the products of your company;
5. Can additional products be sold without affecting the sale of the first product, i.e., there should be no cannibalisation.

If you have taken these safeguards or cautions, you are almost fully prepared for cross-selling, up-selling and combination selling.

The most appropriate timing for cross-selling or up-selling or combination selling may be soon after you have successfully concluded one sale. This is opportune time because you have already established your credibility, and, the additional sale or benefit accrues at a low incremental effort and cost.

TURNING NEGATIVE INTO POSITIVE

The final step or strategy in ABC of closing may be turning a negative into positive. *You can also call it turning a setback into a comeback*. Both mean almost the same thing.

Turning a negative into a positive means, in other words: How can you turn an objection in your favour or closing? It is not easy. But, nothing is easy in life and selling. You may have to apply your skill, training, and, above all, your salesmanship for this.

After the sales presentation, if your prospect says 'NO' to the offer, your first task is to guess or infer what may be the reason for this. During the presentation, you might guess this from his (her) body language or gestures. Try to probe the reason. You might say: "I accept your 'No' gracefully. But, if you could only tell me one or two reasons for your 'No', I would be grateful. I have to report this to my sales manager....I want to come back and satisfy you next time. For me, you are not a closed prospect or customer. I want to take your 'No' positively, and, not negatively. This is a lesson for me."

The prospect may, then, slowly start melting. He (she) may reopen the dialogue. This means that you have won half the battle. The rest depends on how things move further. If you are confident, you can slowly and gradually turn things in your favour.

If you can turn every negative into a positive, i.e., a setback into a comeback, you are moving closer to achieving ABC goal.

Mantra 10

Understand the Customer

"The customer is the most important visitor on our premises. He is not an interruption on our work. He is the purpose of it...."
—Mahatma Gandhi

"Sell your customers what they want, and, not what you want or what you think they want...."
—Selling Expert

We should first understand the difference between a 'consumer' and a 'customer'. 'Consumer' is the universe; 'customer' is a sub-set or part of 'consumer'. Customer is understood with reference to a company or product or brand. So, customer is more specific. For example, Hindustan Lever (HUL)'s customers for Lux toilet soap.

Customers are numerous and they are very diverse in their buying patterns and behaviours. **Some say that the customer's mind is a 'black box'; some say the customer is an 'enigma'; some others say that the customer is a 'puzzle' or a 'riddle'.** These may be rightly so. Experiences of many companies show that customer behaviour or the decision-making process, on many occasions, is almost inexplicable.

DIFFERENT TYPES OF CUSTOMERS

So, it is almost obvious that there are many types of customers. Nine major customer types can be distinguished:

1. Discerning customers
2. Affiliative customers
3. 'Know-all' customers
4. Authoritative customers
5. Inhibited customers
6. Image customers
7. 'Value-for-money' customers
8. Credibility customers
9. Haggling customers

Each of these customer types is explained below:

Discerning Customers: Discerning customers are those who are knowledgeable about marketing in general and, in particular, about the products and brands they are interested in. With these customers, salespersons should only concentrate on providing the required information about products and selling package and allow time for customers to make up their minds. Any attempt to 'convince' the customers with selling talks and over-enthusiasm in promoting the product may prove counter-productive. Pressure tactics should be avoided at all costs; otherwise, there are very high chances of losing the customer.

Affiliative Customers: Affiliative customers show more of people characteristics—high degree of affiliation motive. They may not have much knowledge about the product or market. May be, they also do not care. They care more for people values. Salespersons may best induce such customers by performing the role of a friend. Such customers might visit a retail shop to buy a product. But they may not have any specific brand in mind. Their final decision to buy or not to buy would depend more on the relaters' ability to win over them as individuals and less on a product appeal.

Know-all Customers: 'Know-all' customers think that they know almost everything about products, brands and markets. They are a contrast to discerning customers who are more sound and reflective. Instead of salespersons trying to impress them with sales talk or sales proposals, these customers believe in impressing salespersons with their 'know-all' knowledge of products and brands they are interested in. Salespersons' listening skills rather than presentation skills would be more effective here. Presentation talks or sales talks can be made intermittently to clinch the sale.

Authoritative Customers: Authoritative customers are assertive or dominating and like to feel important whether visiting a store or talking to a sales representative. They also demand considerable attention. In case of such customers, salespersons should try to satisfy their ego by listening, clarifying doubts and appreciating (at least pretending to appreciate) their viewpoints. Once their ego is satisfied, the salesperson might get a better price for his (her) product as a bargain. Such customers may even be willing to buy an expensive brand because the ego factor will work.

Inhibited Customers: Some customers have a feeling of inhibition. These are customers buying expensive and high involvement products particularly for the first time. The idea of entering a big store with all its sophistications may make the customers conscious and inhibited. The newly emerging middle class may provide such customers. Salespersons should make such customers comfortable. A vital factor here is that customers should not feel that they are discriminated against other customers in terms of attention and hospitality.

Image Customers: Image customers are more commonly found in consumer product categories. With changes in lifestyles, attitudes and perceptions of society such customers look for specific image-based brands which will fit into their self-image or self-concept. They do not mind paying a little more for the image which they perceive as an extension of their personality and lifestyle. Salespersons have to take care of product positioning planned and initiated by the marketing strategists. Image customers are more concerned with product categories which have 'social signalling value'—products which can be conspicuously seen by others in the society (cars, refrigerators, watches, televisions, music systems, etc.).

'Value-for-money' Customers: 'Value-for-money' customers are not image seekers. They do not look for image building. They want value for their money. They may have budgetary problems. Therefore, they are generally price conscious. They generally look for no-frills products which offer competitive price. Haldiram's poly pack snacks are good value-for-money products. These customers look for such products/brands.

Credibility Customers: Credibility customers are those who do not take the credibility claims of salesperson about their brands for granted. They want to be sure about it. Salespersons may have to satisfy the customers about brand performance. This is important because customers in this category may decide purchases through word-of-mouth brand endorsements or recommendations. Salespersons can give evidence of performance of a brand by providing details about a set of satisfied customers who have used the brand. Reference groups may be people with whom the customer is familiar (relative, friends, peers, etc.). If the product/brand is new, salespersons can try to convince the customers on the basis of credibility associated with the store(s). For customers, this can also be a way to exploit competition among the brands.

Haggling Customers: Haggling customers are typical in Indian situation. Haggling has almost been a traditional aspect of consumer behaviour in India. Till recently, consumers had a limited choice in the selection of a product because it was more of a sellers' market or closed market. The changed marketplace today offers wide choice of brands and extensions. Godrej offers a variety of soaps to suit the consumer need. Chinese brands offer a variety of audio/video products for price-conscious customers. The same is true about BPL in the telephone system.

Companies have introduced variety to accommodate different price preferences. The price notion existing in the minds of customers have to be understood and matched. If their price expectations are correctly judged and customers are satisfied, salespersons would ensure that the right kind of image has been created in the minds of customers about the company, the store and the price factor. Then, they would not have to face the embarrassment of having to convey to the customers that the store does not encourage haggling.

MANY FACES OF A CUSTOMER

Another way to look at types of customers is in terms of various roles played by them.

The customers generally play six different roles:

1. Teacher or leader
2. Catalyst for competition
3. To be wooed/pampered
4. Ordinary buyer
5. An exploiter
6. Quality killer

The customer can be a **teacher** because, many times, he can guide or be an instrument for quality and service improvements. A number of Indian companies have worked out elaborate schemes to learn from the customers. These include training of sales personnel at customers' sites, inviting customers' delegations to visit the plant or the shop floor to communicate directly with the workers for quality management or quality perfection.

Customers also teach or excite the sellers to compete. In a generalised way, all customers are **catalysts for competition.** But, some can be real catalysts; they can engineer competition through instruments like tenders. Although tenders are traditional and safe methods for government departments or agencies like DGS&D for procuring stores and consumables, in the corporate world, tenders are generally squeezers. Through the tender, the buyer tries to marginalise the sellers. The customers become quite ingenious in laying down tough tender terms to extract maximum out of a competitive situation.

From competition, we move to total customer orientation—the focus is on fringes and cutting edges. Of course, this happens typically in buyers market or under oligopolistic market structure (few sellers, many buyers). Customers **need to be pampered** because of the nature of competition. We shall illustrate with some examples. Several companies are launching exclusive clubs to woo customers with irresistible bargains and inducements. General Motors India (GMI) had set up the Opel Club for all Astra owners, which entitles all members to a host of privileges. Philips India launched Power Circle, a special club for special members. Bullet Club of Royal Enfield even organised social welfare activities for club members.

The 'rich' (a select few) customers always look for priceless goods, and for them price is no consideration only if they can be wooed enough to be convinced about the pricelessness of a particular good (an antique, a painting, a Belgian crystal).

With these exceptions, every customer wants to get the best product at the lowest price. But there is always a segment of customers whose product knowledge is always incomplete. Many customers cannot tell the difference between fine Asian silk and Bounty paper towels. No matter how flat your product is, there is always somebody who can't tell the difference, or, is not interested in knowing the difference or exploring the alternatives. These are 'out of market' customers. Call them indifferent or ***casual customers*** if you like. One can see many of them in the consumer goods markets like soaps, detergents and many other consumables.

Then there are customers who are ***exploiters***. Not to mention the traditional flesh trade, there are a host of customers in the industrial and business world who are market exploiters. This happens typically in monopsony (one buyer, multiple sellers) as a seller does in a monopoly. Glaring examples are Railways, State Electricity Boards (SEB), Director General of Supplies and Disposals (DGS&D), Department of Telecommunications (DOT) and many others. All these agencies usually buy through tenders, and a tender, to put it bluntly, is an instrument of exploitation, or to put is more euphemistically, it is exploitation in disguise.

And finally, there can be customers who are ***quality killers***. There are customers who are too price conscious. The decision to buy is based on price-product parity, and there is inevitably, a price-quality trade-off. This happens, selectively, for both consumer products and industrial products. For consumer products, sometimes compromises are made because of household budgetary controls or constraints.

The conclusion, therefore, is: **Try to identify the face of the customer, and decide the selling strategy**. Learn from some customers to sell to them; declare a price war to sell to some other; 'club' together some customers to woo them; decide strategy for tender bidding; sell discounts and not quality to price hungry customers; preserve quality for pricey customers; and, sell price-product combinations to 'walk-in' customers and the like.

CUSTOMER FEEDBACK AS A TOOL

Customer feedback can be used as a tool for understanding the customer more closely and making sales and rendering customer service. Irrespective of the product or service, properly planned customer feedback on different aspects of sales or marketing on regular basis makes the company more customer focused. This is a good way to feel the pulse of the customer. Such feedback can also be quite useful to the company in fine-tuning its marketing mix and sales strategy.

Customer feedback can be obtained in a number of ways: Five major types of feedback may be distinguished:

1. Post purchase feedback
2. Complaint feedback
3. Ghost shopping feedback
4. Focus group feedback
5. Trend type feedback

Post purchase feedback gives an opportunity to every customer to express his (her) satisfaction or dissatisfaction level over a product or a brand. The frequency of such feedback may vary from one product to another. A user of a car, motorcycle or scooter may require more than six months to form and give an opinion about product performance and after-sales service. A banking service may call for a different frequency of feedback. A beverage like tea, coffee or soft-drink may require much shorter time-span, may be almost instantaneous, for a feedback. Depending on the feedback process, companies should devise a system for obtaining such feedback on regular basis.

Complaint feedback is the most common form of feedback. This helps resolving grievances of customers. Resolving customer complaints efficiently improves a company's image and enhances its brand equity. General Electric (US) sends out 7,00,000 response cards every year to record different kinds of complaints with a view to get closer to customers. Citibank has a continuous system of monitoring complaints on three aspects considered critical by the company—accuracy, responsiveness and timeliness. McDonald's has a system of recording customer reactions on quality, service, cleanliness and value. Franchisees against whom complaints exceed the prescribed norms are dropped.

To pre-empt complaints, questionnaires can be sent to a cross-section of customers periodically to solicit information on product, quality, sales and service. By analysing the responses, management can find out if there is any specific pattern of complaints, and if so, they can take appropriate corrective actions. For example, Modi Xerox found that jamming of papers in copiers was caused by humidity and low quality of papers. The company took steps to ensure that this aspect is taken care of for product development in future.

Pre-emptive complaints can also open up areas for action and improvement not otherwise envisaged by a company. General Electric, for example, reduced the size of one of its divisional sales forces when it found that sales personnel were calling on customers too often, making redundant calls. Monitoring complaints can also help a company to evaluate its standard of performance in terms of product, quality, distribution, service, etc., over a period of time.

Ghost shopping feedback is also a pre-emptive feedback method. This method is often employed by companies to get regular feedback on customer perceptions about company's products and services. This may involve employing 'ghost customers'—individuals engaged by the company to shop in stores as customers to give feedback on different areas which may require improvement. British Airways was regularly flying a 'ghost passenger' in randomly selected flights to give feedback on in-flight services.

Ghost shopping may also involve surprise visits by sales managers or salespersons to the retail outlets and enquiring from the customers present about their perceptions and suggestions.

Focus group feedback is a random sample customer feedback. Focus group approach is quite useful in understanding customer expectations. More specifically, focus group feedback helps companies to ascertain the gap between company's perception of a product or service and the customer's perception of the same after the product has been used and services utilised.

The focus group method involves organising feedback session of a cross-section of customers who have used the company's product and collecting, analysing and synthesising diverse views and suggestions of these customers. Focus groups can be organised either on the basis of size, importance of customers, brand homogeneity, regional clustering or some other criteria.

Trend type feedback focuses on identifying the trends emerging in a specific product/service category. This type of feedback is both necessary and useful in a market environment where changes are often introduced or guided by consumer behaviour. Such feedback would help the companies anticipate and implement product and marketing changes. A number of changes have been introduced in the services of banks through customer feedbacks. Messaging and WhatsApp may affect mobile telephone services. It is, therefore, important for manufacturers to know how customers perceive a new product and positioning of various brands in their product categories. This helps immensely in planning sales strategies.

So, you have to understand the customer in the right way or perspective. **Try to understand each customer in his (her) own individual pattern or behaviour or peculiarity either by analysing the type or role or through the feedback process.** Then, selling becomes easy for you.

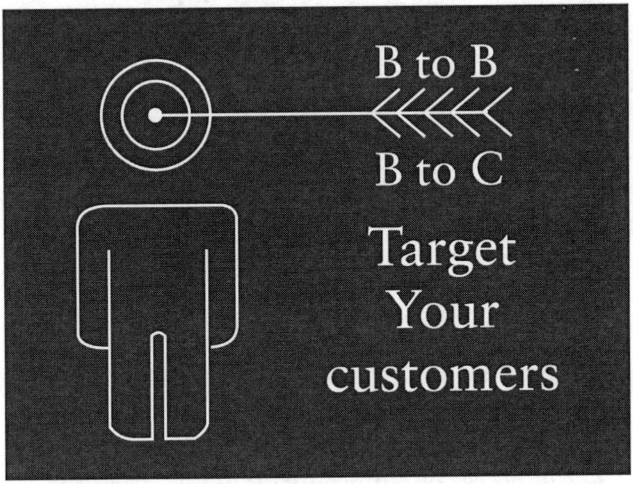

Mantra 11

Remember: Price Product Combination Sells

**Is selling all about product (quality) or price?
Or, is it product and price both?
Which is more important-product or price?...**

In the market, there is always a trade-off between product (quality) and price; knowing the right trade-off is the key to selling success....

A general misconception, even among salespersons, is that, if quality is good or high, the product sells almost automatically. This is not true. If the quality is high, price is also high. But, every customer does not like high price. Many customers may be willing to compromise on quality; they want low price. This is particularly true for daily necessities like soaps, detergents, etc. So, it is usually a price-product combination which sells.

PRODUCT, QUALITY AND PRICE

The general principle in marketing and selling is: higher the quality of product higher is the price, lower the quality, lower is the price. All premium products like Mercedes car, Sony colour TV, Ray-Ban sunglasses have high price. Customers pay for high or premium quality. At the other extreme, there are low quality, low cost products like Ghari detergents or local brands of detergents, Thermoking (local brand in Delhi) air conditioners, various local brands of electrical and electronic products, and, above all, most or all Chinese products. In all these, price is the most important consideration; there is a close trade-off with quality.

PRODUCT, PRICE AND CUSTOMER VALUE

The pricing strategy of most companies have three major objectives:

1. Choose a price point for your product to attract large volumes;
2. Sacrifice margins from premium pricing in favour of higher revenue;

3. Add more and more customer value to push up sales and profit despite smaller margins.

What is customer value? Or, what is creating value for the customer? Does customer value creation come from quality or price? Does the best quality or the lowest price create maximum value? Most often, it is neither the best quality (which is not affordable) nor the lowest price (the quality may not be acceptable). The norm or basis for optimal or maximum value creation is:

Affordable Price Plus Acceptable Quality

Such value creation does not exclude high or premium quality. If a customer can afford a Bentley or Ferrari, then why not? Similarly, a low income group customer may buy a soap or detergent of very low quality. That is his affordability, and, he accepts or compromises on the quality. But, for the vast majority of the buyers—whether in consumer goods, or industrial products or services—it is the golden rule of affordability plus acceptability. This is the price-product combination. This can be clearly seen in consumer goods, industrial products and also in services.

PRICE-PRODUCT COMBINATION IN CONSUMER GOODS

The Indian consumer goods market is dominated by price-product combination practices or strategies by companies. This is true of both FMCGs and consumer durables particularly FMCGs. This is primarily explained by two factors: first, market penetration strategy in a highly competitive situation and, second, the Indian middle class syndrome.

For market penetration, companies deliberately set low price with acceptable quality. Nirma and Ghari detergent powders, Babool toothpaste, Hero cycles, Videocon television, T-series cassettes, Maharaja mixie and United pressure cooker are some of the products/brands which have successfully used product-price combination for market penetration. T-series could outflank leaders, Music India Ltd. (MIL) or HMV, by offering low-priced audio-cassettes, improving the product mix and expanding the distribution channels to non-conventional outlets like cigarette shops and similar other vendors. Nirma is a classic example of using price-product combination for market penetration and securing market share by successfully exploiting the Indian middle class. It posed a serious challenge to detergents of HUL.

This brings us to the middle class syndrome. The Indian middle class is very large and diversified with different income levels—the upper middle class, the middle class and lower middle class. To fully exploit the middle class, which constitute the vast majority of Indian buyers/consumers, companies need to create as many product categories or brand extensions as possible with different price brands.

Surf was a *premium brand* with *commensurate* price. Nirma exploited the price segment with commensurate quality for the typical Indian middle class. HUL later responded to Nirma with product/brand extensions—Rin, Wheel and Sunlight. Ready made garments offer a big product-price range—from those sold in weekly bazaars to small stores to organised retail outlets like Pantaloons and Shopper's Stop. Even rice, the most staple Indian food in many states is available in a price range of ₹ 30 (lowest quality) to ₹ 80/90 per kg. (high quality basmati rice). Tata's Nano is also a classic example of price-product combination for the middle class. In consumer goods, the Chinese products have made price-product combination a *global* phenomenon.

PRICE-PRODUCT COMBINATION IN INDUSTRIAL PRODUCTS

Industrial products are of two types: *finished* products which are ready for use or consumption, and, *intermediate* products which are used as inputs in finished industrial products (B to B) or final consumer goods (B to C). Finished products are sold to business organisations and the replacement market; intermediate products or inputs are sold to original equipment manufacturers (OEM) and to manufacturers of consumes goods. For marketing each of these types of products, price-product combination is extensively used.

Finished industrial products are sold to organizations—companies, educational/research institutions, government departments/agencies, NGOs, etc. These include highly diversified products ranging from capital goods or sophisticated equipments to machine tools or simple hand tools. Sophisticated equipments like elevators need to conform to high quality; price is also high. These are cases of high quality-high price combination.

But there is a whole range of equipments or products like printing machinery in which there is a big product or quality range with commensurate prices. This is a typical example of product-price combination. Another good example is copper wire which is used for house wiring or other electrical purposes. Copper wire is available in various qualities and prices. The Kotla market in Delhi is a classic example. For Kotla market, they say: "you tell the price, we have the quality".

For industrial inputs or intermediates also, product-price combination sells well. For some critical inputs or accessories like car carburcttors, quality variations are less acceptable, and, therefore price variability is also less. But, for majority of other inputs or intermediates, product-price combinations are commonly used. This is true of the OEM market, and, more so, of the replacement market. Let me take the example of the automobile market. Automobile manufacturers have different vendors who can supply components or accessories of different qualities and prices and the automakers make quality compromise on 'cosmetic' parts or components. In the replacement market, 'original', 'local' and 'duplicate' components are regularly available with appropriate price differentials or product-price combinations.

PRODUCT-PRICE COMBINATION IN SERVICES

Services are intangibles, and, therefore, quality assessment or measurement is the most difficult. Quality depends upon perceptions of buyers or customers. Only in some cases like hotels, there are ratings like 7-star, 5-star, 4-star, 3-star, etc. For vast majority of services, product quality is perceptual or in the buyer's mind and price has direct relationship with it. This becomes clearer from examples of various service products.

Let us start with hotels. Hotels have product or quality rating of stars or non-stars. Star rating ranges from 7-star (more regular rating is 5-star) to 2-star with progressive differences in facilities and comforts and cost or prices. In the progressively declining scale, non-star hotels (also known as lodges or even *dhramshalas*) have much less facilities and comforts and much lower prices. A 7-star (or even a 5-star) hotel may charge tariff of about ₹ 10,000 per day. Most of the Taj group and Oberoi group hotels have tariff structure like this. In drastic contrast to this, non-stars may have tariff of ₹ 1,000 per day—going down upto, say, ₹ 500.

Restaurants are not very different in terms of product-price variability. Most of the restaurants in five-star hotels are at the top. Then, there are restaurants of different types and grades. There are fast food restaurants like McDonald's which is real value for money. The line ends with roadside restaurants or *dhabas*. Product-price combination is at its best.

Let me take another service product or category—courier services. Federal Express (FedEx) and DHL are international courier companies, and most dependable for fast and most efficient service. This is the premium category with premium price for premium quality. Then, there are national courier companies like Blue Dart, which also give fast and good service. Then, there are regional or local courier companies (like Blazeflash in Delhi) which are not so efficient, but, may be reliable and the charges are much less. Price-quality trade-off justifies the service.

LOOK FOR THE BEST PRODUCT-PRICE COMBINATION

The conclusion is clear: *The notion of high or best quality for maximum customer value or satisfaction is a myth or mistaken hypothesis.* Customer value or satisfaction comes from a particular product-price combination.

The real strategic task of companies and salespersons is to identify, establish and exploit the ideal or best product-price combination. This is true of all the three product categories: consumer goods, industrial products and services. This is most typical in services with highest variability followed by consumer goods and industrial products.

Companies and salespersons should constantly search for the ideal or optimal product-price mix to maximise sales, market share and profitability.

Mantra 12

Know Your Competitor

"We are not afraid of competition; let competition be afraid of us"
—Aditya Birla

Let you be the strongest competitor in your competitors' minds....

Remember, these is no selling without competition. Only in monopoly (one seller, many buyers), there is no competition. But, monopolies are rare. Under all normal market conditions, there is competition. So, if you are in selling, you have to face and deal with competition to survive and grow. Don't be afraid of this.

IF YOU IGNORE COMPETITION ...

Most companies are busy with making their own marketing plans and strategies. Plans and strategies are made for both the present and the future—how to increase sales, market share and profitability. In this process, either they ignore competitors, or, do not consider or measure their full potential or impact. *This is one kind of marketing myopia.*

The outcome is: targets are only partially achieved or not reached at all. This has happened through decades. In the '70s, Raymond, Bombay Dyeing and Khatau (Voiles) ignored the emergence of Vimal fabrics; in the '80s, HUL (Surf) was overlooking the entry of Nirma and Premier Automobiles (Padmini) could not weigh the full impact of emergence of Maruti (Suzuki); and, in the '90s, HMT (Watches) could not measure the full impact of Titan. Weston, Uptron, Salora, Dyanora could not correctly anticipate the emergence of Sony, LG and Samsung. Some of the companies have completely perished.

EXISTING COMPETITORS

Primary, Secondary and Tertiary Competitors

Existing competitors of a company can be of three types: Primary, secondary and tertiary. *Primary competitors* are competitors in the *same product category* (with different brands) and are the most immediate ones; these are more clearly visible and easily identifiable. If we take the Indian soft drinks market, Coca-Cola and Pepsi are the most immediate (primary) competitors followed by Thumps Up, Sprite, Fanta, Limca, etc.

Secondary competitors are in the *substitute product* categories and are not so clearly visible. Again, if we take the soft drinks market, lemon soda, canned and packaged fruit drinks (like 'Fruity') and slush are substitutes for soft drinks and compete with different brands of soft drinks.

Tertiary competitors are more *distant substitutes* which are not easily visible or identifiable, but, those also compete with the product or brand. Tertiary competitors of soft drinks are cold milk/butter milk, cold coffee, lassi, etc. During different times and situations, consumers substitute them for soft drinks.

Therefore, any company in any business (product) must try to identify all its existing competitors—primary, secondary and tertiary—who always vie for part of the market or market share.

POTENTIAL COMPETITORS

Existing competitors are more immediate threats to a company, but, potential competitors are potential threats and, if not foreseen properly or in time, can pose more serious problems than the existing competitors. *All existing competitors are potential competitors of yesterday.* There are many examples: Titan to HMT, Maruti to Premier Padmini, Nirma to Surf, etc.

COMPETITOR THREAT: FIVE FORMS

Threats from competitors, either existing or potential, can come in different forms. Five major types of competitive threats are possible and are often seen in practice:

(a) Threat from existing competitors.

(b) Threat from substitutes.

(c) Threat from buyers.

(d) Threat from suppliers.

(e) Threat from new entrants.

Threat from *existing competitors* actually implies the battle for market share. It is the most immediate concern of a company particularly if it is a market leader or challenger. Ongoing battle between Coca-Cola and Pepsi, Surf and Ariel, Colgate and Pepsodent are good examples.

Substitute products reduce demand for a product or category of products because some customers switch over to alternatives. Packaged fruit drink and juices have substituted soft drinks to a large extent; e-mail has substituted postal services to a great extent; mobile phones have substituted many landlines; laptops have substituted desktop computers to a significant extent.

Threats from buyers come primarily through *backward integration*—a current buyer of a product starts manufacturing the product itself. This can sometimes be a major threat in consumer durables and industrial products. Examples: a truck or a car manufacturer beginning to make components or accessories like Tata Motors or an air conditioner manufacturer also making compressors like Carrier Aircon or a colour TV manufacturer also making picture tube like Sony or Samsung.

Threat from suppliers may appear rather strange because suppliers are mostly at the receiving end, but suppliers can be tomorrow's competitors. This can happen through *forward integration*—today's suppliers of inputs for a product starts making the product itself. Sony was initially a manufacturer and supplier of picture tubes to colour TV manufacturers, but now Sony is a leading manufacturer of CTV. TVS (earlier Lucas-TVS) traditionally a component or accessories maker has entered into production of motor cycles (TVS-Suzuki). There are other examples also.

New entrants can pose a major threat to the existing market players and even market leaders. Toyota and Honda's entry in the US car market (and also in the global market), Maruti Suzuki's entry into the Indian car market, Vimal fabrics in the Indian textile market and Titan in the Indian watch market are well known. In fact, most of the established products and brands in consumer and industrial markets today were new entrants at some point of time. Foreseeing or forecasting the emergence of new entrants is vital for existing market players/competitors, and, it is also one of the most difficult jobs. But, companies which fail to foresee the new entrants or ignore them may even face disastrous results as is evident in the examples of Padmini (earlier Fiat) cars, HMT watches, Weston TV, etc.

Before making marketing plans and strategies, it is essential for companies to analyse and assess the nature and magnitude of competition particularly the current competitors who are a constant threat to a company's business.

COMPETITOR INTELLIGENCE

One important way to do this is competitor intelligence—knowing more and more about competitors: their business plans and strategies. For effective competitor intelligence, companies should try to gain access to *information* about competitors—what they say about their plans, policies, strategies and other competitors. For this, it is important to have knowledge about various sources of information about one's competitors—primary as well as secondary. Six major sources for information about competitors are:

- *Public sources*: Newspaper reports/press releases, articles, promotional materials of companies, etc.
- *Trade and professional sources*: Annual reports, seminar papers, technical articles and materials prepared by companies.
- *Channel members*: Distributors, wholesalers and retailers.
- *Customers*: Most primary sources of information on competitors' products/brands, perceived value, price/discount policies, etc.
- *Investor, bankers and shareholders*: Discussions in AGM, investors' (non-equity or debt) meetings, bankers' reports.
- *Government (Central/State)*: Offices/departments of excise, customs, income tax, sales tax.

Strong company intelligence can exploit all these sources of information about competitors for formulation of strategy.

Ghost Customer

In addition to the above sources, an effective way to do competitor intelligence is to use the 'ghost customer' approach. Many companies in industrial products and consumer durables use this approach. A company may pose as a customer to a competitor to elicit information about the product, pricing policy, payment system, any special scheme, etc. This way the company obtains first-hand information about competitors' marketing policies and strategies.

COMPETITOR SWOT

Competitor intelligence helps to make competitors' SWOT (strength, weakness, opportunity, threat) analysis. Companies commonly analyse their own strengths and weaknesses for formulating strategies. But, it is equally important, if not more, to analyse the strengths and weaknesses of the competitors for developing appropriate competitive strategies.

Every company should have a competitor intelligence unit which should scan all available information about a competitor's strengths and weaknesses—resource strengths, strategic capabilities, competitive shortcomings, etc., and make a comparative SWOT analysis. The objective of such analysis is to exploit competitors' weaknesses, and, try to convert company weaknesses into strengths.

COMPETITOR MARKETING MIX

Like competitor SWOT, competitor marketing mix analysis is equally important. In fact, it is more important from the strategic point of view. Marketing strategies are expressed in terms of a particular marketing mix, i.e. mix or blending of different Ps in a particular way. Companies do this to obtain the optimal or most efficient marketing mix, and, consequently the best marketing strategy.

To make the marketing mix effective or competitive, companies must do parallel or comparative marketing mix analysis of major competitors. If a company is a market leader, it should conduct the marketing mix analysis of the challenger. The challenger obviously has to do marketing mix analysis of the leader, and, also of No. 3 player if he is a close competitor. The framework for comparative marketing mix analysis should be like this:

Marketing Mix	Company	Competitor 1	Competitor 2	Competitor 3
Product	a_1	x_1	y_1	z_1
Price	a_2	x_2	y_2	z_2
Promotion	a_3	x_3	y_3	z_3
Place (Distribution)	a_4	x_4	y_4	z_4
Total	a	x	y	x

$a_1 \ldots a_4$, $x_1 \ldots x_4$, $y_1 \ldots y_4$, $z_1 \ldots z_4$ are scores or rankings. These give the comparative assessment of each of the elements of the marketing mix of the company and the major competitors. a, x, y, z show the total or overall marketing mix scores. This is primarily subjective exercise. But, properly done, this can be an effective method of analysing the company vis-à-vis the competitors.

MARKET SIGNALS

Market signals given by companies from time to time can be a good source for competitor intelligence and analysis. Market signals are direct or indirect indications given by companies about their intent, motive, plans, etc. Properly tracked, these can give very useful, sometimes vital, clues to competitors' business plans and strategies.

These may even sometimes help a company to take pre-emptive action to block a competitor's proposed plans for business development. Here is an excellent example of this. IBM had announced its intention for production of 3½" discs for PCs. Sony was already manufacturing these discs, and, to prevent IBM to enter into production of this, they increased their production fivefold. IBM had to finally drop its plan. This is a very strategic use of a market signal.

PREPARE FOR COMPETITION

Analyse the competitors particularly the more immediate competitors. Understand the competitors and prepare yourself for competition. *Preparedness is very important. Then, there is nothing to be afraid of competition.*

Take it as a challenge. **Try to adopt the right strategy. You can beat the competition and emerge winner or successful.**

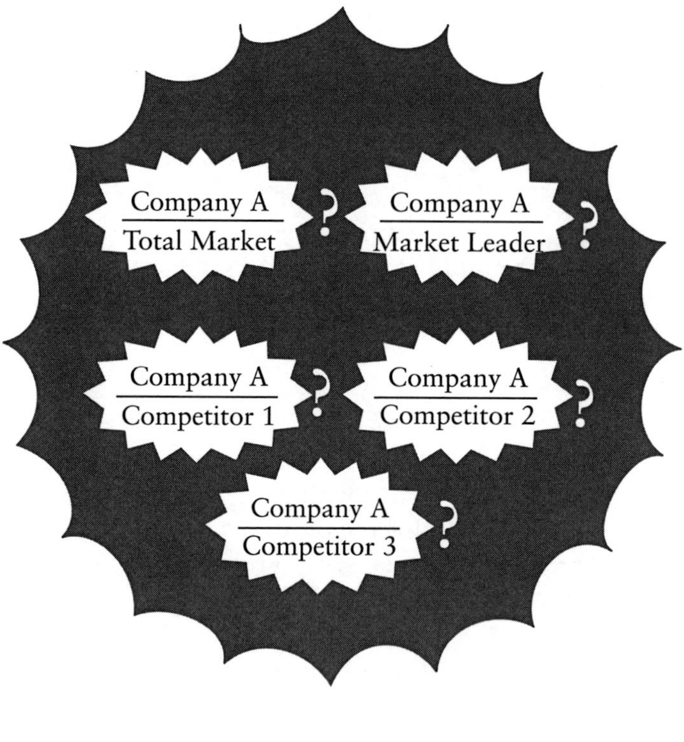

Mantra 13

Know Why Salespeople Fail

The men who try to do something and fail are infinitely better than those who try to do nothing and succeed....

—Lloyd Jones

Failures are the pillars of success....

—Old Proverb

Failure can occur in any sphere of life, personal or family life, business or selling. We can say that failure is almost a way of life like success, but, of course, with lesser frequency. Sometimes, failure and success alternate like darkness and light.

So, **failure should be taken as a temporary setback and, not a permanent roadblock.**

It is important, rather essential, to understand the reasons for failure, analyse them and fake necessary corrective steps or actions and get back on course. The show must go on, that is, selling must continue.

COMMON REASONS FOR FAILURE

There can be many reasons or ways because of which salespeople may fail. Let us try to understand and analyse them.

Sixteen common reasons for failure in selling are:

1. Lack of clarity of goals
2. Not being organised
3. Lack of commitment
4. Lack of motivation
5. Lack of openness/transparency
6. Lack of coordination
7. Lack of monitoring
8. Absence of proper systems/procedures
9. Lack of proper training
10. Over-confidence
11. Lack of confidence

12. Fear of rejection
13. Poor communication
14. Lack of team spirit
15. Too little follow-up
16. Too much follow-up

"Lack of clarity of goals" may be the first reason or cause of failure in selling. The salespersons may not be clear about what is actually to be achieved—territories, products, customers—or which are the priorities.

"Not being organised" means not getting or going prepared for a sales presentation or meeting with a prospect.

"Lack of commitment" and "Lack of motivation" are closely correlated. Lack of motivation causes lack of commitment. These two factors always cause salespersons to underperform or fail frequently.

"Lack of openness or transparency" imply ambiguity. The prospect may feel that the salesperson is trying to hide or conceal some information or details about the company or the product.

"Lack of proper systems and procedures" is another important factor. Salespersons might not be given clear or complete instructions or drills about allocation of territories, prospects/customers, discounts, etc. These may result in failure in execution of sales.

"Lack of proper training" particularly skill-based training, ill-equips the salespersons in selling skills and this becomes a reason for them to under perform or fail.

"Poor communication" can be of two types; first, between the salespersons and the sales manager or headquarters, and, second, between the salespersons and the prospect/customer. Poor communication with the sales manager or headquarters may be in the form of incomplete brief, guidelines or instructions relating to a prospect/customer or sale. Poor communication with a prospect/customer may be in the form of non-supply of information or details about the product or offer or inadequate or incomplete follow-up with the prospect/customer.

"Lack of coordination" is almost an extension of lack of communication. Lack of coordination is more often an issue with the sales manager/headquarters. This can also be with the prospect/customer. Lack of coordination with the sales manager also implies or includes "lack of monitoring".

"Overconfidence" of salespersons can be another cause of failure. Overconfidence can border on the thinking that the prospect/customer will come to them.

Equally bad or damaging is "Lack of confidence". Lack of confidence often leads to "fear of rejection".

Salespersons may sometimes have to work as a team for selling certain products particularly consumer durables and industrial products. "Lack of team spirit "in such cases may cause failure in execution of sales.

FAILURE BECAUSE OF FOLLOW-UP FACTORS

Timely follow-up with the prospects is very important or essential for conclusion of a sale. But, too much follow-up may spoil the broth, i.e., sale. Also, too little follow-up may result in loss of sale. Both may be self-defeating or counterproductive.

There are a number of ways too little or too much follow-up can damage a sale or result in failure.

In actual sales situations, there are more reasons or causes for too little follow-up than for too much follow-up.

Ten common ways too little follow-up takes place are:

1. Laziness/Lethargy
2. Non-caring attitude
3. Habit of not pursuing or finishing the task
4. Lack of commitment
5. Overconfidence
6. Creating a big time lag for follow-up and then feeling embarrassed to call or follow-up
7. Taking a break or holiday in the middle of a pursuit.
8. Not keeping/maintaining regular diary
9. Not keen/conscious about target achievement
10. Feeling that they are chasing the prospect too frequently/ feeling that they are pushing the prospect too much

Six common reasons for too much follow-up are:

1. Too eager to sell/close a sale
2. Attitudinal problem: "I want to prove that I can close a sale faster than others"
3. Lack of patience
4. In a hurry to take a break
5. Too independent to follow proper norms or protocol
6. In a haste to receive a special reward

FAILURE IN SELLING AND BEHAVIOURAL PATTERNS

It has been observed that salespersons with high rate or frequency of failure show certain common behavioural patterns. In other words, failure in selling and salespersons' behavioural patterns are closely correlated.

Eight observed common behavioural patterns are:

1. Salespersons with high rate of failure have an attitude problem;
2. Such salespersons have no clarity of goals;
3. Such salespersons mostly go unprepared for appointments or meetings;
4. They do not practice their sales presentations in advance;
5. They waste time in loose talks and gossips;
6. They think that prospects/customers will wait for them;
7. They generally suffer from overconfidence syndrome;
8. They are never proactive; they are always reactive.

So, the reasons or causes of failure in selling can be many and varied. To shield their failures, most of the salespersons try to shift the blame to the state of economic conditions in the country, environment or circumstances, the company, the sales manager, the product and, often their stars or bad luck. Don't do this. **Don't shift the blame to others.** It does not help your cause or solve your problems.

Take the failures objectively rather than subjectively. Analyse the failure. Prepare your mindset to take appropriate steps for correcting your course, and, look forward to success.

Abraham Lincoln failed nine successive times before he became the President of the United States of America. This is a classic example of how failures can be turned into success.

I am sure you will not have to fail nine times before you make a comeback. You can come back much before that. You have to have hope. **Take inspiration from those who have failed and come back successfully.**

Mantra 14

Learn from Mistakes

When everything seems lost, the future still remains....
—Old Saying

I would never promote a man into a top-level job who has not made mistakes....
—Peter Drucker, Management Expert

The old proverb: "To err is human". To err or make a mistake in selling is also human. So, don't be afraid of or get dispirited if you make a mistake. Instead, learn from the mistakes.

A common perception is that making mistakes in management goes against professionalism. This is far from truth. Mistakes can and do happen in professional management.

Peter Drucker, the management expert, had said: "I would never promote a man into a top-level job who has not made mistakes...otherwise, he is sure to be mediocre. Worse still, not having made mistakes, he would not have learned how to spot them early, and, how to correct them.... The better a man, the more mistakes he will make—for the more new things he will try."

We can interpret Drucker's statement or observation with reference to selling as: The fact that a salesperson has never made a mistake shows that he (she) has never taken initiative, showed boldness and innovativeness in selling and decision making.

MISTAKES IN SELLING

During the selling process, mistakes can occur during different stages and in different ways or forms.

Ten major types of mistakes can be identified. These are one or more of the following:

1. Mistake in goal setting or target setting
2. Mistake in sales planning/planning stage
3. Mistake in communication
4. Mistake in preparation for sales presentation
5. Mistaking "hearing" for listening
6. Mistake in understanding the prospect

7. Mistake in timing
8. Mistake in follow-up
9. Mistake in closing
10. Mistakes in post-closing protocol

Mistake in Goal Setting/Target Setting

Mistake in goal setting or target setting can occur in two ways: setting too ambitious or high target and setting soft or low target. Some salespersons are over-ambitious, and, they like to set high targets for them for reward for achievement. There are others who are conservative, and, want to set soft or low targets for themselves for fear of failure of achievement. The sales manager has a role in target setting in both cases. But, in most cases, the problem of high target setting and, low target setting remains. The mistakes involved in these are revealed later during the monitoring or evaluation stage.

Both over-targetting and under-targetting have implications for sales achievement of the company.

Mistake in Sales Planning/Planning Stage

If there is mistake or mistakes in target setting, these can lead to mistakes in sales planning. Even if target setting is correctly done, mistakes can occur during the sales planning stage. The selling process consists of a number of stages from prospecting to closure of sale. Each stage has to be planned properly in terms of strategy and timing. A mistake can happen because of lapse or lapses during any of the stages.

Mistake in Communication

Communication is vital in any activity or operation. Mistake can take place in the communication process. In selling, mistake in communication can occur in either of two ways or both—communication with the sales manager, and, communication with the prospect.

Salespersons should be in constant or regular communication with the sales manager during different stages of the selling process. Communication with the prospect should also be regular and timely whether before, during or after the sales presentation. If the salesperson is not alert, mistakes can creep in here. Communication with the prospect/customer becomes particularly important for consumer durables, may not be so much for FMCGs.

Mistake in Preparation for Sales Presentation

Preparation for sales presentation is another area in which mistake can often happen. Such preparation may relate to product demonstration and/or negotiation (for non-FMCG products) or may particularly involve objection handling in anticipation like "I had a bad experience with your company." Every salesperson should follow the steps or drill for a good sales presentation. If he (she) does not make adequate preparation for the sales presentation, mistakes can occur.

Mistaking 'Hearing' for 'Listening'

Mistaking 'Hearing' for 'Listening' means not paying proper attention to the person who is speaking to you; in selling, it is the prospect.

Listening is active mode; hearing is passive mode.

The difference between listening and hearing can be explained with an example. You are watching a TV. Your wife comes and talks to you. She is asking you a question. You say "Yes". She says: "What Yes?" I am asking you a question. You say: "Sorry, say it again". You are hearing, but, not listening.

During sales presentation, the prospect is speaking. He (she) asks you a question. You respond by saying "Yes". He (she) is surprised. He (she) says: "I asked you a question". You reply: "Sorry, please say it again." You have heard something, but, you have not listened. The damage has been done. The mistake has been committed.

Mistake in Understanding the Prospect

Mistakes can occur in understanding prospects because it is a difficult and tricky job. Prospects, like customers, can be of different types: discerning prospects, 'know-all' prospects, authoritative prospects, 'image' prospects', 'value-for-money' prospects, credibility prospects, and, above all, haggling prospects.*

* For detailed explanation or description of different types of prospects/ customers, refer, among others, A. Nag, *Sales and Distribution Management* (Second Edition), McGraw Hill Companies, 2022 (Ch. 6).

Before and during the sales presentation, you have to infer and ascertain what type of prospect he (she) is and proceed accordingly. If you do not do this mental exercise properly, you may make a mistake in understanding the prospect, and, the selling process may suffer.

Mistake in Timing

Timing in a sales presentation is very important. Mistake(s) can occur, if your timing is not proper, let alone perfect.

You will obviously not go for a sales presentation without prior appointment. Even after going with prior appointment, your timing issue starts now. You have to quietly observe the receptivity. If you notice that the prospect is looking inattentive, then don't start the presentation Wait till he (she) asks you to start.

After you have started the presentation, you keep quietly observing him (her). If you notice that his (her) attention is getting diverted (may be a telephone call, may be his (her) nature), stop and give a pause. Ask him (her): "Should we take a break?" If he (she) says: "Please continue", then you restart the presentation and try to complete it. If you are not moving cautiously, you are making a mistake.

Mistake in Follow-up

Every sales presentation may not lead to or calumniate in immediate or instant sale. Some follow-up may be necessary. Follow-up should be carefully done. It should be timely follow-up. Too much follow-up and too little follow-up both are unwarranted or bad.

There are many reasons why timely follow-up may not be done like impatience (too much follow-up) or overconfidence (too little follow-up). All such extremes should be avoided. Try to follow the prospect's desire for timing of the follow-up. Otherwise, mistakes will occur.

Mistake in Closing

Closing is the final, and, the most important stage in selling, and, this should be judiciously handled or executed. There are many ways to close a sale: simply ask for the order, summarise the presentation and ask for the order, suggestive close, concession close, side close, alternative close and others. You have to choose the most appropriate method for closing according to the situation and response pattern of the prospect. You can try more than one trial close before you finally close or conclude the sale. It depends on your salesmanship and sales acumen. You should know how much to push when. It's a tricky game. Move smartly; otherwise, mistakes ill occur.

Mistakes in Post-closing Protocol

It is often rightly said that *a sale is not totally closed even after closing the sale.* The after-sales protocols and actions still remain.

After successful closure of a sale, the salesperson should follow the closure routine of thanking the prospect, now turned buyer or customer, for his (her) cooperation and placing an order on the company. During the thanks giving session, do not over-react or become too emotional.

After closing, there is after-sales service particularly for consumer durables. The intelligent and smart salespersons will talk about or seek new business or referrals. Through these, the salesperson will try to build relationship for the future. This is like *a free investment for future business*. All these should be intelligently carried out so that there are no lapses or mistakes. These may be less serious mistakes, but, mistakes are mistakes. There may be difference of degree.

If more mistakes are made during the selling process, it becomes compounding mistakes. The challenge becomes more for the salesperson to correct the mistakes and learn and proceed.

MISTAKE-AVOIDANCE COMPLEX

Some salespersons suffer from mistake-avoidance complex. Their approach to their job is passive or negative: don't take initiative and a decision, and, therefore, don't make a mistake. The fear of a mistake haunts them with the result that they hardly perform. They are never ambitious.

Such salespersons remain very average or mediocre all their life. They become static or stagnant. This is an attitude problem.

Training and motivational programmes also may not work on them. Companies may not like or want such salespersons.

A professional and aspiring salesperson will not lose courage or spirit because of making mistakes. He (she) will analyse the mistakes and learn from those so that he (she) does not repeat the same again.

Every salesperson should have the mindset and desire to learn from mistakes. *His (her) determination plays an important role in this.*

So, we can say, in conclusion, that **making mistake in selling is not a crime. On the contrary, it may often reveal some special characteristics of a salesperson. These characteristics may finally drive him (her) to success.**

Sometimes Salespeople have to Pull Strings together to ensure Sales Growth

Mantra 15

Take Training in Selling

Training does not create capability; it only fills a void in skill or capability....

In selling, training is an input; the output is a successful sales career....

People, including salespeople, are a resource. The use of salespeople, as a resource, should be planned, coordinated and controlled in the same way as any other resource. But, traditionally, in almost all companies, far more attention is being paid to development and fuller utilisation of material resource than of human resource. Companies are, however, now realising the need for organised development of human resource including those in selling. This is where training comes in.

WHY TRAINING IS NECESSARY

The new or raw recruits in a company as salespersons should be trained. They do not have any idea about the company, its products, prices and selling systems or strategies. They need training to be oriented towards and adopting the organisation's culture and style of functioning.

This basic or induction orientation helps the sales manager to prepare or grow the salespersons for actual selling. The salespersons learn to think in one direction and work towards achievement of organisational objectives or goals. All the training inputs or modules would mould the salespersons into successful sales professionals.

Training, including sales training, has significance in another way. Training helps people to learn and remember things better. Scholz has mentioned different ways people remember things with different degrees of remembrance. These are mentioned in the table below.

Different Ways People Remember Things

Way to remember	How much is remembered
By reading	10%
By hearing	20%
By seeing	30%
By hearing and seeing	50%
By what they say	70%
By what they say as they do	90%

Training helps both 'hearing' and 'seeing', and sometimes also 'doing' (on-the-job training) for salespeople in addition to 'reading'.

SALES TRAINING PROCESS

The objective of sales training is to improve productivity, output and efficiency of sales managers and salespeople and, ultimately, of the organisation as a whole.

The sales training process consists of three major stages. The three stages are shown in the figure.

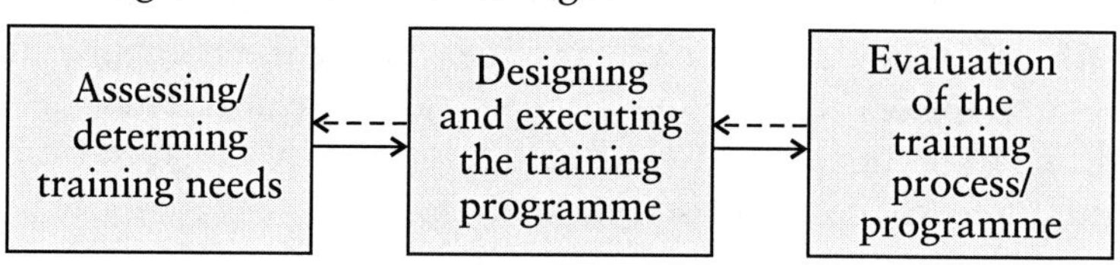

Sales Training Process

In all organisations, training programmes, whether for sales managers/staff, marketing managers, production managers/ supervisors, or any other functional group, are organised by the HR department.

ASSESSING TRAINING NEEDS

The sales manager has to assess the training needs of different salespeople on the basis of their knowledge, skill or capability gaps and send the same to the HR department for organising the training programmes.

Training needs of salespeople are of two types: first, orientation or induction training and, second, skill development training and job-specific training for capability improvement.

Orientation or induction training is a basic/compulsory training given to all new salespeople before they start their jobs. This training consists of five major needs or inputs. These are:

(a) Knowledge of the organisation
(b) Product knowledge
(c) Job profile of the salesperson
(d) Hierarchy and reporting system
(e) Field or territory acquaintance

Skill development training and job-specific or capability improvement training is given to salespeople who are working with the company for sometime. These training programmes should be organised after careful assessment of the training needs of the salespeople. The sales manager/sales department should take into account all relevant factors or inputs for correct assessment of training needs. Six such factors or inputs are:

(a) *Job description*: Job description directly helps identification of skill or capability gap.
(b) *Sales manager's observation*: Area or regional sales managers regularly interact with the salespeople in the field and, therefore, their observations form very important inputs.
(c) *Skill/capability testing*: In many companies, aptitude, skill and capability tests are conducted to assess the gaps or needs.
(d) *Salespeople's inputs/opinions*: Salespeople's own opinion about their training needs for capability building can be an important input.
(e) *Customer feedback*: In products where personal or direct selling is important (industrial products, consumer durables), customer feedback on their experience with salespeople is important.
(f) *Sales audit*: Some companies, as part of sales audit, assess training needs of the salespeople. This is a new method.

SALES TRAINING METHODS

After assessment of training needs, the choice of an appropriate training method is the next important step. This includes both design and execution. Training methods can be many ranging from classroom teaching to on-the-job training.

Demonstration is one method. *Demonstration* is a method to give knowledge about the product and its features by demonstrating its operation and use. Whirlpool used demonstration in an innovative way. The company asked its newly recruited salespeople to live for two months in a house furnished with its home appliances. The salespeople learnt about the products by using them during these two months. Product demonstrations are more commonly done for industrial gadgets and consumer durables.

Role play is another method. *Role play* is a practical method for assessing selling skills or techniques. In this method, one salesperson plays the role of a seller of a company's product and either another salesperson or a group of salespeople play the role of buyers. Through this 'mock' transaction, a salesperson can be taught (tested) about the company's product, competitors, customer expectations, quality, price, etc.

Of late, on-line training is also becoming an important method. *On-line training* methods are electronic performance support system (EPSS), interactive multimedia training and distance learning. On-line training has the advantage of being much less expensive and much faster than the conventional off-line or face-to-face methods.

Different methods of training are not used in isolation. Two or more methods are combined to make a complete package of training. For example, classroom lectures on selling techniques, consumer behaviour, competitor analysis, etc. may be combined with case studies and role plays.

This is how a training package can be made effective and serve the learning objectives. *On-line methods can be useful supplements to the direct or face-to-face methods.*

EVALUATION OF TRAINING PROGRAMME

It is important, in fact essential, to ascertain whether the sales training programmes are producing the desired results, i.e., whether the programmes are justified in terms of costs and benefits. Every programme has a cost—financial as well as loss of working hours/days of salespeople. The benefits from a programme should compensate for these costs.

To ensure this, a proper evaluation and review of every training programme is necessary. This should be, and is usually done through a structured feedback form or questionnaire. The most important part of the questionnaire contains salespeople's feedback on the programme.

The feedback is taken on four important aspects:

(a) Programme content or training inputs
(b) Effectiveness of training methods
(c) Suitability and quality of faculty
(d) Contribution of the programme to enrichment of knowledge, development of selling skills, better performance, etc.

The sales manager/HR department should analyse the salespeople's feedback and other assessment factors mentioned in the questionnaire for correct evaluation and review of each training programme. Evaluation/review may reveal some shortcomings or deficiencies in design or methods of training. Review may indicate some follow-up action. Deficiencies should be removed and follow-up actions undertaken for improvement, reinforcement or reorganisation of future programmes. This completes the sales training process.

Appropriate Sales Training: Firestone Ltd.

Firestone is one of those companies which, through experience and feedback inputs, have evolved an appropriate training programme for all new salespeople.

Firestone had been conducting training programmes for its salespeople for many years. All new salespeople would join the company at Mumbai and would be immediately sent for induction training. The training programme included visit to the factory for shop-floor training and classroom training at the head office. The classroom teaching consisted primarily of addresses by, and interactions with, senior managers from different departments. The sales manager was also one of the speakers/trainers.

In spite of a well-designed/executed training programme, the sales manager found that 60 per cent of the salespeople failed to deliver results for the first three to six months. This indicated that there was some drawback in the programme design. The sales manager's interactions with the last batch which was trained revealed the shortcoming. The salespeople/trainees being fresh from the institutes, felt inhibited when sent to the field because they could not understand many of the terms used in the trade. This resulted in their inability to interact with dealers/customers with confidence.

As a solution to this, the trainee salespeople suggested that, first, they might be allowed to spend some time in the field for initial exposures or familiarisation. The training programme should be conducted after this so that they could clarify many trade terms/doubts during the programme. This would equip them to deal with the distributors, dealers and customers with enough confidence and produce better results.

The sales management/training department found this suggestion/feedback very logical and practical. Accordingly, the training programme for new salespeople was re-designed as follows:

1. First two weeks in the field with senior salespeople for familiarisation
2. Next one week at the factory for shop floor/production process training
3. Last two weeks at HO for classroom training.

The feedback from the sales manager/sales department confirmed that the redesigned programme was producing right results and should, therefore, continue.

TRAINING, GOOD TRAINING

So, the significance of sales training is clear. Its necessity is indisputable. But, training should be well conceived, planned and conducted in the proper way taking into account the full requirements of salesperson. Then, it increases skill, capability and productivity of salespersons. This helps to improve sales performance. Salespeople should always look forward to such training.

Firestone's model is good for most companies and salespersons. This is almost a participative model or module or participative approach to training. This is like a win-win approach or model. Most companies should adopt such model to maximise benefits for the company as well as salespersons.

So, go for training. Go for right kind of training. Go more for tailor-made training. This will enable you to achieve excellence in selling and earn rewards.

We can, therefore, say

Appropriate training

(Ideally participative)

→ Success or excellence in selling

→ Rewards in selling

Mantra 16

Motivate Yourself: Motivation is Key to Performance

Self-motivation is the best motivation....

Motivation mix is like marketing mix; different elements should be blended optimally for optimum result....

To do or perform a job, ability to do the job is essential. To perform their sales job, salespersons have to have the ability or credibility to do it; this may be either inherent or acquired through training. They also require the motivation or inspiration to perform the sales function properly or successfully.

So, performance is the outcome or result of ability and motivation. We can put it like this:

Ability + Motivation = Performance

COMPANY'S ROLE IN SALESPERSONS' MOTIVATION

Every company has a role in motivating its salespersons. This can be done in different ways or forms.

Motivational Elements and Mix

Different factors or rewards act as different motivators. It depends, to a great extent, on the perceptions of salespeople and their positions in their hierarchy of needs and, therefore, the way each salesperson values a particular reward. Because of this, the sales manager or the management needs to work out a motivational package or mix consisting of different motivational factors or tools or elements.

Ideally, a separate motivational mix should be designed for every salesperson to suit his (her) requirements.

Broadly speaking, motivational factors or elements can be of two-types: financial and non-financial. Major elements of a motivational mix are presented in the table below.

Major Elements of Motivational Mix

Financial	Non-Financial
• Salary	• Promotion
• Commission	• Personal growth opportunity
• Incentive bonus	• Recognition/special award
• Perks/Fringe benefits	• Training programme
• Paid holiday	• Seminars/Workshops/Conferences
• Sales contest	• Sales contest

Most of the elements in the table are self-explanatory; sales contest needs some clarification or explanation.

In many companies, sales contests are organised at regular intervals to serve both organisational objective and salespeople's interest. Objectives of sales contest can be many: to foster competitive spirit among salespeople, clear off stock, increase sales, introduce new products/brands, etc.

Rewards for sales contest can be both financial and non-financial. Financial rewards can be cash prizes or awards and also paid holidays. Non-financial rewards can be free or highly discounted merchandise, gift vouchers, etc. Paid holidays are generally given in many companies as a reward for extraordinary performance. The State Bank of India has a system of paid holidays for rewarding special performances.

Factors Motivating the Salespersons

Financial factors or rewards can be easily quantified. Those are usually included in or form part of the compensation package.

Non-financial factors or rewards are qualitative and cannot be quantified. These have to be perceived. Also, all the factors may not motivate all the salespersons the same way; different factors may motivate different salespersons differently. But, generally speaking, ten major non-financial factors way be identified which motivate the salespeople.

These factors are:

1. Organisational culture
2. Opportunity for self-expression
3. Recognition of work

4. Appreciation of work
5. Spirit of competition
6. Job satisfaction
7. Pride in selling
8. Opportunity for growth
9. Job security
10. Post-retirement benefits

Job satisfaction may lead to or culminate in pride in selling. Job satisfaction should inculcate in the salesperson the feeling of pride in his (her) profession—the profession of selling. Such feeling increases his (her) dedication, and, also motivation. He (she) should develop the feeling of belonging to the organisation, and, the fraternity of the company' salespeople.

SALES MANAGER'S TOOLS FOR MOTIVATION

The sales manager can use many tools or methods to inspire or motivate salespeople for better performance for achievement of organisational targets or goals. The sales manager can adopt both financial and non-financial tools—primarily non-financial. The sales manager can utilise these tools at two levels:

1. Individual level
2. Group level

Motivators at Individual Level

Every salesperson, as an individual, is almost unique in terms of his (her) personality, nature, desire or aspirations. The sales manager should have interaction with each salesperson at regular intervals to understand his (her) individual peculiarities and likely motivational factors or requirements. This will enable him to identify the right stimulus or incentive for each salesperson.

Specifically speaking, at individual level, there may be three major motivational tools:

1. Personal meeting and counselling
2. Personal communication/correspondence
3. Personal award or reward

Motivators at Group Level

For working out motivators at group level, the sales manager should ideally start by understanding and analysing group psychology and behaviour. The salesperson behaves or acts in a particular way as a group. Understanding of this psychology or behavioural pattern is very important. Peer pressure or performance exercises a lot of influence on a salesperson's action or performance.

The sales manager can adopt or use many motivators at group level. Six major motivators are:

1. Sales meetings and conferences
2. Sales campaigns
3. Sales contests
4. Training/orientation programme
5. In-house circulars/publications
6. Motivation building films

Zero-cost or Low-cost Motivators

All motivators, whether at individual level or group level, do not have financial implications. There can be many zero-cost or low-cost motivators.

Sam Deep and Lyle Sussman have suggested fifteen zero-cost or low-cost motivators. These are:

1. A pat on the back.
2. A smile.
3. A simple, sincere, "thank you".
4. A personal letter to the salesperson.
5. Public recognition in front of peers.
6. Public recognition in front of salesperson's immediate boss.
7. A letter of praise from a customer or vendor posted on the company bulletin board.
8. Listening to a salesperson who has an idea for improving efficiency.
9. Arranging salesperson's discounts from your vendors or customers.

10. Allowing the salesperson to work on an especially exciting project or product.
11. Asking a salesperson what non-monetary reward he (she) would like to have and, if possible providing it.
12. Issuing a "You were Mentioned" certificate to a salesperson whenever you hear something nice about him/her, whether from a customer, co-worker, or superior.
13. Electing a high-achieving salesperson to a quality circle or to a company wide task force.
14. Providing free lunch for salespersons for act of victory.
15. Rotating the "company flag" or other symbols of excellence from one deserving unit to another on a quarterly basis.

To sum up, a company can play its role in different ways to motivate salespeople. It can use an appropriate mix of financial and non-financial motivational tools. It can offer many non-financial stimuli. The sales manager can use motivational tools or methods at individual level and also group level for inspiring salespersons and generating competitive spirit for better performance. Many of these can even be zero-cost motivators.

SELF-MOTIVATION TO COMPLEMENT COMPANY MOTIVATION

Companies may offer several packages to motivate salespersons. But, those, by themselves, may not be enough. Salespersons also have to motivate themselves.

It has been rightly said that ***self-motivation is the best motivation.*** It is like this: you can motivate and take the horse to the pond to drink water. But, the horse will drink water only if it is finally self-motivated. This points to the *complementarity of company motivation and self-motivation by salespersons.*

In a sense, **motivation or self-motivation is like fire.** It is not enough to just kindle the fire. We have to keep putting fuel to it; otherwise, it will die out. Fuel for a good sales professional is commitment, determination and perseverance. These keep the fire, i.e., motivation burning. If this is not done on regular basis, do motivation creeps in. True sales professionals will not allow this to happen because they are self-motivated.

So, a salesperson's self-motivation should complement the company's motivational programmes or packages. Only then, motivation will be complete or sustainable. We can, therefore, say.

Company motivation + self-motivation = Total motivation

If there is total motivation, it will keep inspiring salespersons constantly for continuous performance—high performance without break or discontinuity. Without this, performance may slip.

Always remember

No motivation, no performance, i.e., no sale

A Salesperson Inspired by Motivation

Mantra 17

Try for Higher Compensation Through Higher Performance

Compensation is the most direct form of motivation....

If salespeople always look for compensation, they can never perform.....

Motivation, compensation and training are three key contributory factors for the performance of salespeople. Some salespersons are self-starters; they show enough initiative and commitment. Such salespeople may not require much motivation.

But, the vast majority of salespeople need to be motivated to perform better. One of the most direct methods of motivation is compensation—financial and non-financial, mostly financial. Training also helps to motivate, but, not as directly as compensation.

COMPENSATION: COMPANY VIEWPOINT VS SALESPERSONS' VIEWPOINTS

Objectives of compensation plan differ depending on whether we are looking at the objectives from the company viewpoint or the salespersons' point of view.

Every company wants to recruit and retain competent and high performing salespeople. They offer a suitable compensation plan. But, the compensation plan may not always be the most attractive to the salespersons. This may happen because the management would like to offer a competitive package, but, it should also be cost-effective from the company's point of view.

Salespeople, on their part, expect regular incentive schemes in addition to fixed monthly income or salary. Also, they expect a fair and equitable payment plan. This may often be in conflict with the management's plan, because, the management may like to give special rewards to high performing salespersons, and, this may appear discriminatory to other salespeople.

Whatever be the expectations of the salespeople, it is the company or management who finally decides or determines the compensation plan or package. They should, however, take into account salespersons' perspective or point of view as much as they can. This will make the compensation plan more balanced or unbiased and acceptable to the receiving party. This is imperative because this has important implication for their motivation and performance.

DESIGNING AND IMPLEMENTING COMPENSATION PLAN

Because of different viewpoints and other reasons, a company should proceed in a cautious and systematic way in designing and implementing the compensation plan for the sales force. It should develop the plan in steps or stages.

A model compensation plan is presented in the figure below.

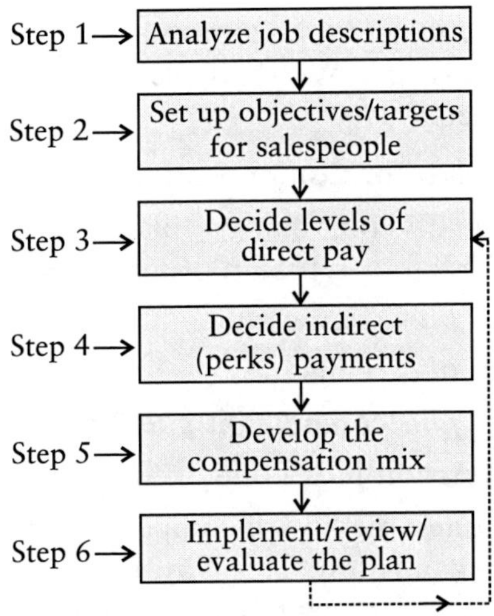

A Model or Framework of Sales Force Compensation

The final and the most important task of the management is to implement the compensation mix and see if it works as per their plan and expectation and produces necessary results in terms of performance and productivity. Implementation and results are the real test of any plan including a compensation plan. If implementation reveals some drawbacks or shortcomings in the mix or plan, the drawbacks or shortfall should be identified and rectified. The management may have to go back to the basic pay level and rework the compensation mix as shown in the figure.

COMPENSATION PLANS IN PRACTICE

Compensation plans used in practice by companies are of four types:

1. Only salary
2. Only commission
3. Combination of salary and commission
4. Combination of salary, commission and bonus

According to a survey, only about 32 per cent of all companies adopt either 'only salary' or 'only commission' method; the remaining 68 per cent of the companies use a combination formula. Out of 32 per cent, a larger percentage of companies use only salary as compensation; a smaller percentage pay only commission. We shall discuss here the combination plan in some detail.

Combination Plan for Compensation

Four types of combination plan are generally used by companies. These four types, in order a usage, are given below:

(a) Salary *plus* commission
(b) Salary *plus* bonus
(c) Salary *plus* commission *plus* bonus
(d) Commission *plus* bonus

The commonest method of compensation used by companies is salary plus commission. This way, the compensation package has both a fixed component (salary) and a variable component (commission), the variable component being related to performance. Some companies link bonus to customer satisfaction and customer potential. IBM follows this practice. In salary plus bonus method, salary is the predominant component. Incentive bonus is given for achievement of special objectives or targets. Salary plus commission plus bonus scheme is not very common. However, companies like Siebel Systems pay a monthly salary plus commission plus a quarterly bonus based on customer satisfaction survey for each salesperson.

MARKET BASED COMPENSATION

Before deciding and implementing a particular compensation plan, the company or the sales manager should take into account the prevailing market factors or conditions for salespersons' salaries and allowances and incentives.

The company or the sales manager should consider the current market rates being paid to salespersons for the age, educational qualifications, skill and experience the company is looking for.

The company has to analyse the demand and supply situation in the market. In a country like India with high level of unemployment even for educated youth, supply or availability may not be a major problem. But, aspiring salespersons with certain level of education, skill and experience, particularly MBAs, would consider alternatives and try to go for the best available option.

Willingness or ability to pay may differ from one organisation to another. It depends on their budget allocation and products/brands, sales policy and systems. It also depends on job descriptions and responsibilities including sales targets assigned to particular salesperson. These are not uniform or standardised for all salespersons.

However, the market factor remains. This provides a standard or benchmark for fixing salespersons' compensations.

BALANCED COMPENSATION PLAN

No compensation plan is perfect, because no plan can satisfy everybody. If the sales manager or management is happy, the salespeople may not be satisfied. If salespeople are satisfied, the management may find the package as costly or overpayment. Sometimes a section of the salespeople may be happy, but not others. However, all efforts must be made to strike balance between different competing factors to arrive at the most desirable or optimum compensation plan. Such a plan should have the following features or characteristics.

(a) *Objectivity and Fairness*: Objectivity generally ensures fairness.

(b) *Adequacy*: Adequate financial protection of the sales staff through established norms/benchmarks.

(c) *Flexibility*: No compensation package should be very rigid.

(d) *In-built Incentives*: Incentives should be more regular and not very occasional.

(e) *Budget-friendly*: The package should be compatible with the overall budget (expenditure) of the company.

(f) *Practical*: The compensation plan should be easy to understand and implement.

SUCCESS OF COMPENSATION PLAN

The objectives, design and implementation of compensation plan determine the degree or level of effectiveness or success of particular compensation plan (figure below).

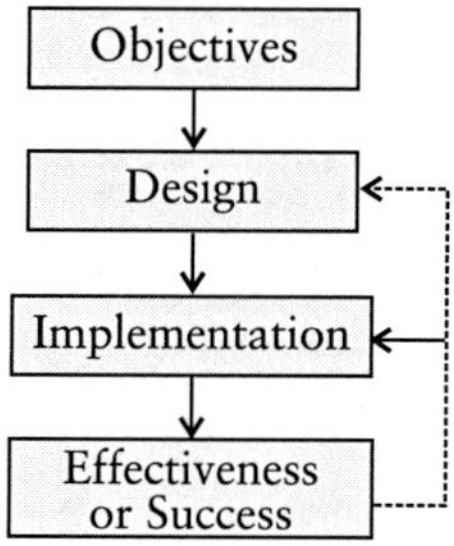

Objectives, Design, Implementation and Success of a Compensation Plan

Major factors which contribute to the effectiveness or success of a compensation plan may be enumerated as follows:

1. Defining the sales job
2. Matching sales job with skill and experience and compensation level
3. Internal consistency of the plan
4. Salespersons' participation in the plan
5. Following industry norms or standards
6. Cost-benefits of the plan
7. Performance-linked incentive
8. Scope for future growth

HIGHER PERFORMANCE, HIGHER COMPENSATION

Some debate may go on about what is market-based compensation; debate may also go on about what is a balanced compensation plan; or, even what is an ideal compensation plan. Sales experts and companies may keep deliberating on this.

The company may have a particular view about what should be the correct or optimal compensation package for the salespersons. The salespersons may have their own perception about the right or optimal compensation plan or package. There may be differences in the perceptions of the two sides.

But, the fact remains that *total compensation package varies with performance of individual salespersons*. The fixed or monthly salary may not very much. But, the variable component may keep changing from one salesperson to another. The variable component may keep changing because of changes in elements like commission, incentive bonus, paid holidays and some other elements—mostly financial.

The variable component can sometimes be quite significant. For star performers and sales superstars, the variable component can be, and, often, is higher than the fixed monthly salaries. This also shows what salespersons can achieve through better or higher performance.

So, strive for higher performance. Motivate yourself, take training, take counselling from the sales manager. Do all these and gear up yourself. This will help you to achieve your goal of becoming a successful salesperson.

Let your motto be:

High Performance, High Compensation

Keep reminding yourself of this every day, every week, every month.... This is a continuous process.

Mantra 18

Make Use of Mobile Commerce

M-commerce is a logical successor of e-commerce....

M-commerce means explosion of applications and services accessible from Internet-enabled mobile devices....

Mobile commerce (m-commerce) is a large area of activity comprising transactions connected with or delivered through different mobile devices—mobile phones, communicators, palm size computer, tablet computers, PDAs (personal digital assistants), etc.

WHAT IS M-COMMERCE?

Mobile commerce relates to new ways of doing business—buying and selling. This is quite different from traditional e-commerce.

A functional definition of m-commerce is given below:

"M-commerce (Mobile commerce) is the buying and selling of goods and services through wireless hand-held devices such as cellular telephone and personal digital assistants (PDAs). Known as next generation e-commerce, m-commerce enables users to access the Internet without needing to find a place to plug in."

Mobile commerce or mobile sale provides salespersons access to customer data and applications when they are on the move. The genesis of mobile commerce is that all the information and transactional needs are transmitted to the mobile sales force for faster decision making for sales execution.

INCREASING USE OF M-COMMERCE

Technological developments have helped mobile commerce. Wireless technology is facilitating increased use of mobile commerce and its applications. Wireless technology enables companies or sales managers to develop mobile applications for their sales force. The sales force can communicate, and, more importantly, integrate their information inputs with organisational database while they are on the move. This enables them to create a cohesive data bank for decision making in the field.

Mobile phones, iPhones, tablet PCs and PDAs support or sustain mobile communication anywhere any time with wireless network. Mobile commerce have made it possible to close sales faster and better. This is almost like a mini revolution in selling.

New horizons are emerging for mobile commerce. These will make possible sales planning, order booking, sales management, and, also sales closure on the same platform through hand-held or mobile devices. Newer dimensions and possibilities are developing.

In the days to come, mobile computing will emerge and this will introduce new platform and enable salespersons to perform their functions faster with greater precision and accuracy.

M-COMMERCE IS THE FUTURE

For really taking off, it is important for m-commerce to build on established habits, practices and infrastructure and add specific mobility value. The added value should be in the form of "instant access and delivery, flexibility, convenience, personalisation, location awareness and better customer service."

The key drivers of m-commerce service adoption are ease-of-use and convenience keeping the security issue intact. The challenge is to implement a simple, secure and fast working commerce module.

This is happening. M-commerce is coming of age. FMCG majors like Hindustan Lever (HUL), Procter and Gamble (P&G) and also ITC are making more use of m-commerce for increasing their sales. Many other companies are doing the same. Some more to follow.

Today is the age of sales force automation. M-commerce is one of the important ingredients of this.

Enter this field if you have not already entered. Use the technology. Use this to your advantage and grow in this field.

So, ***be modern, and, make more use of mobile commerce for selling.*** You can supplement your conventional methods of selling with mobile commerce selling. This will help you to increase your total sales, and, may also improve your success rate in selling.

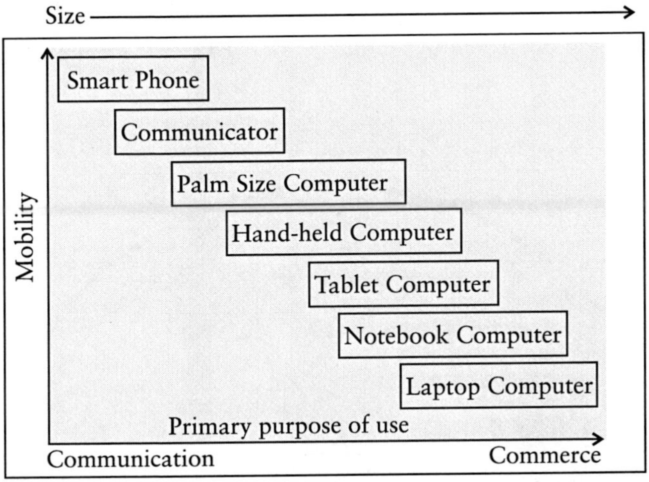

Mobile Information/Commerce Devices

Mantra 19

Develop Virtual Selling Skill

Virtual selling is one of the latest innovations in sales force automation....

With lock-downs and social distancing, 'virtual' is the order of the day....

Virtual selling is a new, in fact, one of the latest dimensions in selling. The transition to virtual selling is in process in many countries. In countries like the US, this has already gained enough ground.

WHAT IS VIRTUAL SELLING?

In simple terms, *virtual selling* may be defined as: *How to get a purchase order (PO) or make a sale without being there.*

In extended terms, *virtual selling* may be defined as: "Running a sales process where you can take many months to do it; you got phone calls, proposal presentations, and, even the contracting process; and, all of that, or 95% of that, is done virtually", i.e., without being there in person.

Till recently, it was thought that it is not possible to get a PO without some sales presentation in person. But, things are changing; this is because of changes in buyer behaviour. All buyers do not insist that you have to be there in person. They accept you not being there. This signals transition to virtual selling. The transition to virtual selling is being facilitated by new technologies like Calendly and Uber Conference which make scheduling and conference calls smooth and easy. New tools for virtual selling are emerging.

HOW TO MAKE VIRTUAL SELLING SUCCESSFUL

Selling is not easy. Virtual selling is also not easy. Companies or salespersons have to acquaint themselves with the ways virtual selling should be conducted or concluded. Certain tools or techniques are available for virtual selling. These have been used by companies who have been successful in virtual selling.

Some call these tips or guides or techniques for winning the virtual selling game.

Ten proven tips or guides are mentioned below:

1. Choosing right tools.
2. Alignment with marketing.
3. Ensuring Internet speed.
4. Setting the video.
5. Setting the sound system.
6. Remembering that the sales process is important.
7. Client's questions are important.
8. Sales process should be educational for the prospect/customer.
9. Wrapping touch points.
10. Tracking performance of virtual selling or outcomes or sales results.

A number of tools or techniques are now available for virtual selling. These are essentially video conferencing software. These include Zoom, Microsoft teams, Skype, Go to Meeting and WebEx. Some of these softwares are tested and proven tools for virtual selling. A number of new softwares are also emerging.

A company or salesperson needs to choose a particular tool or tools based on features, cost and suitability to the organisation. Choice of an appropriate tool is important. This is almost the first step in successful virtual selling.

With the sales process under way, the next logical step is to plan out every single touch point within the sales process which wraps around the virtual meetings. Touch points include phone calls, video calls, text messages, sales-generated e-mails, follow-up e-mails and, any other documents used with the prospects.

By properly designing the wraparound touch points and, making them distinct in the communication process, a company can differentiate itself from the competitors. The touch points exercise can help a company to shorten the sales cycle and increase close rates or closing ratios.

VIRTUAL SELLING RESULTS

All virtual sales processes and tools should lead to desired outcomes or sales results. These are tracked through performance parameters or criteria. Many performance parameters or criteria can be thought of and tracked. The more important ones are:

1. Actual sales vs quota or target
2. Close rate (closing ratio)
3. Sales cycle in days
4. Average revenue per client
5. Percentage of sales opportunities to close

These should be tracked and reviewed ideally weekly, but, definitely monthly. The results can then be aggregated quarterly, half yearly and annually. These will suggest course corrections or improvements whenever necessary to make virtual selling successful.

Virtual selling assumes special significance during periods of social distancing, restrictions on personal meetings and travel as India and the whole world is facing today (2020-21).

Try to develop virtual selling skill. Your company should adopt virtual selling as a corporate policy and support you with necessary tools and facilities. This will give you another avenue for selling and an edge over other salespersons and also your competitors.

Mantra 20

Remember: Results are Rewarded, Efforts are Not

The relationship between efforts and results is like input-output relationship: efforts produce results....

Efforts, results and rewards are a three-stage progression: Effort → Result → Reward....

This is a fundamental truth: results are rewarded, but, efforts are not. This is true in every sphere of life including selling. But, this is not always clearly understood. Salespersons have to accept it, face it and prepare for it.

DIFFERENCE BETWEEN EFFORTS AND RESULTS

Let me give some live examples of this. These are facts or truths of life.

Example 1

A king had his *mantri* (minister). He had attendants. The mantri was obviously paid much higher than the attendants. One of the attendants asked the king: "*Maharaja*, both *mantri* and I work for the whole day. I put so much of efforts. I work very hard. But, why do you pay mantri so much higher salary?" The king said: "You want a reply for that?" The attendant: "Yes, *Maharaja*." The king said: "Just wait for few days."

After few days, the king called the attendant and said: "A *saint* has come. He is on the riverside. Go, see him and tell me about him." The attendant came back after seeing the saint. The king asked: "Have you seen the *saint*?" Attendant: "Yes, *Maharaja*." The king asked: "Is the *saint* tall or short?" Attendant: "I did not notice it." King: "Go again and see him." The attendant goes running and comes back running and says: "*Maharaja*, he is tall." King: "Is he fair or mixed complexion?" Attendant: "I did not notice it; I will just go and see him again." He goes running and comes back running and says: "Yes, *Maharaja*, I have seen; he is fair." *Maharaja* asks: "What will be his age like? Is he young or old:" Attendant: "I did not notice it;

I will just go and see." He again goes running and comes back running. He says: "*Maharaja*, he is middle-aged." This way, more than half-day was spent.

Maharaja told the attendant: "Just wait." He called mantri and told him: "A saint has come on the riverside. Would you go and see him and tell me about him?" Mantri says: "Yes, Maharaja, I will go and see him and tell you about him." Mantri goes and comes back in an hour. Maharaja says: "Describe the person." *Mantri* replies: "The *saint* is middle-aged, tall and fair."

Maharaja turns to the attendant and says: "Have you understood why I pay mantri so much salary?" Attendant: "Yes, *Maharaja*, I have understood."

The attendant had put plenty of efforts, but, he could not produce result in time. *Mantri* did. This explains the difference between effort and result and consequently reward.

Example 2

Let me give another example.

In a race, whether national competition, Commonwealth Games or Olympics, ten to twelve runners run (after initial screening). All of them put their best efforts according to their abilities. But, only three runners are rewarded: first (gold medal), second (silver medal) and third (bronze medal).

This is how results are rewarded, but, efforts are not. ***Results are visible; efforts are not.***

EFFORTS AND RESULTS IN SELLING

The company or the sales manager assigns you monthly, quarterly, half-yearly or annual targets. The targets are usually in terms of territories, products and customers. The achievement of the targets is a test of your selling skill and capabilities; in other words, a test of the difference between making efforts and producing results.

If you cannot achieve the targets, you are an under-achiever or have produced poor results. If you achieve the targets, you are a good achiever or have produced the desired results. If you have overshot the targets, you have produced excellent or outstanding results and you get suitably rewarded financially or otherwise.

In every case, you have put enough efforts. But, if you are an under-achiever, you lack the ability or capability to produce results. The company may not appreciate your efforts because you have failed to produce the result they wanted. You should have now understood the difference between effort and result and reward. You have to work on yourself to improve.

A Case in Selling

Let us take a case or situation or test in selling. Your company have a bad territory. But, they want to sell there. They have tried two salespersons earlier, but, they have failed to penetrate. The competition is very high. It is difficult to sell there.

The company feels that you are a good salesperson. They have assigned you the territory. The sales manager has given you necessary guidelines, instructions and strategy to be adopted. But implementation is in your hands. You can use your training, skill and capability to produce results. This depends entirely on you. Nobody is going to help you in the failed. You have to sail all by yourself.

If you can achieve the target/goal, you have understood the difference between efforts and result. The company will reward you adequately. But, if you cannot produce the result, you have still to work on it and move towards the result or goal.

SPECIAL ATTRIBUTES/CHARACTERISTICS FOR RESULTS

To convert efforts into results and rewards, you need to possess or develop some special attributes or characteristics. Six such attributes or characteristics are:

1. Burning desire to produce result
2. Self-motivation to succeed
3. To be passionate about results/success
4. Belief in yourself
5. Desire to improve/be perfect
6. Pride in result/success

These six attributes or characteristics are prescriptive, and, not necessarily conclusive or exhaustive, some other sales trainers or sales experts may suggest some alternatives or additional attributes or characteristics. But the spirit of these attributes are important.

Keep these on your agenda for self-improvement. ***Self-improvement is a continuous process.*** It does not end with one result or achievement. Keep regularly reminding yourself about such attributes. These are imperatives. These should drive you every moment or everyday.

So, if you are in selling, you must put your best efforts well directed towards your targets; otherwise, results will keep evading you. Take that additional step or make the extra stride to convert your efforts into results to get recognised and earn reward.

In most of the actual sales situations, you have to successfully combine efforts with selling skill or acumen to cross the margin or fence to achieve the goal. ***You may call it the marginal booster dose.***

If you have done or achieved this, you have fully understood the difference between effort and result. Then, you have also reached your goal.

Mantra 21

Learn How to Break a Dry Spell

A dry spell in sales should not be treated as a failure; it may be the forerunner for a new beginning....

In selling, as in any other activity or profession, there can be setback. A salesperson can have a dry spell. This is not uncommon. This should be taken as part of selling. There may be disappointment. But, salespersons should not get frustrated or break down. They should know how to break a dry spell and get back to course with confidence and continue selling.

WHAT IS A DRY SPELL

Meaning of a dry spell seems obvious to most of us. *It is a time or period when no sale takes place, i.e., you can't close a sale.*

In an extended sense, dry spell may mean a period when you do not get an opportunity or call to make a presentation. It can be a period when you can't even schedule a meeting or appointment.

We often describe such period as: "It is a bad time of the year"; or, "the area (territory) is all worked out...nothing left for me (us)"; or, "It is my bad luck." You can console yourself by saying all these, but it does not solve your problem. The sale has not taken place. That is what matters to you and the company.

According to some sales experts, the real reason for a dry spell is either or both of the two:

1. *We are not working*, i.e., we are not engaging with our prospects or customers;
2. *We are not working properly*, i.e., something important is missing in our selling effort or process.

What is the period of a dry spell? Most salespeople consider three, four, five or more days without a sale a dry spell. But, to be more realistic, dry spell should be understood like this:

1. *One day* without a sale should be considered a *dry spell*;
2. *Two days* without a sale should be considered a *long dry spell*; and,
3. *Three* (*or more*) *days* without a sale should be considered a *crisis*.

HOW TO BREAK A DRY SPELL

A dry spell is unavoidable in selling (except for exceptional salespersons). We should work on how to break a dry spell.

There are many ways to break a dry spell. The way or method to be adopted or actions to be taken depend on what kind of dry spell it is—one-day dry spell, two-day dry spell or three (or more) days' dry spell.

Breaking a Dry Spell: One-day Dry spell

If you have one-day dry spell, you are advised to do the following:

1. *Clean up your briefcase*: Remove business cards you have been accumulating and do not consider important. Throw away those call back notes which you have been considering as your future appointments. Forget about those old customers who you hoped would come around and make a purchase some day. Remember this is the time for action now. Give yourself a fresh start tomorrow.
2. *Check your supplies*: Ask yourself 'Am I really ready to sell?' 'Do I have enough supplies I would need for every call?' Obtain any additional supplies you need. This will step up your confidence and put you more at ease on the next call.
3. *Have everything ready for the next day*: Plan your visits thoroughly and carefully. Do not allow yourself to wander aimlessly. Develop a plan of action and stick to it faithfully.
4. *Put yourself into a serious mood*: A dry spell is to be taken seriously. Dry spells can kill salespeople. You should never take a dry spell, even a short one, lightly. If you do so, more dry spells will follow.

5. *Go to work and do not stop until you sell*: If that means working twelve hours straight without resting, let it be so. Do not stop till you sell. Of course, you should have breaks to recharge your batteries.

Breaking a Dry Spell: Two-day Dry Spell

If you go two days without a sale, you should think that you are approaching a crisis situation. It is time for you to review your actions and change yourself. To break the dry spell, in addition to the five steps mentioned above, do the following:

1. *Review your presentation*: Have a second look at your presentation. Make sure that the sales manager or a co-salesperson evaluate your presentation. It is natural for us to fail to see problems in our presentation that are obvious to others. So, listen to your sales manager or somebody else concerned with your sales and change your presentation, if necessary.
2. *List out ten reasons for not selling*: Sit relaxed, for a while, think and list ten reasons why you feel you are not selling. You will find the answer to your dry spell.
3. *Now go to sales*: If you have found an answer to your dry spell, go and implement it. It would also be a good idea to discuss this with your sales manager and take his (her) guidance.

Breaking a Dry Spell: Three (or more) Days' Dry Spell

Three or more days without a sale is a genuine crisis. Something is definitely, or, rather seriously wrong. It is, therefore, time for a major review. Do the following:

1. *Take a break*: Take a break for a day or two for review. Review your approach, your customers and your market or territory. Sit down and analyse closely.
2. *Prepare a list of things that could have gone wrong*: Write them down honestly. Try to arrange them in order of importance. Ask yourself questions as:
   (a) Am I accepting 'No' too quickly or too easily from my customers?

(b) Am I failing to make my proposition clear to my customers?
(c) Am I selecting wrong prospects?
(d) Is there no excitement in my presentation?
(e) Am I failing to create urgency?
(f) Am I losing confidence in myself?

Discuss all these with your manager.

3. *Check any physical or emotional problems*: Some physical or emotional factor may be hindering your selling efforts. Are you having problems with your health, family, co-workers or friends? Are you a person who becomes easily upset, angry or distressed. Check out on all these. Whether your problems are physical or emotional, you must resolve them before you return to sales.
4. *Take a new road*: Take a new route—new area, place or territory where you have not yet sold. This will give you a feeling of freshness and a new perspective on every call you make. Maybe, this will help you to break your dry spell.
5. *Take sales leads from others*: Ask for sales leads from co-salespeople, sales manager or some other salespeople you know. It will help you particularly if you take leads from people who have gone through similar dry spells. They all can give you very useful leads.
6. *Plan your day in different way*: Write down your new work plan. Give a copy of your new plan to your manager, discuss with him, if necessary, and take his approval or advice before you start action on your plan. Make sure your manager is aware of your commitment to follow the plan sincerely. Keep interacting with him (her) if necessary.
7. *Review/Reassess your prospects*: You might not have chosen the right prospects. So, have a second look at the prospects. These include your old and existing customers also to whom you are trying to sell again.
8. *Check if you have lost sight of your goal*: May be you have lost sight of your goal. You have to remind yourself

that you have to achieve certain goals or targets during a specified period. **Goals are not to be reset.**

9. *See if you have a financial problem*: Most of us face financial problem sometimes or the other. So, if you have a financial problem, don't get too upset over this. Just getting upset does not solve any problem. Tell yourself that you will get over this if you start selling and sell more.
10. *Rework your sales strategy*: Your sales strategy may require some reworking. It is possible that you are not focusing on the right price-product combination. Your discount policy or strategy may not be very clear; therefore, it has to be made more clear or require some change. You may have to have a second look at your closing method or technique. Discuss with the sales manager if you feel like.
11. *Let someone in your organisation grade your presentation*: Someone in your organisation may be a salesperson—your peer or senior—assess and grade your presentation, and, give you suggestions for change or improvement. This may help you.
12. *Take counselling from your sales manager*: A counselling session with your sales manager may be a good idea. This may be a refresher for you. This may give a new or right direction. Counselling can be through an audio call or video call or conferencing or personal meeting.

If you have a dry spell, act according to the situation. Take steps depending on whether it is a one-day dry spell or two-days' dry spell or three (or more) days' dry spell.

If you do that, you can change or transform any dry spell into or refreshing and successful spell. *Remember, a dry spell is never an end in itself.* It can be and should be the warning for a new beginning. Take the warming and start again. Be on the move.

Dry spells should be viewed as an opportunity for all salespeople to develop newer and more creative work habits, a better lifestyle, and, finally, recapture the lost dreams.

This is the positive way of thinking. Any negativity may only prolong the dry spell. That should be avoided at all cost. **And, you have to come back strongly.**

Mantra 22

Take Operating Tips in Selling

Operating tips are a "tool-kit" for sharpening edges in selling....

Operating tips are catalysts for perfecting implementation....

Sales operations play a vital role in sales performance. This fills the void or provide the link between sales planning and execution. The result of sales efforts may depend, to a large extent, on how well the sales operations are conducted. Salespeople should be fully aware of this.

OPERATING TIPS IN SELLING

Sales experts, sales trainers and successful salespeople have suggested many ways for effective selling. They have given many *practical tips*. These are essentially different ways of self-management by salespersons. These relate to or can be classified into six different aspects of selling. The six aspects are:

1. Attitude
2. Approach/outfit
3. Sales presentation
4. Quoting price
5. Relating to customer
6. Closing the sale

"Practical tips" in these six aspects of selling are given below.

1. Attitude

(a) Try to remain cheerful and cheer people up. It is many times difficult, but we have to strive towards it.

(b) Always speak well of other salespeople, your competitors, your colleagues...everyone. This shows your class.

(c) Say everything that you have to say in a positive way. Eliminate negativity from your approach. It always pays.

(d) Do not be afraid to let your customers know that you are a professional; and if you can't do things in the right way, you do not want to do business with them.

(e) If you do not know the answer to a question your customer asks, never be afraid to tell him or her the truth. Chances are that the customer will find out in any case. Make sure, however, that you assure the customer that you can and will get the answer if some time is given to you.

(f) Do not let anyone waste your time. You should never be afraid to tell your colleagues, competitors and customers that you would like to get down to business and they should appreciate it.

2. Approach/Outfit

(a) Keep your briefcase neat, well stocked and well organised. You should clean it every night and keep it ready for use all the time.

(b) Always keep your brochure book, samples and other materials clean and in good condition. Treat all your props and sales aids as if they were very important.... because they are!

(c) Anticipate unplanned or unusual sales opportunities and carry with you whatever sales material you need to make such sales possible. Do not ever allow yourself to be caught unprepared or unaware. Sometimes, this may be unavoidable. But, keep it to the minimum.

(d) Never allow your customers to take control of your samples, props, sales materials and aids. You may feel dispossessed.

(e) Whenever you enter a house or place of business, look around for a 'dog dish'. Look closely. If you see one, proceed with caution.

(f) Know as much as you can about your product(s) and service. Make sure you know and understand all aspects and are able to explain those to your prospects customers.

(g) Do not ever make promises either for yourself or for your company which you cannot keep.

(h) Compare and associate yourself with winners. Form your opinion about your company, the opportunities it offers, its people, policies and programmes by talking to winners in the organisation. *Never form opinions by talking to losers.*

(i) Study the careers of great salespeople, and let them both inspire and teach you.

3. Sales Presentation

(a) Think through each sales presentation before you start. Ask yourself: "What am I going to say to this customer?" and "How am I going to sell to this customer?" Then, focus on the presentation.

(b) Before a presentation, examine your customer's surroundings. This will give you a good idea of your customer's tastes and preferences in design, colour and many other aspects that can help you sell your product or service better.

(c) Let your customer take care of his business before you begin your presentation. This establishes you as a gracious person in the customer's mind. It also allows your customer to clear his (her) mind of his (her) own immediate concerns so that he (she) can concentrate on your presentation better.

(d) When you enter a customer's premises, look around and select the most ideal spot for your presentation. Select a spot that commands attention. Also try to make sure that you are not interrupted during you presentation.

(e) Remember that you are like an actor (actress) and your presentation is like a 'set speech' in a play. You are the star of the show. **Your customer is your co-star.** The difference between your presentation and a stage play is that your co-star does not know his (her) lines. You, therefore, have to carry through the show by putting the lines for the customer, that is, impressing or convincing him (her).

(f) Whenever you make a presentation, acknowledge everybody present other than your prospect and involve him (her) in the presentation/selling process. This includes any guests, family members, existing customers or anyone else who may matter.

(g) Never prejudice a customer on the basis of his (her) initial objections. An objection at the beginning of a presentation usually means that the customer can be sold the product or service you are offering. The customer is taking interest.

(h) Movement during your presentation, either you or your customer's is good. Do not hold yourself down. Do not also let an animated customer make you feel nervous during your presentation.

(i) Practice the fine art of regaining control during presentation if someone interrupts or tries to distract you. One good way to regain control is to stop speaking, stand perfectly straight, raise your hands into the air and remain motionless till everyone near your stops speaking. Seize control and continue.

(j) Do everything you can to avoid awkward movements in your presentation. Practice using gestures and telling stories that illustrate a point to help you move smoothly from one part of your presentation to another.

(k) You can always make better impression with gestures, sketches, graphs and physical objects during your presentation than with words, numbers or statistics. So, try to make more use of these.

(l) Do not read every caption, every explanation or every illustration in your printed material to the customer. Just explain each key point briefly and move ahead. Explain second time only if asked or required.

(m) A long explanation is usually difficult, and sometimes impossible, to follow. Keep every explanation short, to the point and easy to understand. This way, your customers will never miss your important points and will not lose interest.

4. Quoting Price

(a) Do not be in a hurry to quote price to your customers. **Build value liberally, but quote price sparingly.**

(b) Use the opportune moment to quote price. An opportune moment is when the customer is showing interest or willingness to buy.

(c) Do not quote a very high price and provide for a big discount. This raises suspicions about your offer.

(d) **Do not ever quote a fixed price.** There should be some room for negotiation. The customer feels happy if he (she) can reduce the price.

(e) Try to relate price discount to volume.

5. Relating to Customer

(a) Do not try to qualify your customers to determine if they will buy. Customers cannot really know whether or not to buy till you have built a lot of value. Qualify customers only to know if they can buy.

(b) Pursue your customers. Let them know that they are important to you. If they are sick, visit them. You can even make courtesy calls.

(c) Let the customers know that you want to make the sale and need to make the sale. Make sure they always know how important the sale is to you.

(d) Always accept any courtesies or favours offered by your customers such as a cup of tea or coffee or a cold drink.

(e) If your customer tells a joke, try to participate in it and appreciate it. But, then, do not tell another story of yours to 'top' the customer. The customer should remain at the top.

(f) Do not argue with a customer. If you argue with a customer, you can never win. On the other hand, if you acknowledge any objections you hear, you smile and then build value; you cannot lose.

(g) Respect your customer's property. Be careful not to scratch their furniture, spoil their carpet(s), leave the door open or do anything that might annoy or irritate the customers.

(h) Allow your customers to tell about themselves—what their plans are, what they like and what they do not like. Try to appreciate people for what they are, and you will find that you are also appreciated.

(i) Develop the habit or art of listening to your customer. Listening is not always as easy as it seems. Listening requires patience and attention.

(j) Avoid anything that might make your customer nervous. Do not get too close to customer's cash or any valuable thing. If you are a male, do not strike up a casual conversation with the customer's adult daughter.

(k) Make your customers think and dream about their future. Get them to think about fixing up things, building and expanding. This almost always puts them into a buying mood.

(l) Appeal to your customer's ego in one way or another.

(m) Remember to stay in touch with your old customers and do not hesitate to ask them to help you to find and sell to new ones.

6. Closing the Sale

(a) Remember: closing the sale is the most important step in selling.

(b) Closing the sale is the final measure of your success.

(c) Never be in a hurry to close the sale. Choose the right moment or time to close the sale.

(d) Master the art of closing the sale. Closing a sale means income for you. *If you really think of it, you could have 365 pay days a year*!

FOLLOW THE OPERATING TIPS

The operating tips just mentioned are quite exhaustive. This cover all important practical tips in six major factors relating to successful selling: attitude, approach, sales presentation, quoting price/discount, reaching the customer and closing the sale.

The number of tips mentioned may be large. You can prioritise the tips depending on your trait, personality and style of functioning. You can use ABC analysis for this as shown below:

A: The most important tips

B: Important tips

C: Less important tips

This analysis or classification may be purely subjective. But, ultimately, it is you whose selling or performance is at stake. So, you decide which are the more important tips.

Try to memorise the 'A' category tips; keep handy, and, almost daily, go through 'B' types; and, regularly visit the 'C' category tips.

If you follow the tips as a practice, in every sales situation, your success rate in selling will definitely increase.

Mantra 23

Manage Your Time

Work expands to fill the time available for its completion....
—Parkinson's Law

We all have a waiting time in life—winners wait for their destination and losers wait for their destiny....
—Shiv Khera

"Go, Sir, gallop, and don't forget that the world was made in six days", wrote Napoleon to one of his aides, "can ask me for anything you like except time." He said. Management experts and practitioners only echo this.

Time management is a perennial issue in life and management and, also in selling. Much has been written and talked about this. But, the issue persists.

HOW IMPORTANT IS TIME MANAGEMENT?

Every one of us—no matter how rich or poor, young or old, intelligent or ignorant, successful or struggling—has the same 365 days a year, 24 hours a day, 60 minutes an hour and 60 seconds a minute.

With 365 days a year, let us see what it means if you are asking for a day off:

A Day Off!

- There are 365 days per year available for work.
- There are 52 weeks per year in which you have two days off per week, leaving 261 days available for work.
- Since you spend 16 hours each day away from work, you have used up 170 days leaving only 91 days available.
- With 1/2 hour's lunch break every day, you have used up another 23 days leaving only 68 days available.
- A gracious holiday of 31 days by way of Earned Leave is allowed to you. This leaves you with only 37 days available.
- You are off for 16 closed holidays per year. So your available working time is down to 21 days.

- You enjoy very causally 14 holidays per year as Casual Leave, thus leaving 7 days available.
- You are generously allowed 15 minutes grace period every day; thus you have used easily another 7 days a year.

  And, still you want to take a day off!

  (If sick leaves are added, you will be clearly running a debit account!)

This may seem to be an exaggeration, but, it signals to a lot of truth about time management or time rationing.

Time is inelastic and not elastic; you cannot stretch or expand time.* You cannot store time; *it is perishable; time lost is lost forever.

According to many, of all the resources of production, time is the most precious resource. So, utilise this resource. Don't waste it.

The success of a salesperson depends, to a large extent, on how well he (she) manages his (her) time. This applies to managers and all salespersons. But, this becomes more important for a salesperson as he (she) moves up the ladder, because, there is more demand on his (her) time. Do the salespersons realise this and practice proper time management?

COMMON TIME WASTERS

There are many time wasters—be it in general management or selling. We should know them.

Where Time Goes

Alec Mackenzie has studied time management for over a decade. He has interviewed managers at hundreds of companies around the world. He concludes that reasons for time scarcity and waste "are remarkably similar across management levels, industries and national borders."

Five biggest time wasters according to his study are:

1. Telephone interruptions
2. Inadequate planning
3. Trying to do too much
4. Drop-in (unscheduled) visitors
5. Crisis management

Personal Time Wasters

Sales managers and salespersons often blame external factors like meetings, drop-in visitors and telephone calls to be time wasters. But, studies have shown that the "man within" or the internal factors are the major time wasters. Here is a list of ten such wasters:

1. Lack of self-discipline
2. Indecisiveness
3. Insecurity
4. Personal habits
5. Excesses—stretching too much
6. Going round a point
7. Overcautious approach
8. Unnecessary paperwork
9. Procrastination
10. Obsession with routines

Time Mismanagement

Time mismanagement is an extension of time wasting. We can even say that time mismanagement is worse than time wasting because it is often more deliberate.

TIME MANAGEMENT IN SELLING

Everything in time management is important in selling. But, salespersons should, in particular, follow certain principles or practises to manage their time. Ten important principles or practices are:

1. Always take appointment with prospects/customers in advance to avoid waiting or wastage of time;
2. Let your actions in selling show that, for you, time is very important;
3. Let your behaviour/posture show that you respect prospects'/customers' time;
4. Find time to take break in selling; relax and try to enjoy; labour-leisure parity is very important;
5. During leisure time, read motivational books or see motivational films;

6. Prioritise your prospects. Divide them into three categories: hot leads, lukewarm leads and cold leads. Take up the hot leads first, then lukewarm leads, and, at last, cold leads. Plan and manage your time accordingly;
7. Plan your follow-ups with prospects judiciously. Spend more time in follow-ups with those prospects where there are more chances of business/success;
8. Schedule your daily time. Prepare a time table for the day—for calls/appointments, sales presentation, closing and customer service/follow up. Try to stick to the time table;
9. Deal with interruptions—telephone calls, paperwork, unscheduled callers/visitors. These may be unavoidable. Dispose of promptly, but, pleasantly;
10. Follow the 80 : 20 rule in selling. Spend 80% of your working time for revenue generation and 20% on administrative jobs/official routines.

HOW WELL ARE YOU MANAGING YOUR TIME

Are you satisfied with the way you manage your time? Or, does your time keep running out on you? Are you a time-waster, time-sensitive or a time-planner? Use the time quiz to find out:

TIME QUIZ

Time use	True (√)	False
I always apportion my day so that I can do everything I want to	☐	☐
I usually build in extra time in my schedule to cover unforeseen eventualities	☐	☐
I find it easy to refuse to participate in unimportant activities	☐	☐
I know my best times for concentration and always make good use of them	☐	☐
I do not rush through tasks in hand, but work steadily at my own pace	☐	☐

Time use	True (√)	False
I always tend to work according to well-set schedules	☐	☐
I have an accurate and clear idea of how best to use my time	☐	☐
I work at my best when I am under pressure and have to meet a deadline	☐	☐
I almost always finish most of my task well on time	☐	☐
I meet self-imposed deadlines by sticking to specific time-slots	☐	☐
Total 'True'	☐	

0-4 trues: Time waster
4-7 trues: Time sensitive
7-10 trues: Time planner

MAKE A TIME PLAN/TIME CHART

Prepare and maintain a time plan or time log or time chart for everyday—from morning till evening. This is particularly important if you are a time 'waster' or even 'time sensitive'.

A framework for a time chart is given below.

Time slot	Activity	Performed on time (Yes/No)	If 'No' Reason
9.00-10.00			
10.00-11.00			
11.00-12.00			
12.00-1.00			
Break			
2.00-3.00	...	...	...
3.00-4.00			
4.00-5.00			
5.00-6.00			

(You can make your own time slots)

Follow the time chart. It will save time. Review the time chart everyday in the evening. See where your time planning went wrong. Use this as input or feedback for your next day's plan and so on.

TIME CAN BE ETERNITY

If you can really plan, you will have time under your control. "Time" for any person whether in office or at home, is how one looks at work and life:

Time is

Too fast for those
who wait,

Too slow for those
who fear,

Too long for those
who idle,

Too short for those
who work,

But for those
who plan,

Time is eternity..

So, plan your time. Manage your time in life and selling. This will give you more time to produce results—more achievements.

Mantra 24

Know the Roadmap to Success

The quality of a person's life is in direct proportion to their commitment to success, regardless of their chosen field of endeavour....

—Vince Lombardii

Success is 95 per cent perspiration and 5 per cent inspiration....

—Thomas Edison

Let me make it very clear in the beginning: **There is no textbook or copy book formula for success** in any field including selling. It is not that you swallow a pill and success comes automatically. Every one of us, including those in selling, has to work the hard way to achieve success.

But, we can learn from those who have achieved success. We can learn how to succeed. We can know what is success in selling, essential qualities for success, laws of success, and, finally, a recipe for success.

WHAT IS SUCCESS IN SELLING

Success in selling can be looked at or understood in different ways. Therefore, success can be defined or measured also in different ways.

We give below definition and measurement of success as commonly done:

Success is commonly defined or measured in relation to task, target or result. If a salesperson is asked to sell 100 units or pieces of a product, and he (she) sells all the 100 units, he (she) has achieved success.

There are two other related factors here; first, the cost or expenditure incurred to achieve the target and, second, the time period. The sales target should be achieved within the budget or resources allocated, and the prescribed time period.

Success, so defined, can be shown as below:

Success in Selling and Defining Constraints

Using these three factors, success can be measured as a weighted average or a composite index using a five-point scale. This way, success can also be rated. This is shown in table below:

Measurement and Rating of Success

Factor	Rating 1	Rating 2	Rating 3	Rating 4	Rating 5
Target achieved	5	5	5	4	3
Cost/ resources	5	5	4	3	2
Time period	5	3	3	2	2
Total	15	13	12	9	7
Average	5.0	4.3	4.0	3.0	2.3

5.0: Outstanding, 4.5: Very good, 4.0: Good, 3.0: Average, 2.3: Poor

Based on the scores in the table, the level of success can be rated as follows:

Score	Level of success
5.0	Outstanding
4.3 – 4.5	Very good
4.0	Good
3.0	Average
2.3 or less	Poor or failure

The above scores and rating are hypothetical. In actual situations, scores and ratings by different companies would be different indicating different levels of success of salespeople.

ESSENTIAL QUALITIES FOR SUCCESS

One may be a leader in sales or a follower. But every salesperson must possess certain qualities to succeed.

The question is: which are the qualities or characteristics the salespeople should possess for success? Or, which are the essential qualities or attributes? This is an issue many sales analysts have been debating on, many companies have been seeking an answer to, and, often, sales managers and salespeople have been asking themselves. Is it qualification, knowledge, skill, training, ambition, aggressiveness or something else? All or some of these are definitely important, but which are the more important or essential ones?

Steeve Reeves, with 30 years of sales and sales management experience, offers an answer to this. According to him:

"Successful salespeople display the same characteristics in my experience, but those characteristics aren't the one most people would expect. They don't include ambitious, aggressive, gregarious, social, pushy or any of another 20 we might think of. But they include the qualities we would look for when wanting to buy from somebody."

Reeves contends that every successful salesperson he has worked with, combines four qualities or characteristics in certain proportions. These are:

- Honesty: 30%
- Efficiency: 30%
- Empathy: 30%
- Luck: 10%

We may add skill to this. Then, the five qualities and their weights or proportions will be reworked as follows:

1. *Skill: 20%*
2. *Efficiency: 30%*
3. *Honesty: 20%*
4. *Empathy: 20%*
5. *Luck: 10%*

1. Skill: For success, salespeople must acquire or develop required skills for selling a particular product. Skills required for selling consumer goods, industrial products and services are usually different because of the nature of products and the target customers. Skill development can be done through proper training. Skill grows with experience and gets perfected over time.

2. Efficiency: *Efficiency is all about application, determination and perseverance.* These virtues are essential for success. Efficiency is also about delivery of products the customer wants at the right prices, quality, and on time with assured service. All these require high level of efficiency.

3. Honesty: Successful salespeople tell customers the truth—about their company, product and sales policy. They do what they say they will do. They also understand their customers well—their buying habits, likings, dislikings, emotions, etc. If a salesperson misleads a customer for buying something, he (she) can do it only once; and, his and his company's dishonesty may be established through words of mouth.

4. Empathy: Empathy, and not sympathy, is what customers want. *Empathy*, in a simple language, means understanding the customers in their own way. Customers want to buy from salespeople who understand the problems of deciding to buy, choosing who to buy from and why. This way, they get inspired or induced to buy from salespeople who show the right empathy.

5. Luck: Every one of us needs a bit of luck in our life. So do salespeople. Some people may believe it or not, luck does play some role in success. It offers or provides that "extra something" which makes skill, efficiency, honesty and empathy produce result.

TEN LAWS OF SALES SUCCESS

A recent Gallup poll on the honesty and ethical conduct of business professionals found that insurance salespeople and car salespeople ranked last. But it does not seem to be only the insurance salespeople and car salespeople who have a bad reputation. Bill Brooks of the Books Group estimates that more than 85 per cent of customers have a negative view of all salespeople. This perception may be generally true. This is primarily because of the way majority of salespeople present and conduct themselves in sales presentations and meetings with customers.

To change this perception, salespeople need to learn and develop right skills and techniques which may make customers think differently about the selling process. And, this would increase the success rate in selling significantly.

Len Foley suggests ten principles—he calls them "tactics" or "laws"—which prepare salespeople better for success. These ten principles or laws are:

Law 1 Talk less and listen more: This is particularly important during the first few minutes of the sales meeting/interaction with the prospect/customer. It is true that the salesperson wants to introduce himself (herself) to the prospect/customer. He (she) likes to tell his (her) name and the purpose of his (her) visit (phone call). But, he (she) should not try to talk much about the product or service. At this point, the salesperson does not have any clear idea about what he is offering is of any interest to the prospect. So, the salesperson should talk less and listen more to find out the prospect's interest and need.

Law 2 Sell with questions, not answers: Instead of immediately trying to sell the product or service, the salespeople should focus on understanding what or why the prospect wants to buy. To do this, the salespeople should try to get close or intimate with the prospect. They need to ask carefully phrased questions to know more and more about the prospect's mind and thinking.

Law 3 Pretend that you are on a first date with your prospect: Salespeople should try to get curious about the prospects/customers by asking about the products and services they are presently buying. Are they happy with those products? Sometimes, customers buy products they are not really happy with. They use them because of lack of suitable alternatives. Therefore, salespeople should try to find out what they really need or are looking for.

Law 4 Speak to your prospect just as you speak to your family or friends: Salespeople should try to create an air or atmosphere of informality and move/proceed slowly. They should not quickly switch to sales mode with formal sales talks. They need to avoid exaggerated tones. Instead, they should speak normally and, of course, appropriately to let the sales points or issues emerge automatically or spontaneously.

Law 5 Pay close attention to what your prospect is not saying: In selling, we normally expect the salespeople to pay close attention to what the prospect or customer is saying. That, of course, is important. But what is equally, or may be more, important is to pay enough attention to what he (she) is not saying, but is trying to express through his (her) mood or visual revelations. Is he (she) looking upset or agitated? If this is so, the salesperson may ask: "Is this a good time to talk? Or we should meet some other time or day?" Very few salespeople do this. Most salespeople are so occupied with what they are going to say next that they forget to pay enough attention to the mood, posture and possible reaction of the prospect.

Law 6 If you are asked a question, answer properly but briefly, and move on: If a prospect is asking questions, it generally means that he (she) is showing interest in the salesperson's approach or talk. The salesperson has to reply to the prospect's query to his (her) satisfaction and move on. He should not get stuck in that question, even if it is a tricky or difficult one. The art of answering, and not avoiding, difficult questions comes into play here.

Law 7 Correctly assess the needs of the prospect, then you make your offering: Product offering should not be made in a haste; salespeople may end up in wrong offering. It is, therefore, essential to correctly assess the prospect's requirements, and then make the product offer. This enhances the chances of concluding the business.

Law 8 Refrain from making a very long sales presentation: In industrial products, sales presentation can be little long because it involves greater details on product features, performance, maintenance, etc. But for consumer goods (except for consumer durables to some extent), talks or presentations should be short and precise. Individuals and households do not generally like long presentations. The salespeople should focus on those points or aspects which have a direct bearing on the prospect's thinking, and liking and the particular situation. This also includes the positives or benefits of the offering.

Law 9 Ask the prospect if there are any barriers to taking the next step: After the salespeople have gone through the first eight steps, they should have a good understanding of the prospect's needs in relation to the company's products or service. The salespeople would have also developed mutual trust and belief. They should now be in a position to bridge the gap between the prospect's needs and their offering, or, find out from the prospect if some gap or barrier still exists. They are now actually getting ready for Law 10 (closing).

Law 10 Invite your prospect to take some decision or action: This means that conventional closing techniques are not necessary because the salesperson is not trying to close the sale, but inviting the prospect to do so. The ball is in the prospect's court. And, he or she has to take the final view or decision. The salesperson should lead him (her) to that. If the salesperson can successfully lead or guide the prospect to the decision, he (she) is well on his (her) way to becoming a successful or even outstanding salesperson.

RECIPE FOR SUCCESS

Here is a known recipe for success:

Right/Proper goal setting

+ Great attitude/mindset

+ Correct planning

+ Appropriate sales strategy

+ Hunger for result

+ Proper implementation

+ Determination to succeed

= **Success**

This is recipe and not formula for success. There is no fool-proof formula for success. The recipe gives the direction or road map for success. The rest is in your hands.

Follow the laws of success as far as possible. Remember and put in practice the recipe for success. Hurdles will come. *Work hard*. Try to cross the hurdles.

You have to perspire. Success will come your way—if not today, by tomorrow. ***Keep hope.*** You will succeed.

Team Building for Sales Success

Mantra 25

Master the Recipe for Winning

Winners don't do different things. They do things differently....
—Shiv Khera

Winning means pushing yourself a little differently, a little harder and a little further....

Success means winning. To succeed is to be a winner. All of us want to win. And, we want to win always. This is more true of salespeople because every time they win, they secure an order or business, and they may win some reward.

If you are tired of your mediocre performance, try winning. Also, if you want to exploit your potential to the full, try winning. Trying to win means doing more than the next person (your colleague). Trying to win means pushing yourself a little harder, a little further and little longer than you have done before. This means making a sustained effort to find out what you are and what you can do. You can start by finding out what winners do or how they do things.

HOW TO BE A WINNER

Eight-step Recipe for Winning

Here is an eight-step recipe for winning:

1. Hope to Win

Our actions depend a lot on what we think, what we expect or what we hope to do. *Hope is a great driving/motivating force as despair is a great demoralising force.* If you hope to win, you will start thinking in terms of winning. This will keep any thoughts of losing away from you.

2. Decide to Win

Convert your hope into decision to win. This means moving a step further from just hope to win.

Corporate and selling programmes are products of decisions. Sales techniques and strategies are also matters of decisions. Similarly, winning in sales is, first, a matter of decision to win.

Commitment follows almost automatically. Many times, the difference between these who win and those who do not is the decision to win or the lack of it.

3. Plan to Win

The next stage is planning or the plan to win. Without a well-defined plan to win, you will lose directions, and may probably only succeed in losing. On the other hand, you may be able to achieve almost any objective in life if you develop the right plan and implement properly. *It takes many time as much energy to get something moving as it requires to keep it moving. Planning makes the difference.*

If you want to beat the competition almost every time, you must start with a plan and commitment to win. So, sit down and prepare a plan for winning. Your plan for winning should be a plan with focus. *Remember, it is focus that makes all the difference between the light of a candle and the power of a laser beam*. In your plan, you should focus on three important things:

√ Focus on your objectives or targets

√ Focus on your strategy or tactics

√ Focus on your time or timing

4. Prepare to Win

Planning is not enough. You have also to prepare yourself for winning.

Average salespeople prepare for their jobs only as much as they must to get their job done. Their preparation is just in proportion to their attitude towards their performance. They usually do not achieve much. When such people see the winners and their achievements, they usually feel and say: "They have just been lucky." Through this, they are actually voicing the frustration of losers.

Fate or destiny has its own role/place in everybody's life. We cannot deny this. But we cannot also just take shelter in destiny. Some people decide their own destiny. At least, they prepare for it. As Anthony Robbins put it: "The meeting of *preparation* with *opportunity* generates the offspring we call *luck*."

In most jobs or professions, a person must have some special education or advantage to excel. For example, in business you will have to start with some capital (and, of course, entrepreneurial ability). In law, medicine and engineering, you must have a specialised education. In art, you must possess the innate talent that enables you to do creative work. But selling is not so specialised. **To succeed in selling, you do not need specialist skills.**

Selling may also be an art (as we have said earlier). But most of the skills or tools required for successful selling can be acquired or those are already available with many salespeople. That is why **many feel that almost anyone can succeed in sales if he or she is prepared for it.**

5. Work to Win

Preparing oneself for winning is not enough. One has also to work to win.

We hear people talking about "workaholics." "Workaholics" may either mean sloggers—people who burn the midnight oil unnecessarily without any clear purpose; or, people who really do hard and serious work with a target to achieve or an objective to be fulfilled. If you wish to win, you should belong to the second category.

Many feel that winning has lot in common with a public auction. At an auction, the person who is willing to pay the highest price walks away with the reward (the object in auction). Similarly, the person who wins in sales is the person who is most willing to pay the highest price in terms of planning, preparation and hard work.

Hard work may not usually be very exciting. *The result of hard work is exciting*. One has, therefore, to wait for results. That is why it requires tremendous conviction and energy to continue with hard work. Losers may give up. They become quitters. But winners do not quit. They never give up the chase.

6. Act to Win

Work is a continuous process, but the ability to act has a lot to do with timing. You have to act to win. And, you have to act in time to win.

The ability to act also means to be proactive or pre-emptive rather than reactive. When you are reacting, you are not showing any 'initiative.' You are only responding, or forced in responding, to somebody else's initiative. **To act to win is to act with initiative.**

All actions in business or selling may not be pre-emptive or proactive. Sometimes you may have to react. Even if you have to react, act or react positively. That is the way to act to win.

7. Have the Will to Win

Finally, and the most important, you must have the will to win. Will or determination is the final driving force.

Will to win is not the wish to win. There is an old saying which many of us know: "If wishes were horses, beggars would be kings." But wishes are not horses. Just wishing is not enough. It must be backed by a strong will to win. We should always remember the great saying: "Where there is a will, there is a way." We should have the will to find a way to win.

8. Adopt a Role Model

For winning, it will always help if you adopt a role model. Your role model will be a winning sales professional—a star performer or a sales superstar. He (she) is a person you can emulate to overcome your shortcomings, learn new things and get on to the winning track.

THE WINNING ATTITUDE

We should also remember another truth about winning. This is about the winning attitude. *The difference between winning and losing, many times, is not your company or resources or your position or your customer or your competitor, but your mindset or attitude.*

All the factors just mentioned are very important, but your attitude is vital. It depends on how strong your conviction is. You have to face failures and emerge winner. We should derive inspiration from people like the great American President Abraham Lincoln. Abraham Lincoln failed nine times in succession before he became the President of the United States.

Winning Attitude: A Self-evaluation

Every salesperson can make a self-evaluation of his (her) winning attitude. Here is a self-evaluation exercise. Twenty statements are given below, each relating to winning. Read each statement carefully and assign scores/values of 1 to 5. Assign 1 if you 'strongly disagree' with the statement; assign 2 if you 'disagree'; assign 3 if you 'agree'; assign 4 if you 'quite agree'; and assign 5 if you 'strongly agree' with the statement. See the statements below:

	Statement	Score
1.	I always expect to win	—
2.	I plan to win	—
3.	I have a plan for today, this week and this month	—
4.	I know exactly what I must do to win	—
5.	I have developed a formula for winning	—
6.	I prepare to win	—
7.	I believe that I am so important that I should win	—
8.	I work hard enough to win	—
9.	I have the will to win	—
10.	I refuse to lose	—
11.	I never allow myself to make excuses for not winning	—
12.	I never allow others to make excuses for me when I do not win	—
13.	I pay the price to win	—
14.	I do not allow routines like car problems or traffic problems or any others to delay the start of my day	—
15.	I consider the costs as well as the benefits of winning	—
16.	I would not be surprised if I win a national sales contest	—
17.	I increase my will to win if others win national or other sales contests	—
18.	I can accept failures to finally emerge winner	—
19.	For winning, I am able to summon all my resources	—
20.	I want to make winning a habit	—
	Total Score	—

You add up all the scores (total score) to evaluate or ascertain your winning attitude. If total score is 80 or above, you have a strong winning attitude; if the score is between 50 and 80, you have a positive winning attitude; if the score is below 50, you have a losing or defeatist attitude.

Once you know your winning attitude or orientation, you can work on this to improve and prepare yourself for winning.

SIX CS FOR WINNING

Also know the six Cs for winning.

Adopt six Cs for practising and developing winning as a habit. The six Cs are: clarity, competence, communication, character, courage and conviction. These are made clear below:

1. *Clarity*: Clearly spell out objectives or goals.
2. *Competence*: Possess/acquire required skill and capability to sell.
3. *Communication*: Develop persuasive skill and the ability to convince prospects.
4. *Character*: Show integrity and determination even during setbacks.
5. *Courage*: Demonstrate braveness to move ahead fighting failures.
6. *Conviction*: Make your belief anchored in the organisation and profession.

The six Cs are made more focussed with the diagrammatic presentation:

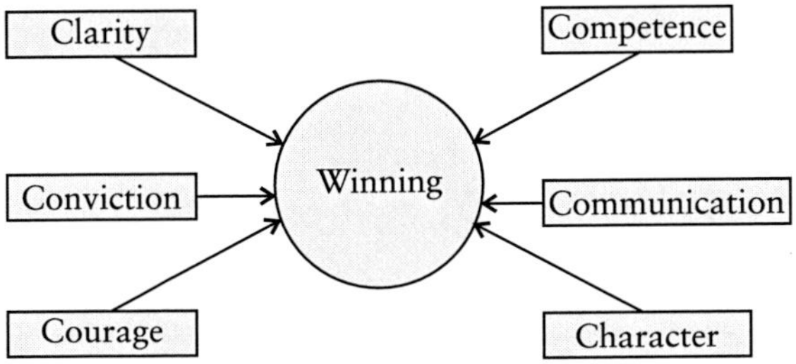

Keep a photocopy of the diagram in your pocket. This is your recipe for winning.

The six Cs mostly complement each other and can be viewed as integrated Cs. Develop the six Cs and try to reach perfection in them. Winning will be yours. **Keep winning!**

Mantra 26

Be Ambitious, But Not Over-Ambitious

Ambition is the seed for success in life....

Beware! Over-ambition may end in downfall....

Every one of us should have ambition in life whatever be our profession. Ambition leads to dream; dream leads to goal(s)—something to look forward to for fulfillment. But, over-ambition is bad. It may be unrealistic. Over-ambition can result in shattered dream(s). It may even lead to disaster.

AMBITION AND OVER-AMBITION IN SELLING

This can be best illustrated by the examples/stories of two salesmen. The two salesmen are Smart and Steady. Steady is ambitious; Smart is over-ambition. Let us see how ambition of Steady and over-ambition of Smart unfold and result in their selling careers.

Smart and Steady Go to Sales

Smart and Steady were working on the shop floor of a local factory in their hometown. One day, their lives changed suddenly. Their shop foreman called them into his office and gave them the bad news. 'Sorry gentlemen,' said the foreman, 'our business has been very bad, and we have to make some cutbacks.' So, Smart and Steady were sacked. This was a fact of life, and they had to accept it.

Both Smart and Steady were depressed, but *remaining depressed does not help in life*. One has to seek solutions to problems, and so did Smart and Steady. They started searching solutions, that is, jobs.

Both spotted the same Ad for jobs in sales. They decided to go for a career in sales. Both got jobs in the same company and were given sales positions that promised ₹ 8,000 to ₹ 15,000 a month. Smart and Steady were very excited about the new challenge.

Setting Goals

Goal setting by Smart and Steady is very interesting and this had implications for their sales careers.

To start with, Steady set his goal only for the first year. He set three clear and specific targets for himself. First, he decided to practice and rehearse his sales presentation so that he could make them perfectly. Second, he planned to save some money from his salary or earnings to complete payment of his car loan. His third goal was to earn promotion to the position of senior salesman.

Smart's goals were more ambitious and grand. First, he set his target for earned commissions at lofty ₹ 1,50,000. His second goal was to break all sales records his company had so far. His third goal was to take a month's holiday to Switzerland with his family.

Two Contrasting Courses

Steady's thinking was that even though selling was new to him, he was going to commit himself to the job. He said to himself: 'I might have to work long hours, nights and weekends for a while. It will be hard, but I will do whatever it takes to succeed.' Smart assured himself that he could outsell any of the other salespeople he had met so far. He said, 'I just don't see why they expect me to spend so much time in those boring sales meetings.'

Steady set certain specific goals for himself to be accomplished during first few years in sales. He planned to practice and fine-tune his sales presentation till he could make it perfect and convincing. His aim was also to be promoted to the position of senior salesman. Smart's goals were rather grand. He intended to break every sales record his company ever had. His target for earned commissions was a lofty ₹ 1,00,000 per month.

Learning processes adopted by Smart and Steady were also contrasting. Steady closely observed his fellow salespeople in action. He watched the most successful salespeople presenting themselves to their customers. He experimented with all the sales techniques suggested to him. He perfected the ones that worked and abandoned the others.

Smart wanted to get jump on Steady and other new sales staff. He decided to get some hot tips by reading the new best-selling book on salesmanship *Buyers are Liars* by B.S. Brothers. He also studied, on audio cassettes, the famous sales seminar *How to Manoeuvre your Customers through Subliminal Body Language*. He also bought *One Hundred ways to Manipulate your Customers* written by the reverend Mr. Slim, the seminar developer. Smart continued his sales education by buying another series of tapes. His newest programme offered insight into another popular new technique: How to influence your Customers by avoiding eye contact.

Doer and Dreamer

Steady would reach office early for every sales meeting. One could almost set his watch by him. He would work long hours every day. He spent many evenings and weekends studying and perfecting his skills. He spent several evenings a month with his sales manager. He used this to practice a variety of sales techniques and perfect his presentation. He dedicated himself to learn everything he could about his trade.

Smart enjoyed his new found freedom. He continued to believe that he should get his sales training from the 'professionals'. He invested in another programme and slept through the entire series of subliminal tapes by Super Sell Smith titled *How to get Back a Million Dollars on your Income Tax*.

During the first few months, Steady averaged only about ₹ 8,000 a month. Before the end of the sixth month, however, things changed dramatically. He was earning over ₹ 20,000 per month. He had also accomplished one of his key goals—promotion to senior salesman.

Smart was getting frustrated. He did not think he could ever learn anything useful from his fatheaded sales manager and those other 'stiffs' in the office. He also felt that it was foolish for a man of his talent to work as Steady did for peanuts. After all, he had got into sales only for big money.

Smart's frustration prompted him to look for better opportunities. Soon, he came across a really big deal. The deal was: if Smart invested ₹ 1,00,000, he would receive an exclusive goat milk franchise. Literature on the subject provided statistical evidence that goat milk use was fast trending upwards. Available literature also proved that by leveraging his mental power, he could work five minutes a day and earn million rupees a year without even getting out of bed!

The Winner and Loser

Steady is now the manager of a large sales force. He has an unlimited expense account and a six-figure annual income. He is a very busy executive with great deal of responsibility and authority. Still, Steady tells people about the freedom, the big commissions, the excitement and the adventures he had when he was a direct salesman.

For Smart, the goat milk franchise also fell through. He is now working once again in the same factory where he and Steady had worked together earlier. After the goat milk scheme fell through, Smart felt that this was the wisest thing for him to do—at least till he is out of debt. Once again he is putting in eight hours a day on the shop floor. Once again he is punching a time card. He feels this is his destiny.

AMBITION IN REALITY

So, don't be ambitious like Smart; don't do only day dreaming. This may doom you. Be realistically ambitious like Steady.

Your ambition should be according to your preparedness and capability. Understand the steps for progress or growth. *Move step by step*. Strive for achievement—one after another. Don't try to jump.

Avail of or exploit opportunity which comes your way. But, you have to prepare and work for it—work hard. Use all your resources. But, use judiciously. *Resources are not unlimited*. Do not misdirect or drain your energy or resources.

Be a dreamer who does. Be a dreamer who does knowing wall his (her) capability and constraint. Don't be one who is a dreamer and only dreams.

Be a dreamer like Steady. Translate your dream into reality with your skill, capability and perseverance. This is another name for success.

To be ambitious in reality, every salesperson must develop the virtues of 'self-commitment' and 'self-evaluation' during every sale and growth of sales. This will provide the base for further growth. This is the winning process.

We can put the whole thing like this:

Mantra 27

Learn from Sales Superstars: Indian Superstars

The best salespeople seem to have a sixth sense....

Sales superstars, like winners, do not do different things; they do things differently....

In every profession, there are some outstanding performers whom everybody regards as superstars. David forward, in his book *Sales Superstars: How They Made it and What They can Teach You*, narrates the success stories of nineteen sales superstars (both men and women) in diversified products and services—life insurance, real estate, courier, photocopiers, textiles, aircraft and automobiles.

Sales superstars include both Indian superstars and international superstars. Success stories of three Indian sales superstars are narrated below:

A. Dhirubhai Ambani

B. Bharat and Vijay Shah

C. Karsanbhai Patel

INDIAN SALES SUPERSTARS

The sales superstars presented here are not typical or 'life-long' salespeople as many international sales superstars are. But they rose to greatness or stardom by showing extraordinary instinct and love for selling. They are like born salesmen. And, they were constantly conscious of, rather driven by, profit or profitability—the ultimate objective in selling and business.

All of them exhibited great entrepreneurial skills. And, it is the combination of their zest for selling, entrepreneurial skills and profitability goals which made them successful and exemplary business magnets in later life. Three such superstars are: Dhirubhai Ambani, Bharat and Vijay Shah and Karsanbhai Patel.

DHIRUBHAI AMBANI

All of us remember Dhirubhai Ambani as one of the greatest entrepreneurs and visionaries. Most of us may also know his rags to riches story. But many of us may not be aware of his instinct and passion for selling which finally culminated into his future success.

Dhirubhai was born in 1932 in a humble Gujarati family in Chorward village, Junagadh district, Gujarat. Born to Jamna and Hirachand Ambani, he was the middle of five children—three boys and two girls.

School teachers get lowly—if not meagre—salaries particularly in villages. With these salaries, they cannot afford much or higher education for their children. Therefore, as soon as Dhirubhai matriculated, he, like his elder brother, Ramniklal had to leave books (which Dhirubhai felt very much in his later life) and go to work.

Right from those days, Dhirubhai showed a penchant for selling and earning money. As Ramniklal put it: 'During the Mahashivratri fair, Dhirubhai got together with some friends and sold *ganthia*, a Gujarati savoury.' According to a Chorward contemporary: 'Dhirubhai was a familiar sight here, cycling from village to village. All he needed was the whiff of a business opportunity and he was off to book the order.'

Sales and business instinct kept chasing Dhirubhai. He took a loan and started a trading company—the Reliance Trading Corporation—with a capital of ₹ 15,000. He could not afford to buy or rent office space; he, therefore, had set up his office in the corner of a borrowed space in Bharat Bazaar, Bombay.

Reliance Trading Corporation was an export house dealing primarily in general merchandise—sugar, ginger, cashewnut, cardamom, pepper, etc. Exports were mostly to Aden where Dhirubhai had developed many connections when he was working there. He fully exploited the connections. Aden was also a free port. These two factors tremendously helped Dhirubhai's export business. Dhirubhai's selling skill was the real driving force.

Dhirubhai was also exporting ghee, sand and soil. Soil? Yes—'anything that had the potential.' Soil export was to an Arab country. An Arab Sheikh had placed an order for a consignment of Indian soil for growing roses in the desert. The soil export was successfully made. But, was this a legitimate business? We may keep on seeking answer to this. But Dhirubhai's approach and answer to this was: 'See the opportunity and strike.' The sale should be made and profit should come.

In the domestic market, Dhirubhai focused on yarn trading. The struggle continued. During the initial years, there was very little to distinguish between him and other yarn trades. Like many others, he was working hard in Bombay's hot and teeming yarn markets, living on tea shop snacks, endlessly chewing *paan* and selling yarn.

Gradually, but surely, things changed for better for Dhirubhai. Business was growing and profit was also increasing. Highly entrepreneurial and insightful Dhirubhai would grab any opportunity which came his way for selling and making profit.

During the year 1971, the Government of India introduced the High Unit Value Scheme. Through this scheme, polyester filament yarn (raw material) could be imported against export of nylon fabrics (finished product), which was a 'high value added' product. Dhirubhai exploited this opportunity very successfully. Reliance Export Corporation accounted for more than 60 per cent of export under this scheme. Handsome profit was made. During those days, polyester was called *chamatk* in the local market, and Dhirubhai became the *chamatkar* (wonder).

Later stories of Dhirubhai's success are well known—ONLY VIMAL, Reliance Industries (Petrochemicals), telecommunications, etc.

ONLY VIMAL gives an exemplary account of Dhirubhai's sales acumen and innovativeness. Reliance was a late entrant in the already crowded Indian textile market—Raymond, Grasim, Bombay Dyeing, Khatau Voiles and S. Kumar were all established players. But Reliance's spectacular growth leaving behind many traditional leaders makes a fascinating story. Marketing and sales strategy of Vimal (Vimal is the name of Dhirubhai's nephew—Ramniklal's son) fabrics is a combination strategy—a unique blending of a product strategy, a pricing strategy, a promotional strategy, a distribution strategy, and a market segmentation or selection strategy.

Intelligent/innovative exploitation of the showroom or exclusive retail-outlet—that is an independent channel of Reliance's own—was the cornerstone of Dhirubhai's distribution strategy. Other textile mills also had resorted to selling through showrooms, but there was something unique about the way Reliance used it. Reliance organised this on a massive scale with a very extensive nationwide network of exclusive Vimal showrooms. In fact, the 1800-strong Vimal showroom network became the largest retail network of its kind in the country.

Dhirubhai was not content with using the showrooms as a means of distribution only; he exploited the showrooms also as a means for promotion. In effect, he converted the distribution strategy into another powerful platform for product promotion. Reliance management kept constantly talking to its customers and prospects about the showrooms. A catchy slogan always accompanied all Vimal ads:

VIMAL SHOWROOMS

The largest nation-wide retail network

There is one near you

Through innovative ad campaigns and sales promotion strategies the ONLY VIMAL slogan was almost made a household name among the target audience.

In short, ONLY VIMAL portrays complete marketing and sales strategy; in other words, total salesmanship of Dhirubhai Ambani!

BHARAT AND VIJAY SHAH

Bharat and Vijay Shah, two brothers and both college dropouts, started from scratch like Dhirubhai Ambani. But within ten years, the brothers built a ₹ 35 billion international empire selling an Indian speciality product—cut and polished diamond—which has a global market and is highly competitive. They became the world's diamond czars with cutting and polishing factories in Bangkok, Antwerp, Tel Aviv, Bombay, Surat and Palanpur.

Bharat and Vijay started by going to the bottom end of the diamond market—buying, cutting and polishing rough diamonds which the Jews had rejected. Buyers liked the products, but Jewish wholesalers were prejudiced against Indian.

The Shahs had to break the shackles. How did they do it? What were their special skills? According to Van Loovaren, a large international diamond broker: “To be a successful diamantaire, you need to be intelligent—that goes without saying. But, you need to have the right combination of the abilities of a banker, manufacturer, a marketer (seller) and to have a good judgement of people. If there is a misjudgment in any one of these qualities, the combination goes wrong; it goes without saying that both Bharat and Vijay have the right combination of these qualities”.

Bharat and Vijay had nicely balanced their job handling or operations. As Bharat puts it: “I started handling the manufacturing activity in Bombay and meeting the buyers; Vijay kept sending foreigners, the roughs, and also the clients (buyers) to me.” They were perfect complement to each other.

The secret of competitive international pricing of polished diamonds by Shahs was their aggressive and cost-effective sourcing of rough diamonds. Vijay ‘roamed markets of the beaten tracks’—markets which would give better margins than the common diamond procurement centres, but those which others may not easily tread.

Vijay used to buy large quantities of rough diamonds from Africa. For going to Africa those days and buying rough diamond, one had to be both confident and adventurous and also a shrewd price bargainer. One had to literally fight for prices. It was the most difficult thing to do because the Africans had a strange and dubious approach to pricing. If the roughs are worth \$ 10, they may ask for \$ 100. “...if you understand the goods, you will start with \$ 5, ...but if you don’t understand, what are you going to offer? If I was lucky, sometimes finished it at \$ 6 or \$ 7”, says Vijay.

From Bombay, the entrepreneurial and self-motivated Shahs ventured into Tel Aviv. In Tel Aviv, they set up a state-of-the-art cutting and polishing centre. In 1981, Vijay received the highest export award of the Israeli Government. In just within a year, sales galloped from $ 2 million to $ 21 million—an increase of more than 10 times. The story goes on.

The real test of a marketing or selling company or salesman is during market downtown or recession. Bharat and Vijay Shah set a great example of how to thrive in diamond selling during a global recession.

The international diamond industry and trade was in the grip of a recession during the mid '70s. Demand had fallen and prices were down. Both Indian traders (who mostly operate at the lower end of the market) and Jewish firms (who primarily operate at the top end of the market) were equally affected. The trading floors (where buyers and sellers meet across the tables) in Antwerp, one of the largest diamond trading centres in the world, were witnessing many brokers and wholesalers/sellers, but very few sales were taking place.

Bharat and Vijay did not take this as a setback, but grabbed this as an opportunity and fully exploited the situation to their advantage. They judiciously used their market research and business acumen and selling skill to generate sales and make profit. The whole market used to wonder: What is Vijay doing? What is the magic? The secret was simple: 'Buy cheap, sell cheap, build up volume, even a rupee's profit is good profit'. This minimalist philosophy went against the grain of most Indian diamantaires.

The profit of B. Vijay Kumar (the company of Bharat and Vijay Shah) increased while that of others decreased. Explains Bharat Shah: "That time we were dealing with very low quality, where the value added is more and we were converting in hard currency ($). So, the profit increased. ...in good period, everyone can run and the profit margin is very low. In bad periods suppose you can do more business, naturally you have more profits.... that is why, whenever the market is weak, that time our business is double".

B. Vijay Kumar could sell polished diamond cheaper because they were buying rough diamonds cheaper through innovative sourcing. But "people were thinking that we are undercutting the market...if you sell the polished 10 percent cheaper, and still are making good profits from the lower (priced) roughs, what's wrong with that? This is the tricks of the business," says Vijay.

This, in short, narrates the story of Bharat and Vijay Shah becoming sales superstars in the diamond trade. They achieved stardom by sourcing rough diamond or feedstock cheap, adding large value during processing and selling polished diamond at competitive prices in the domestic and international markets with attractive margins or profit; and, in the process, took business risks, but, at the same time, showed enough aggressiveness and innovativeness to ensure success.

De Beers, the South African diamond giant, summarises Shahs' success by saying that Bharat and Vijay Shah are the world's biggest diamantarires, annually cutting, polishing and selling several billion diamonds. A true czar of carats (diamonds)!

KARSANBHAI PATEL

Karsanbhai Patel is the legendary founder and present chairman of ₹ 3,000 crores Nirma Ltd. (Nirma washing powder). Like Dhirubhai Ambani's, Karsanbhai Patel's also is an astonishing rags to riches journey during which he, like Dhirubhai, shattered many established business theories and wrote/rewrote new ones to establish the supremacy of Nirma. Throughout this journey, he was driven by his instinct and acumen and marketing vision. He dreamt of making Nirma the biggest brand in the world. Today, Nirma is synonymous with Karsanbhai.

Karsanbhai was born in Ruppur village, Mehsana district, Gujarat. He came from a humble farmer family in the same village. In 1969, at the young ate of 25, Karsanbhai moved out of family farming and started a small scale enterprise in washing powder. He was making and selling detergent using indigenous technology (hand-made) at one-third of the prevailing market price without compromising much on the quality or product.

Karsanbhai started his business operations in the suburb of Ahmedabad city. Ahmedabad was then a big soap market. There were about 2000 retail outlets in the city and more than 200 large and small soap manufacturers. So, Karsanbhai made his entry into an already overcrowded and highly competitive market. During that time, washing soap was getting fast replaced by detergent powder. That guided Karsanbhai's product choice. He called the product Nirma after his daughter Niru or Nirupama.

Karsanbhai would himself hand-mix detergent powder in batches and pack into polythene bags (stapled them). He used to load several gunny bags, full of powder packets/sachets, on his bicycle and go from house to house in Ahmedabad selling his product. He was the travelling Nirma salesman for the city residents/households. He used to make 200 kg powder every day and would sell all of them. He had mastered the art of personal selling. This also meant that he was operating with zero inventory carrying cost.

Karsanbhai priced Nirma washing powder at ₹ 3 per kg. The next available cheapest brand in the market was ₹ 13 per kg. With his ingenious cost management and the unbelievable price shake-out, Nirma revolutionised the entire detergent powder market and, in a short span of time, created a new segment in the domestic market. By late 1980s, Nirma became the world's largest selling detergent powder.

During that time, the Indian detergent market was mostly limited to the premium segment and was dominated by MNCs—Surf of Hindustan Level (HLL, now HUL) being the most dominant and the market leader. Nirma gave these brands and companies—particularly Surf and HLL—many sleepless nights.

How was all this possible? How did Karsanbhai achieve this feat? The answer is: developing a unique marketing and sales strategy by revolutionising the marketing mix. All the four Ps of marketing mix—product, price, promotion and place (distribution)—were perfectly blended.

As a product, Nirma was made of an innovative formulation. It was phosphate free and hence environment friendly. The process of manufacturing was highly labour intensive using cheap local labour. This made the product extremely cost-effective with minimal investment in plant and machinery. The global detergent giants were later compelled to emulate Nirma process, to the extent they could, to achieve cost competitiveness.

The cornerstone or crux of Karsanbhai's marketing and sales strategy was pricing. He used flanking strategy, that is, attacking or exploiting the weak aspect or segment of the leader—Surf of HLL. Surf was highly priced. Karsanbhai understood from his experience of door-to-door selling that the average Indian household wanted a detergent which is quite budget friendly, i.e., very competitively or lowly priced, even if it meant certain trade-off with product formulation or quality.

In 1977, Nirma was priced at ₹ 4.35 per kg, about one-third of the price of Surf. This was made possible by highly efficient cost management, rather labour management, by Karsanbhai. He exploited the labour-intensive process to the maximum extent possible. As late as in 1989, the average labour cost of Nirma's 8000 workers was estimated to be in the range ₹ 15-25 per person-day compared to HLL's labour cost (semi-skilled) of ₹ 30-40 per man-day. Karsanbhai did not use electricity in the Nirma production process for a long time. This also added to significant cost saving.

In advertising and sales promotion also, Karsanbhai was very innovative, and he ensured that budget or cost was no limitation. His advertising and sales promotion efforts were directed towards gaining trade and consumer acceptance. He successfully used the "ghost customer" approach; he had hired young women to visit retail shops and ask for Nirma. This had immediate effect as retailers started stocking Nirma to satisfy anticipated demand. He also announced many prize draws for salespeople offering large sums of money as rewards.

The distribution strategy of Nirma fully complemented the product, price and promotional strategies. Nirma's distribution system or network boasts of a 350-strong sales force, 400 distributors and more than one million retail outlets spread all over the country. Nirma detergent powder and Nirma detergent cake are among India's top 20 most distributed brands, and the most widely distributed brands in the detergent powder and detergent cake categories.

The famous war of the mid-80s between Nirma and Surf—then market leader—is well known. HLL could never imagine that they could be challenged by a low image new entrant like Nirma. Nirma was available at all retail outlets including cooperative stores, and had almost become a household name across the country. Surf's sale was steadily declining and, at one stage, the threat to Surf was perceived to be so strong that HLL, almost in desperation, bought out all Nirma stocks in Pune. This move misfired and led to an adverse publicity of HLL. Surf's sale and image continued to decline and at some stage, the fall was so significant that market analysts had almost predicted "demise" of Surf.

This was a great strategic victory of Karsanbhai over a multinational. This story and Nirma's phenomenal growth in the Indian FMCG market had such a global impact that it was taught as a case study in the Harvard Business School.

If anyone asks Karsanbhai about his achievements, he might say: "I am first and foremost a salesman; everything else follows from there". No wonder, then, that he has won many sales awards in addition to other awards for outstanding performance in business.

Mantra 28

Learn from Sales Superstars: International Superstars

If you want to be successful, hang around successful people....
—Clement Stone

Regardless of your educational level, race, industry or age, if you can take one trait from each of the sales superstars, you will be one of the superstars (yourself)....
—D.C. Forward

As there are Indian sales superstars, there are many international sales superstars in diversified product groups.

Success stories of three international sales superstars are presented below:

A. Sid Friedman

B. Frank Pacetta

C. David Koch

INTERNATIONAL SALES SUPERSTARS

Like Indian sales superstars, there are many special traits or distinctive characteristics of international sales superstars. They can be broadly understood in terms of six major characteristics:

1. *Volume or Value*: Sales superstars generate high volumes. They constantly sell significantly higher volume or value of their company's products or services than their peers.

2. *Delivery Rate*: Sales superstars have consistently a higher delivery rate than others.

3. *Eliminating Negativity*: Sales superstars are always positive. They are also able to turn a negative situation into positiveness or advantage.

4. *Profitability*: Sales generated by superstars are consistently profitable.

5. *Customer Satisfaction*: Sales superstars always achieve a very high level of customer satisfaction.

6. *Setting Example*: Sales superstars consistently set a good example to every other salesperson around them. They are like role models.

SID FRIEDMAN: THE ROLLS ROYCE OF LIFE INSURANCE SALESMEN

Sid Friedman started his sales career by selling life insurance in his uncle's agency, and he was selling successfully. But he felt that he should get more recognition. So, Friedman decided to change his job, and he changed job as a junior sales manager with the Phoenix Mutual Life Insurance Company which became Phoenix Home Life after a merger in 1993. Sid had told his interviewers in Phoenix that he was not interested in being a salesman or low-level sales manager forever. His goal was to be an agency manager at one of the company's branches. Phoenix agreed and told him that, if he could attain a certain sales level within two years—a production target they did not expect him to achieve—they would give him his own agency to manage.

Phoenix did not know that when Friedman sets his sights on a goal, it is as good as met. Let as put this in his own words:

> I found out later that they believed the objectives were almost impossible to reach. At the time, my wife, Sue was six months pregnant with our first child, and that put me in supercharge mode. I rose just after 5:00 A.M. and would be at my desk before 7:00 A.M. I never took a day off, and usually got home around 10:00 P.M. I worked with my agents; I went on calls with them, held sales meetings helped with case development—whatever it took six days a week. I was there to help them become successful because I earned an override on every dollar they brought in. Then on the seventh day, I did not rest. I spent it calling on personal clients whom I could not meet during the week.

Six months later, that is, a year and a half earlier than the target fixed for him, Friedman declared to Phoenix management that he had met their goals. It was time for his own agency. The company, as per the agreement, assigned Friedman the Philadelphia office—the lowest producing, the most problem-plagued agency in the country. "When I first walked in here I was shocked," he recalls today. "There was no management, no discipline, no morale—hence there was no business! The 73 agents had collectively generated only $ 28,000 in commissions for the entire previous year. Most of them were characters I would not want to share an elevator with, let alone trust them to sell me life insurance."

But Friedman turned around the Philadelphia office. Friedman's success in turning around the office was due to what he calls the "Sid Friedman success System": Have a dream, plan your work, maintain discipline and have the courage to do whatever it takes. Friedman realised that he had to start from scratch. After a mouth of working with the salespeople in Philadelphia office, he had all the information he needed. He then started acting. He fired all but two of the agents. Sid believed that he could do nothing less to succeed because the office could sink no further.

The news that Friedman had terminated almost the entire agency sales force spread like wildfire throughout the industry. He knew he had taken a drastic step, but he realised that the future success of the entire agency and, therefore, of his own career, was solely his own responsibility. Once again, he took on the challenges of building the agency and his own sales career.

Early in his career, Friedman had coined the phrase "If it is to be, it is up to me", and these ten simple two-letter words have guided him ever since. "You have to take responsibility for yourself, your career," he says. "A sales manager can help you, can be a resource, but ultimately, you are the one who decides what time to set the alarm or what time to quit every day. It was like when I first came to the Philadelphia office. If I failed and became the laughing stock of the company, whom would I blame? I knew I could turn this place around. I accepted the challenge and took responsibility for doing it. If it is to be, it is up to me. The rule applies today just as it did 30 years ago."

Today, Sid Friedman is the ultimate success story. He is the top manager every year, and his agency has the highest sales and commissions in the company for last 15 consecutive years. An outstanding performer in his own right, he enjoys a lifestyle befitting someone whose annual income is \$ 1-\$ 2 million. Yet, he continues selling and motivates others to achieve their own goals. "I have only two speeds," he says, "frantic and stop. Nothing gets in my way while I am working."

FRANK PACETTA: GETTING THEM ALL FIRED UP AT XEROX

At first glance, Frank Pacetta looks like a management guy from one of America's blue-chip companies—white shirt, silk tie, well-tailored suit and gleaming shoes. But when he talks about the challenges confronting salespeople in the real world today, he appears to be from the military background.

"Because it's war out there," he declares, "Being in the sales today is like being in the infantry. You study the territory, you learn to use whatever weapons you have, then you walk right into the battle. That's what it's like competing against an enemy who is trying to get their products into the customer at your expense. That's how it feels when you are on the front line making cold calls." Pacetta's point is that in modern day selling, the use of voice mail, fax machines, E-mail and satellite communications will not win new customers, but an effective, properly trained, well-equipped sales team will.

Pacetta had a mediocre start to his illustrious career. He admits that he had let first three or four years of his career go with mediocre sales because he lacked dedication and organisation. Then he sold a big order of Xerox's 9200 models—their top-of-the-line copier at that time, and that year, he was the top sales representative in the district. But "In the midst of the celebrations as I reflected on how good life was, my manager pulled me into his office and said, 'Let me give you a little feedback. Despite the year's sales, you have not been performing upto your potential...' I decided right there to do something positive and to dedicate myself to building a career as a leader, a manager."

At Xerox, a panel for promotion selects candidates. When a sales manager's job fell vacant, Pacetta applied for it and was interviewed by the panel but was rejected. Sometime later another vacancy fell vacant but the panel again rejected Pacetta's candidature. "I thought it was all their fault," he says today. "After all, my numbers were fabulous."

Pacetta sought his father's advice. The veteran Chase Manhattan Bank executive asked Pacetta what he had done differently in the second interview compared to the first. "I told him that I had not changed a thing. Both interviews were basically the same." His father rebuked him for his lack of foresight. He asked Pacetta if the things he said and did in the first interview were not good enough to get him promoted, how did he expect a promotion by repeating the same thing second time? "As usual," admits Pacetta, "my Dad was right." Next time, when an opportunity for promotion came, Pacetta changed his style and presentation and he was successful. It was time for him to get serious about his career with Xerox Corporation.

On promotion, Pacetta moved from Ohio to Minnesota where he became the number one district sales manager in the country. Then he was offered a position which could make or break his dreams with Xerox: he was asked if he would accept the district manager's position in the Cleveland sales office. At that time, Cleveland was in the last place in the region and almost at the bottom of 65 Xerox offices in the country. Pacetta jumped at the opportunity.

When Pacetta arrived in Cleveland, he found an office totally bereft of motivation. Discipline was poor. Morale was low and a sense of despair hung in the air. Pacetta called a meeting of all the sales representatives and their managers in the district. "The first thing you have to do with your troops is to tell them where they are going," he says, "so I told them that our goal was to make the Cleveland district office number one in the region." But, as he looked into the eyes of the salespeople and watched their body language, he realised that achieving this goal was going to be very tough, but, not impossible.

Pacetta believes that the keys to success are clear communication, empowerment and accountability, and with these keys or tools, he was able to transform the Cleveland sales office and make it number one among all the Xerox offices.

According to Pacetta, *clear communication* is very vital. Wars have been fought, marriages have failed, friendships have turned into enmities and customers have been lost because of inability to communicate correctly or effectively. Pacetta is almost fastidious about communicating clearly and openly with both his sales force and customers.

Empowerment is the next critical factor. Once Pacetta is convinced that a sales representative is reliable and fully committed, he empowers him to take decisions which historically needed management approval. He even allows salespeople to quote terms they need to close a sale. "Our people run their territory as if it were their own small business. They know what they have to do to be successful and it rarely revolves solely around price. If it did, we would not need highly trained salespeople; we could get by a bunch of order takers."

And, finally *accountability*. Pacetta believes that every salesperson should be responsible for his (her) action, and should be accountable to himself (herself), the company and the customers. When he came to Cleveland office, he found sales representatives sitting in the coffee shop even at 10:00 A.M. The first thing he did was to lead by example. He was in the office every morning by 7:00 A.M. If he had to have a sales meeting, it was over by 8:30 and people knew they had to be in their first appointment by 9 A.M. There was also a sales calendar for every salesperson and a fully structured review and reward system.

The *Wall Street Journal* profiled Pacetta in a front page article in which the reporter narrated the "maverick manager's" success in Cleveland. Pacetta also documented his sales philosophy in his (co-authored) successful book—*Don't Fire Them, Fire Them Up: A Maverick Guide to Motivating Yourself and Your Team.* Every salesperson can learn from this book.

DAVID KOCH: FEDERAL EXPRESS SUPERSTAR

David Koch was a professional diver and fishing boat captain. He was deep below the waters when the call came to him to join Federal Express. "I told them I was happy where I was, and that I was not interested. Then a year later, they contacted me again." He decided to go for the interview. "They met me on a Tuesday and I was on board with FedEx Friday." The reason Koch impresses everyone he meets and is able to take decisions quickly.

David Koch says he has always loved selling. "I was successful as a paper boy. I sold in a hardware store throughout high school and worked my way through college." When Federal Express persuaded Koch to join the company's sales force for its new ZAP-mail service, he thought he was on fast track to a great career.

Unfortunately, ZAP-mail was one of the decade's colossal corporate flops. After three weeks of Koch's training, the company cancelled the entire programme. "They put me on a six-month hiatus while the company sorted out the mess," he says, "Then...they asked me to become an account executive for the Federal Express in the Boston South territory." Koch discovered a customer base that had a $ 15-20 million revenue potential and included several large accounts. He devoted himself to building that business. He did not simply make sales calls to his clients. He learnt everything possible about their business and showed his clients how FedEx could help to serve their customers better. Revenue from this territory increased dramatically.

FedEx then transferred Koch to California and, within three months, he was promoted as global sales executive. As global sales executive, Koch had to travel extensively to Europe, Asia, Alaska and South America, "My wife...virtually did not see me from Christmas until May....Fortunately, she is also Federal Express Hall of Famer...so our common pride in the company and her own experience in what the job entails, helped enormously." Koch feels that the priorities in his life are "family first, then FedEx, and me last". He admits that balancing his time between building a superstar sales career, and being home for every family occasion is difficult. "It is a thin line and I have crossed it a few times," he confesses.

In less than ten years in FedEx, Koch has earned the reputation of being the best person to rehabilitate broken account relationships. "I don't know what the big deal is", he says, "I just go in and ask, 'What is the problem here? What do you need us to do?' Then I design a solution to meet their needs." It may seem simple to Koch, but the company clearly saw his talent. So, when FedEx found their biggest customer in the world—worth $ 70 million revenue per annum—was thinking of another overnight delivery carrier, they promptly sent Koch to save it. He is now a member of the six-member focus team devoted full time to serving that one account worldwide.

Like all successful salespeople, Koch believes in building long-term relationships with customers. He calls it "relationship selling". To him, this means that his customers feel like they are giving business to a friend and not a billion dollar corporate giant. This may sound a little cosmetic, but "how many IBM, AT&T or Chase Manhattan salespeople you know give their home telephone number(s) on their visiting cards?" Koch does. He also carries a beeper with him 24 hours. "I tell my customers, 'If it is important enough for you to have to call my beeper at 2 AM', then I know it is as critical to you as dialling 911."

Koch has been successful in preventing many FedEx accounts from defecting. He has also seen the results of competitor's poor selling skills. This dual experience has given him clear ideas on good and bad sales practices. Koch says, "Of all the complaints I have heard about competitors, I think the most frequently voiced mistake—and, dumbest for salespeople to make—is that they don't return phone calls. I have even called customers from airplanes, and do you know what they were still talking about that months down the road."

Koch also sees overselling as one of the biggest barriers to sales success "Too many salespeople talk too much. They need to spend more time listening, more time asking questions and learning their customers' needs." According to him, many salespeople do not think in terms of the business or customers they are trying to sell to. They never try to visualise or analyse the entire scenario. This is a very myopic approach.

Koch never had any formal sales training before he joined FedEx. But, today, he is the first three time winner of Federal Express's President Club Award—an award received by only few salespeople in FedEx. He was finally inducted into Federal Express Hall of Fame—an honour bestowed annually on about 30 out of company's 1,00,000 employees.

LESSONS FROM SALES SUPERSTARS

Each sales superstar is unique in himself (or herself) in terms of personal traits, approach to selling and the way he (she) made to the stardom. But if we closely analyse them, we will find that they teach us some common lessons. Every salesperson will do well to learn from these lessons: Ten important lessons are:

1. Great salespeople do everything that good salespeople do; but they do the same thing differently.
2. Successful salespeople are not only dreamers; they are also great doers.
3. Success is, many times, built on failure; so, learn to live with failures in sales.
4. Never feel shy to learn from others.
5. Everyone in sales should learn to love competition.
6. Try to know your competitor's products better than your competitor does.
7. Make customers feel good about you and your company, not just your product.
8. Meet customer requirements even if it means fighting your office system or bureaucracy.
9. There is no substitute for hard work.
10. Consistency in results is the key to becoming a superstar.

Mantra 29

Try to Adopt a Role Model

Role models inspire, mould and prepare a salesperson to become a role model one day....

A role model is a milestone; it gives a salesperson direction for his (her) journey....

Almost every person in a profession adopts a role model or tries to adopt a role model. It may be cricket, football, athletics, acting or management. It can apply to selling also. You should also try to adopt a role model.

Cricketers think of adopting a role model like Don Bradman or Sunil Gavaskar or Kapil Dev or Sachin Tendulkar. Footballers try to adopt a role model like Pele, Maradona or Messi. Film actors may like to adopt a role model like Amitabh Bachchan. Managers wish to adopt a role model like Y.C. Deveshwar (Chairman, ITC) or Indra Nooyi (CEO, Pepsi), R.C. Bhargava (Chairman, Maruti-Suzuki). Entrepreneurs and salespersons dream of adopting a role model like Dhirubhai Ambani. There can be many others.

TRY TO BENCHMARK YOURSELF

Adoption of a role model should start with benchmarking yourself.

What is Benchmarking?

Benchmarking may be understood as a comparison with and *adherence* to prescribed norms or standards or practices in a business.

A functional definition of benchmarking is given below:

> Benchmarking is a process of identifying, understanding and adopting outstanding practices from the same organisation or from other businesses to help improve performance.

The objective of benchmarking is to emulate or adopt any good practice or the best practice in the same business or any other business or industry. This can apply to selling and salespersons also.

So, by benchmarking, you set a standard for yourself. This is a step towards adopting a role model and improving your performance.

WHO SHOULD BE YOUR ROLE MODEL

Your role model should be ideally a person who is in selling. He (she) may be in your company or in some other company whom you know. He (she) may be selling the same product(s) or any other product.

Your role model should be a person who is known to be performing well or outstandingly, i.e., a high performer. The person has certain attributes or characteristics which attract you and you want to emulate. He (she) is unique in his (her) own way. He (she) sets examples.

Your role model should be one who has attributes or characteristics you do not possess. It may be his (her) commitment or dedication or discipline or hunger for success. You wish to acquire or develop these to reach his (her) level of performance. He (she) is usually senior to you in terms of age and experience. You feel that you can learn from him (her).

CHOOSE YOUR ROLE MODEL

Given these attributes or factors, you try to choose your role model. You may have some alternatives open before you i.e., more than one personality known to you or in your view. The person you choose should be one who inspires you. This is important.

The person need not necessarily be from your company. He (she) can even be from your competitor company.

You should ideally consider or look for the following factors in choosing your role model:

1. He (she) is a high performer.
2. He (she) is a self-starter.
3. He (she) is a self-motivated person.
4. He (she) likes challenges.

5. He (she) is not afraid of failure.
6. He (she) has a hunger for success.
7. He (she) believes in himself (herself).
8. He (she) is loyal to his (her) organisation.
9. He (she) is not a rolling stone, i.e., he (she) does not switch job frequently.
10. You know him (her) for sometime.

You may or may not find all these virtues or attributes in one person. But, the person should be possessing most of them. Overall, he (she) should be a proven or accomplished or outstanding salesperson. He (she) should be your role model.

SET GOALS FOR YOURSELF

To move closer to your role model, you have to set certain goals for yourself. *Goals give you a sense of direction.* Goals drive you to be result-oriented and focussed on accomplishment or achievement.

Goals lead to targets. A professional and result-oriented salesperson sets goals or targets as time-bound plans. Time frame can be broken into different time zones or horizons. Time zones can be:

1. Monthly 2. Quarterly	→ Very short-term
3. Half-yearly 4. Yearly	→ Short-term
5. One year to three years	→ Medium term
6. More than three years/up to five years	→ Long-term

Beyond five years, it should be a *rolling plan*, i.e., at the end of five years, plan should be prepared for the next five years and so on. This gives the right long-term perspective.

In rigorous planning, monthly targets should be broken into weekly and even daily targets.

Remind yourself of your daily targets every day in the morning. **Plan your targets one week in advance.** Any shortfall in daily target should be made good the next day or during the week. Daily fluctuations cannot be ruled out. But, it should be balanced by the end of the week.

Implementation and results of monthly, quarterly, half-yearly and annual plans should be reviewed regularly for any course correction. Keep the milestone always in view. This facilitates goal achievement.

MOVE TOWARDS YOUR ROLE MODEL

Goal setting and achievements will take you closer to your role model.

Through the process of goal setting and achievement, you will gradually acquire the ten virtues or attributes mentioned above. You may already possess some of them. Learn or develop new ones. These will lead you closer to your goal.

Your goal achievement should match your role model in the medium term. Short-term may be too ambitious or unrealistic. If not in the medium-term, you must accomplish your goal in the long-term.

If you are determined for goal achievement, you may one day become a role model yourself. *Keep that as your dream.*

Mantra 30

Try to be a Joe Girard

Joe Girard is the World's best salesman according to the Guinness Book of World Records....

Joe Girards are living examples of rise from commonness to stardom....

Joe Girard worked as a salesman with a Detroit Chevrolet dealership company. His glorious achievement: he has sold more than 13,000 cars for the dealership company for 12 years running. He has achieved this amazing feet by providing unmatchable customer service. 'Service' is actually the summary description. It is the total sales package from start to finish and service after sales. It is long-term relationship building.

MANY SUPERSTARS LIKE JOE GIRARD

For winning in sales, it always helps if you follow the examples of successful salespeople. So, adopt a star performer as a role model. It would be ideal if your role model is selling or has been selling the same product or products you are selling. You can also look for role model whose personality characteristics or traits show certain similarities with those of yours.

You can adopt Joe Girard as your role model.

You can make Allan Domb your role model—Allan Domb is America's number one realtor (real estate salesperson). You can make Phyllis Wolborsky your role model—Phyllis Wolborsky is real estate's $ 40 million woman. You can make Marc McEver your role model—Marc McEver is America's star car salesman. You can make David Koch your role model—David Koch is Federal Express' (courier) superstar. You can make Sid Friedman your role model—Sid Friedman is the Rolls Royce of life insurance salesmen. You can make Ron Rush your role model—Ron Rush is superstar time manager, marketer and realtor. You can make Tony Pallet your role model—Tony Pallet is Ameritech's cellular sales success. You can make Frank Pacetta your role model—Frank Pacetta is Xerox star salesman. You can make Tom Pappert role model—Tom Pappert is Chrysler's big salesman in Detroit. You can make John Leahy your role model—John Leahy is the high flying salesman with Airbus.

There are many star performers in India also—Dhirubhai Ambani and others. You can adopt one of these as your role model. He will always lead you by example.

HOW JOE GIRARD MADE IT

Joe Girard did not become the world's best salesman overnight. He had to work himself up to ascendancy. Every salesperson should try to find a Joe Girard in him (her).

Many times, we do not know our potential. Many more times, we do not know how to exploit our potential. A salesperson, howsoever average he (she) considers himself (herself), has the potential to grow. How or how much he (she) considers himself (herself), has the potential to grow. How or how much he (she) grows depends on a whole host of factors, but the more important ones are attitudinal or behavioural—confidence in the self, willingness to change, winning habits, etc.

This is not to deny the various occupational hazards a professional salesperson has to go through. In practice, things are never very straight. Customers can be difficult; some customers can be very demanding; contracts get signed, but the payment does not come forth, the competitors try to outwit you, and such others. A salesperson has to sail through all these to establish himself. This is what Joe Girard also did.

Joe Girard, in his best selling book, *How to Sell Anything to Anybody*, has a lesson for all salespeople: "Anybody can do it if I can do it". Salespeople should derive inspiration from this. But for doing things the Joe Girard way, you have also to become a Joe Girard.

HOW TO BECOME A JOE GIRARD

To become a sales superstar or a Joe Girard, you should know the difference between success and failure. Many times, the differences are certain "self trade-offs"—some call these "trading nothing for something". *Many of these trade-offs do not cost anything.*

We can call these courses for success or courses to become Joe Girard. These are almost free courses. Ten such courses are prescribed below.

Course 1

Trade your old cynical, skeptical and unhealthy attitude for one that is positive, forward looking and healthy. Every good thing has to start with a good attitude. So, if you want to achieve something, you have to start with an attitudinal trade-off.

Course 2

Trade your procrastination, your inactivity and your daydreaming for real action like out into the field and try to make things happen.

Course 3

Trade the idea of being the peddler for the idea of becoming a professional salesperson. Study, practice and professionalise your skills.

Course 4

Trade your poor work habits for good work habits. Develop a work schedule. Manage your time properly. Plan your work and make your plan work.

Course 5

Trade sloth and flabbiness for active physical fitness. **Physical fitness is an essential requirement for mental fitness.**

Course 6

Trade carelessness and untidiness for dressing and looking smart and sharp. This does not cost you much money.

Course 7

Trade mediocrity for success. **Try to do everything better than you have done before.** You will slowly, but steadily, be moving towards success.

Course 8

Trade a bleak and uncertain future for a prosperous and secure one. Your present may not be prosperous, but **remember that hope lies hidden in the uncertainty of the future.**

Course 9

Trade your poverty for wealth. This means: Do not reconcile to your present financial level. Convert this reconciliation into quest for richness or wealth.

Course 10

Trade your pessimism for optimism. Things may not be happening now. But hope that things will happen in future. That is the best way to make things happen.

The above trade-offs are like price for success. Pay the price for success now. It is not easy. But, what is easy in this world?

Decide and prepare yourself for all or most of the above trade-offs. If you successfully do these trade-offs, you can win. You can become a Joe Girard.

All these modes or courses may not be applicable to all salespersons; because, almost every salesperson is different.

One may add to or modify some of the courses to suit or make tailor-made to one's trait, personality and style of working. But, these are almost sure guides to the path to stardom. And, these can be followed or implemented at minimal cost or investment.

Joe Girard may be the right role model for you. *You may not be aware that you may be a Joe Girard in the making.*

But, for this, you may have to climb many ladders. It may be a ladder and snake game. But, ultimately, you may go to the top, i.e., reach your goal. You may become another Joe Girard.

Let every salesperson culminate in a Joe Girard.

We complete this book with this wish.

All the best!

A Salesperson at the Top of the Performance Pyramid A Sales Superstar?

Index